# PC DOS 4

## *A Self-Teaching Guide*

# Related Titles of Interest from Wiley:

*PC DOS: A Self-Teaching Guide*, 3rd Edition, Ashley and Fernandez

*QuickPascal: A Self-Teaching Guide*, Weiskamp and Aguiar

*DOS Productivity Tips & Tricks*, Held

*The New DOS 4.0*, Christopher, Feigenbaum, and Saliga

*DOS 4.0 Reference*, Christopher, Feigenbaum, and Saliga

*Mastering Enable/OA: Office Automation Software*, Spezzano

*Using dBASE IV: Basics for Business*, Brownstein

*Paradox: A Business User's Guide*, Condliffe

*Ventura Publisher 2.0: Mastering Desktop Publishing*, Jantz

*Using Lotus Agenda*, Goodman

*Desktop Publishing with PageMaker 3.02 for the Macintosh*, Bove and Rhodes

*Desktop Publishing with PageMaker 3.0 for the IBM PC and Compatibles*,
   Bove and Rhodes

*Lotus 1-2-3 Release 2.2.*, Williams

*Lotus 1-2-3 Release 3*, Williams

# PC DOS 4

## A Self-Teaching Guide

Ruth Ashley

Judi N. Fernandez

**WILEY**

**John Wiley & Sons, Inc.**

New York • Chichester • Brisbane • Toronto • Singapore

Publisher: Therese A. Zak
Editor: Katherine Schowalter
Managing Editor: Ruth Greif
Copy Editor: Ron Pronk
Design and Production: Rob Mauhar and Lenity Himburg, The Coriolis Group



**Library of Congress Cataloging-in-Publication Data**

Ashley, Ruth.
   PC DOS 4 : a self-teaching guide  / Ruth Ashley, Judi N. Fernandez.
     p.    cm.
   ISBN 0-471-51712-7
   1. PC DOS (Computer operating system)   I. Fernandez, Judi N.,
1941-  .  II.  Title.
QA76.76.063A844  1990
005.4'469--dc20                               89-28872
                                              CIP

Printed in the United States of America
90 91 10 9 8 7 6 5 4 3 2 1

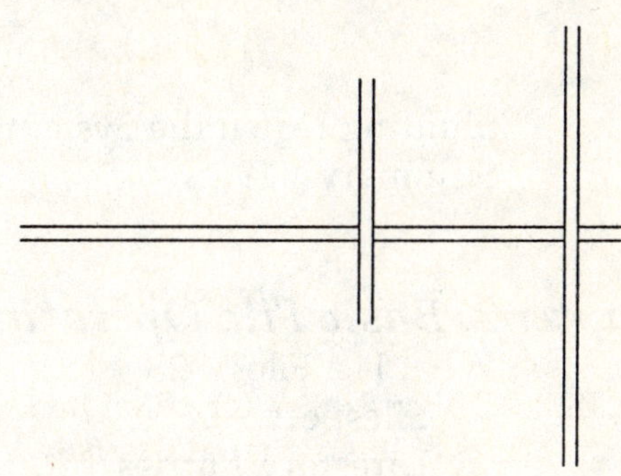

# Contents

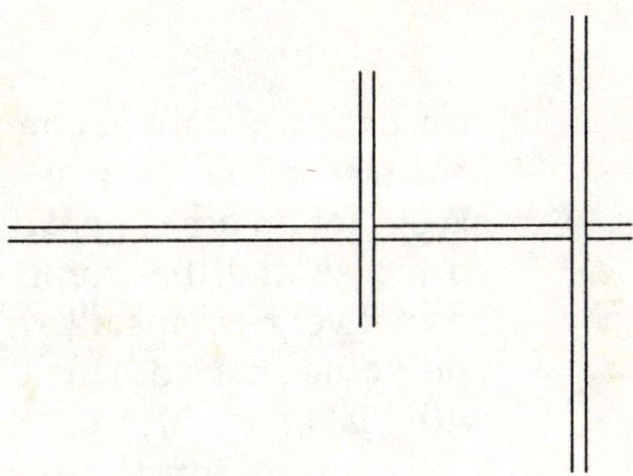

# About This Book

This guide consists of 15 chapters that have been carefully sequenced to introduce you to your personal computer and its operating system and to help you develop a useful set of skills. We have made every effort to organize the material in the best possible learning sequence, so that you can begin using your machine as quickly as possible. It's best to study the chapters in order. You will learn to do easy tasks, then successively more complex tasks, until you have mastered the system.

Each chapter begins with a short introduction followed by objectives that outline what you can expect to learn from the chapter. The body of the chapter consists of individual topics followed by checkpoints that let you test your knowledge. For each set of checkpoints, you'll be provided with questions or hands-on work to review the portion of the chapter you've just read. Answers are provided below the checkpoint questions. To check yourself, place your hand or a sheet of paper over the checkpoint answers. Then try to answer each checkpoint question on your own. After you've come up with an answer, take a look at the corresponding answer provided in the book to see how you've done.

Also be sure to do the exercises provided at the end of each chapter. These exercises help you apply new information at your keyboard. The best way to learn DOS is to use it—hands-on.

This book is written for beginning computer users—you don't even have to know how to boot your computer. Even if you have some experience with a computer, however, you will still benefit from it. The book assumes you have a personal computer and DOS 4, including the shell. Either the IBM or the Microsoft version of DOS will do. Both versions are identical except for an occasional difference in messages. We also assume you have a hard disk and that someone has installed DOS on your hard disk. If DOS has not yet been installed, see Appendix A before starting with Chapter 1. If you do not have a hard disk, see Appendix B for hints on how to use DOS with diskettes only.

This is an introductory book and does not teach everything there is to know about DOS. It is meant to get you started with DOS. Most of the commands and shell functions are mentioned, but advanced options are not always explained. Once you are comfortable with the system, you can learn about advanced facilities by studying your DOS reference manuals.

General command format statements are provided throughout the book. This hypothetical one shows how you should read a format statement:

```
READ [/S or /V] [filespec]
```

Any term in all uppercase letters must be entered character for character as it appears in the command format, except that you don't have to use uppercase letters when you actually type it at the keyboard. All symbols except square brackets ([ ]) must be entered as shown. Any term in italics indicates an item for which you must supply a value. The word "or" indicates a choice between two items; both items may not be used. Items outside of brackets are required. Items inside brackets are optional. Thus, the above format indicates that you must enter the word READ. (You can use uppercase letters, lowercase letters, or a combination of both.) You can enter either /S or /V, but not both. You can also provide a filespec. You don't enter the word "filespec"; instead you enter a string of characters, such as CHAPTER1, that is used by DOS to find a file.

# Getting Started

DOS 4 lets you communicate with your computer. It provides two different ways to accomplish many functions. In this chapter, you'll learn the basics of what DOS can do for you and how to use the two interfaces. Specifically, you'll learn to:

- Boot your system
- Enter and leave the shell
- Pull down shell action menus and make selections
- Perform many shell activities
- Get the command prompt
- Type commands
- Use shell online help
- Shut down your system

## What Is Your Computer?

Your computer is hardware. You probably know what its hardware components are by this time. The *monitor* displays what you type, program output, and DOS messages and screens. It doesn't really matter whether you have a monochrome, CGA, EGA, or better monitor; DOS can handle them all as long as you have installed DOS properly.

The *keyboard* lets you type information into the computer. The keys that resemble typewriter keys in layout are standard. The CapsLock key locks

1

the letter keys into uppercase but has no effect on symbol or number keys. You'll need to use the standard Shift key for those. The keyboard also has many special keys you'll use for different purposes.

The keys labeled Ctrl (control), Alt (alternate), and Del (delete) have special uses. In DOS 4, you'll also have special uses for many of the function keys (labeled F and a number), the Tab key, and the Spacebar.

The arrow keys on the numeric keypad, as well as Home, PgUp, PgDn, and End, control the cursor position. Their exact function depends on the program you're using. The NumLock key works much like CapsLock, switching between keypad numbers and the cursor functions. Separate cursor control keys on the enhanced (101-key) keyboard can also be used; they have the same effect regardless of the status of the NumLock key. So with the enhanced keyboard, you can leave the numeric keypad set to numbers (NumLock on) and have both sets of functions available at once.

The computer also has a *system unit* that contains disk drives, memory, and the control boards and chips that make the computer work. The diskette drives have slots to the outside so you can insert diskettes. If there is only one diskette drive, it is named A:; DOS will also recognize it by the name B:. Two diskette drives are named A: and B:. A fixed disk, also called a hard disk, may also be included in the system unit, but it has no opening to the outside. A fixed disk is usually named C:. It might be partitioned into two or more logical drives named C:, D:, and so on. If your computer has more than two diskette drives or more than one fixed disk drive, you'll have to find out their names. We won't use them in this book, however.

Your *printer* is also essential to your computer. During installation, you have to know whether your printer is parallel or serial. Once it is installed, you access it the same way no matter which type it is.

## Diskette Write Protection

Many of your diskettes contain valuable information that should not be accidentally erased or changed. Diskettes have write-protection mechanisms that prevent diskette drives from writing on them. Figure 1.1 shows how to write-protect both types of diskettes. With 5.25" diskettes, you put a piece of tape over the write-protect notch; to remove the write protection, you pull it off. With 3.5" diskettes, you slide the plastic tab in the corner to open the write-protect hole; to remove the protection, you close the tab again.

When you buy a new program, routinely write-protect all the diskettes, even before you copy the files to your hard disk or backup diskettes. This prevents you from accidentally copying in the wrong direction—from the hard disk or backup diskettes to the program diskettes. You might also want

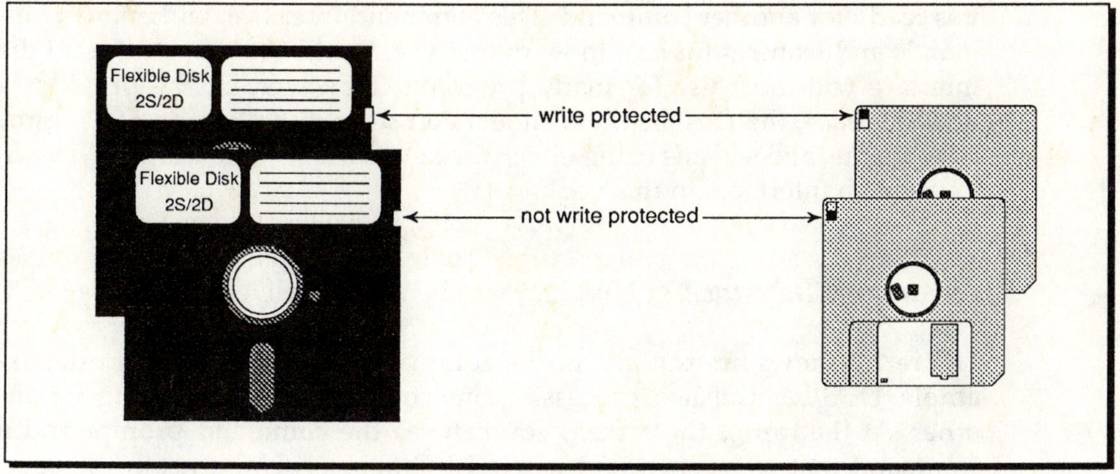


Figure 1.1. Diskette Write-Protection Mechanisms

to write-protect your backup diskettes. But don't write-protect any diskette that you want to copy files to or update the files on.

You can't write-protect the hard disk. But you can protect individual files on it. You'll learn how later in this book.

# What Is DOS?

Your IBM-compatible computer is a marvelous piece of machinery, but without an operating system it is just hardware. DOS 4 is the operating system of choice; it is the software that makes the computer go. DOS is a set of programs that you use to run your computer. PC DOS and MS DOS are basically the same. This book applies to either one.

DOS makes it possible for you to get your computer started. It helps you manage files and programs stored on disks and in memory. It has default values for many features, which work in most situations. Later in this book you'll learn to modify defaults and manipulate many DOS effects. In these early chapters, we'll use only the defaults so you can learn to control DOS in its basic form.

# DOS Interfaces

Ever since the early days of personal computers, DOS has had a command interface. You see a prompt on the screen, you type your command, then press Enter. DOS processes your command, then sends a new prompt when it is ready for another command. This command interface, with many commands and features for you to learn and use, is still available. It is still the interface you must use for many programs. However, DOS 4 provides a new interface, the DosShell, which lets you select functions and programs from menus and screens using either the keyboard or a mouse. You'll learn to use both interfaces in this book.

## Command Interface

Figure 1.2 shows an example of the command interface screen. In the example, DOS has finished processing one command and is waiting for another. At the top of the screen, you can see the command prompt and a command that was typed and entered by the user. Underneath the command, you can see the output, a directory of the A: drive. The last line is another command prompt, indicating that DOS is ready to receive another command.

The basic DOS prompt looks like this:

```
A>_     or     C>_
```

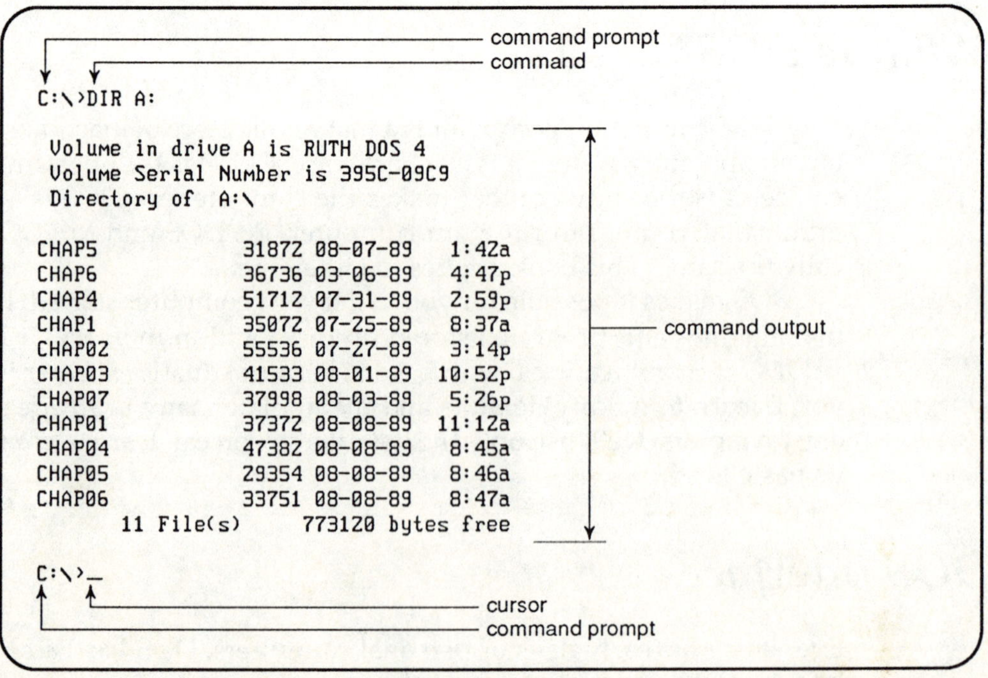


Figure 1.2. Sample DOS Command Prompt Screen

The letter indicates the current disk drive. When you start up the system, the current drive is usually A: for a system without a fixed disk or C: for a system with a fixed disk. The angle bracket indicates the prompt, and the cursor (which looks like an underscore character on most monitors) rests to the right of the prompt.

Your prompt may look like this instead:

```
A:\>_     or     C:\DOS>_
```

Here, the letter still indicates the current disk drive, but is expanded to include the name of the current directory. The colon is considered part of the drivename and the backslash (\) begins the directory name. This style of prompt tells you where DOS is currently working. You'll learn more about drives and directories in Chapter 3.

Your command prompt might be different from one of these, depending on how your system is set up. You'll learn to set up the prompt you want later in this book.

When you see the command prompt, you can type a command. Treat your keyboard as a typewriter. DOS doesn't care whether you use uppercase, lowercase, or mixed case in typing a command. If you make a mistake in typing, just press Backspace to erase and correct it. If you enter an incorrect command, you may get an error message. The most common is "Bad command or file name." This usually means you typed the command incorrectly or that DOS can't find the requested program.

## Shell Interface

The shell takes up the entire screen and includes prompts to let you know what you can do next. You can use either the keyboard or the mouse to perform any actions from the shell. Figure 1.3 shows the initial shell screen. It's called the **Start Programs** screen, as shown in the top line.

The parts of this screen are labeled. The top line is called the title bar; it includes the name of the screen and the current date and time. The second line is the menu bar. The names on the left indicate menus you can see from this screen. At the right end, DOS shows that you can press F1 to get help. You'll find that F1 (that's function key 1) always displays a box with information about the selected item. You'll see how to select items and use the help system later in this chapter.

The body of the screen will vary depending on the type of screen you are using. This one in Figure 1.3 shows the main items that you can access from the screen. It also tells how to select items from the list by using the keyboard. The highlighted item (in inverse video) is currently selected; on this

menu bar         title bar

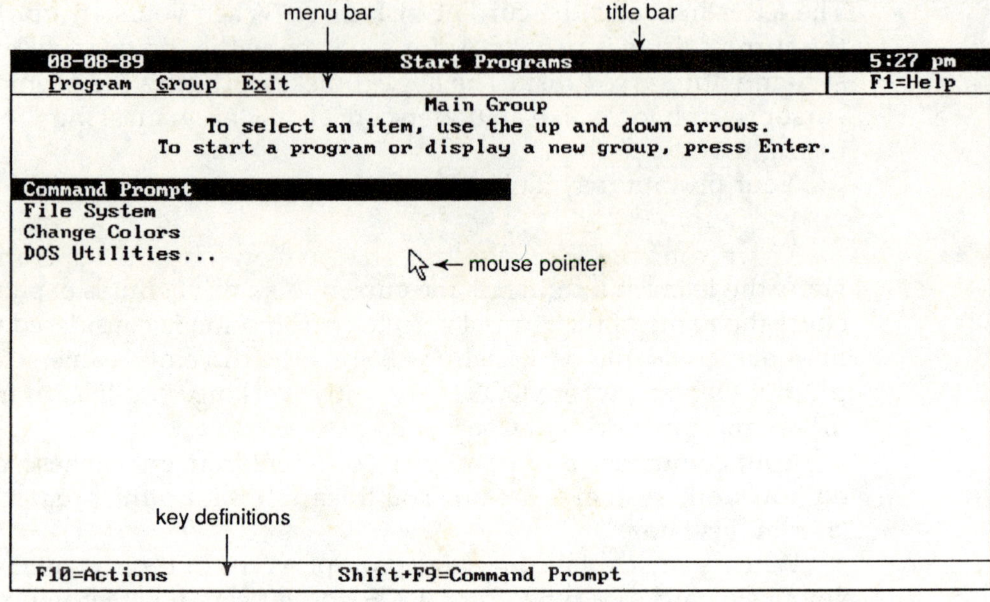


Figure 1.3. Typical Shell Screen

screen **Command Prompt** is highlighted. Later in this chapter, you'll practice selecting items from the list with the keyboard and with a mouse.

The bottom line shows additional key definitions. You can press the indicated keys or click on the definition with your mouse to get the specified effect. On most screens, the F10 key toggles the cursor between the body of the screen and the menu bar. Shift+F9 (press both at once) gets you the command prompt screen; it has the same effect as selecting the **Command Prompt** item in the list.

This book contains many checkpoints in which you can test your knowledge about the commands and techniques you have just learned. In this checkpoint, you'll decide what sort of system you have and consider how to give commands to DOS.

1. Does your system have a mouse installed?
2. How will you use the shell, with the keyboard or the mouse?

*The answers depend on your hardware. If you have a mouse, you'll probably use it most of the time, but you'll still use the keyboard sometimes. If you don't have a mouse, you can skim over instructions about using the mouse.*

# Booting with DOS 4

We are assuming that your computer already has DOS 4 installed on disk. If not, you should follow the directions in your documentation to install DOS before continuing. Appendix A includes some hints and information that will make installation much easier and will relieve some of the stress associated with it.

When you boot your system, you turn it on so that the operating system you want is in control; in our case, that's DOS 4. When you boot, the system checks the memory and many of the peripheral devices, then starts up the operating system. How you boot differs according to where your DOS 4 master system is stored. In this section, we'll explain how to boot with four different types of storage media: fixed disk, 360K diskette, 1.44MB diskette, and 720K diskette. Read only the section that applies to your computer.

Rebooting is restarting the DOS system from the beginning; it doesn't redo the memory check, but the operating system is started from scratch. You'll have to reboot occasionally to make some special command take effect or to interrupt a process gone awry. You don't have to turn the computer off to reboot.

## Fixed Disk

If DOS 4 is installed on your fixed disk, you can boot from it easily. Remove any diskettes from their drives. Then turn on the computer; turn on the monitor as well if it has a separate switch. Turn on the printer also, if you wish. Then watch the screen for messages. The messages vary according to how the system is installed and what commands are processed automatically at startup. Eventually, however, you'll see either a shell screen or a command prompt. Either one means your system booted successfully.

To reboot from the fixed disk, remove any diskettes from drive A:, then press the reset button, if you have one, or press three keys simultaneously: Ctrl+Alt+Del. The computer will start up DOS 4 from the fixed disk again. You'll get some of the same messages on the screen as you see when you boot.

## 5.25″ Diskette

If your version of DOS 4 was installed to be booted from 5.25″ diskettes, it is probably provided on several 360K diskettes. To boot from them, first insert the diskette labeled **Startup** into drive A: (the top or leftmost slot) and close the drive. Then turn on the computer; turn on the monitor as well if it has a separate switch. Turn on the printer also, if you wish. Then watch the screen for messages. The messages vary according to how the system is installed and what commands are processed automatically at startup. Eventually, however, you'll see the command prompt, which means your system booted successfully. If you want to use the shell next, you'll have to switch to the **Shell** diskette.

Later in this book, you'll be able to use the commands needed to combine these 360K diskettes with other DOS programs on a single 1.2MB diskette for easier use. Appendix B includes additional information about working with DOS 4 installed on diskettes.

To reboot from the diskette, make sure the **Startup** diskette is in drive A:, then press the reset button, if you have one, or press three keys simultaneously: Ctrl+Alt+Del. The computer will start up DOS 4 from the diskette again. You'll get some of the same messages on the screen as you see when you boot.

## 3.5" Diskette

If your version of DOS 4 was installed to be booted from 3.5" diskettes, you may have either a 720K diskette or a 1.44MB diskette to boot from. The process is the same, except for the label on the diskette you insert for booting. Use the one labeled **Shell** for a 720K diskette or the one labeled **Startup** for a 1.44MB diskette.

To boot, first insert the appropriate diskette into drive A: (the top or leftmost slot). Then turn on the computer; turn on the monitor as well if it has a separate switch. Turn on the printer also, if you wish. Then watch the screen for messages. The messages vary according to how the system is installed and what commands are processed automatically at startup. Eventually, however, you'll see the command prompt, which means your system booted successfully.

To reboot from the diskette, make sure the appropriate boot diskette is in drive A, then press the reset button, if you have one, or press three keys simultaneously: Ctrl+Alt+Del. The computer will start up DOS 4 from the diskette again. You'll get some of the same messages on the screen as you see when you boot.

Like most of the checkpoints in this book, this one asks you to use your computer as you try out the techniques you have just read about. If you're not sure how to proceed, look below the line for some suggestions; try not to

look at them unless you can't figure out what to do.
1. Find out whether DOS 4 was installed on a fixed disk or on diskettes for your system. If you need a diskette, locate the appropriate one.
2. Boot the system.
3. Reboot the system.

---

1. *If you're not sure how your system was installed, get help from the person who installed it or someone who uses it.*
2. *If you're booting from diskette: Put the appropriate diskette in drive A: and turn on the hardware. If you're booting from fixed disk: Remove any diskette from drive A: and turn on the hardware. If your system doesn't boot, check these diagnostic questions to uncover the problem:*

   - *Was DOS installed correctly? If anyone else uses DOS 4 on that computer, it was installed okay.*
   - *Did you use the appropriate diskette? Check the labels on your diskettes. If you want to boot from fixed disk, make sure no diskette is in drive A:.*
   - *Did you turn on all essential parts of your system?*

   *If you still can't tell why DOS didn't boot, check with a colleague or try reinstalling it. Your documentation and Appendix A will help you.*
3. *Press Ctrl+Alt+Del.*

---

# Examining the Shell

Once you have booted successfully, you have to be able to switch back and forth between the shell and the command prompt in order to use both interfaces. If you don't intend to use the shell, you should at least learn to remove it from the screen if it comes up. For basic functions, especially file and directory management, you'll find that using the shell is much simpler than typing in the required commands.

If the shell didn't appear automatically, you can call it up with the DOSSHELL command. Insert the diskette labeled **Shell** if necessary. At the command prompt, just type DOSSHELL, in either uppercase or lowercase letters, and press the Enter key.

You saw the main shell screen, labeled **Start Programs**, in Figure 1.3. The largest portion of the main shell screen tells you how to select an item and lists the groups already installed. As described earlier, you can select any item or action with the keyboard or mouse as well. While you'll see how to add more groups and programs later, the ones in the figure are added during the installation process. Your screen should contain at least these four choices.

## Pulling Down Menus

The menu bar contains three menu names. You pull down a menu to make its options available.

You can click on any menu name with the mouse; just move the mouse pointer to the menu name and press the appropriate button. That's usually the leftmost button, which lies under your right index finger. The menu is pulled down on the screen. To see a different menu, just click on it. Any already displayed menu disappears, since only one can show at a time. To remove a current menu with the mouse, just click outside the menu.

From the keyboard, you must first move the cursor to the menu bar, then select the menu you want. Pressing F10 toggles the cursor between its current location and the menu bar. Once the menu bar is active, you can type the underlined letter for the menu you want to see or use arrow keys to highlight the menu name and press Enter or the down arrow. Either method pulls down the menu. To change to a different menu, just use the right or left arrow. To remove a menu, press the Escape (Esc) key.

Suppose you select the **Program** menu. Figure 1.4 shows how it looks on the screen. When a menu is displayed, it is automatically active, so you can

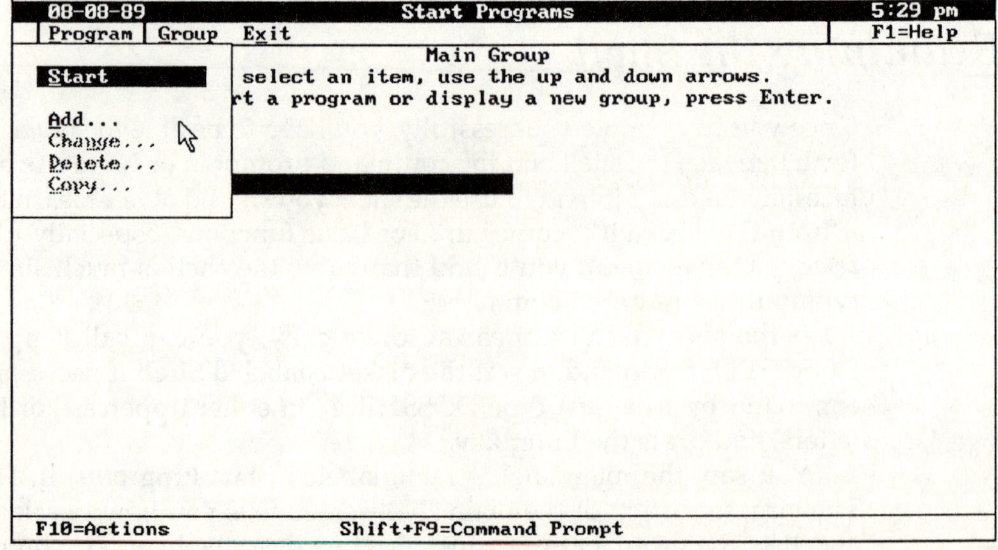


Figure 1.4. Typical Pulled-Down Menu

select items from it much as from the active menu bar or a list of items. Click on the desired option, highlight it and press Enter, or type its underlined letter.

To remove a menu from the screen, you can select another menu to replace the current one. To remove a menu without pulling down another one, just click elsewhere on the screen or press Esc.

## Exiting the Shell Permanently

To terminate the shell and enter the command interface, you select the **Exit** menu from the **Start Programs** screen. With the mouse, just click on the **Exit** word in the menu bar. From the keyboard, first activate the menu bar with F10 or Tab, then type X or use an arrow key to highlight **Exit** and press Enter. The result is the **Exit** menu, as shown in Figure 1.5. The first menu option, **Exit Shell**, confirms the exit request. The other menu option, **Resume Start Programs**, cancels the exit request and leaves you at the **Start Programs** screen.

To select a menu option with the mouse, simply click on it. To select an option with the keyboard, type its key letter (the underlined letter). Alternatively, you can move the highlight to the option by using the arrow keys and press Enter. An easy way to exit the shell with the keyboard is to press F10 followed by two Xs. F10 puts the highlight in the menu bar, the first X pulls down the **Exit** menu, the second X selects the **Exit Shell** option.

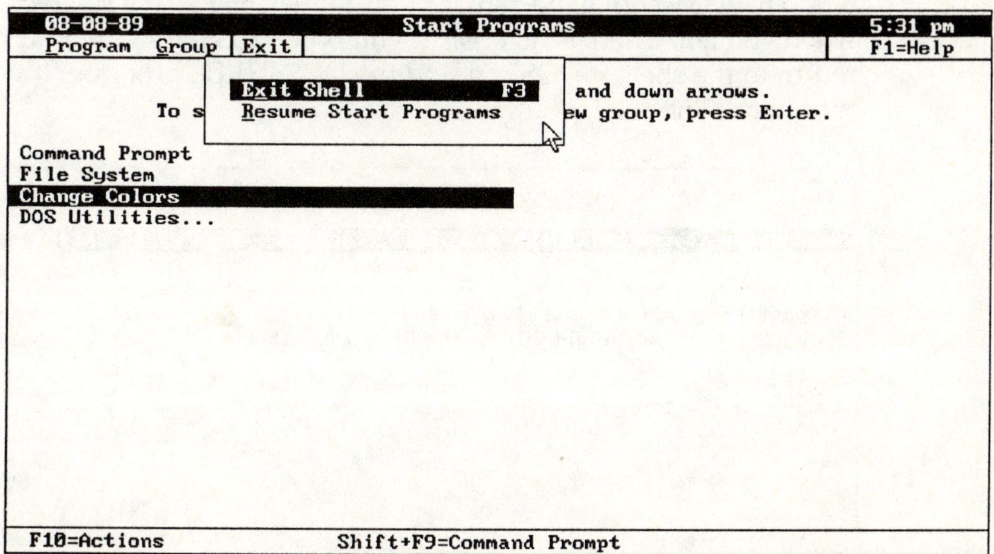


Figure 1.5. Exit Menu

But there's an even easier way to exit the shell. Notice the F3 next to the **Exit Shell** option on the **Exit** menu. This tells you that you can press F3 to select this option, even when the menu isn't pulled down. Whenever you are on this **Start Programs** screen, you can press F3 to exit the shell. This is the fastest way to exit the shell, whether you have a mouse or not.

Exiting the shell in this way gets you completely out of it. It does not have the same effect as pressing Shift+F9 (see the bottom screen line) or selecting **Command Prompt**. When you use the **Exit Shell** option, the shell is terminated. You'll have to use the DOSSHELL command to restart it.

## Exiting the Shell Temporarily

To exit the shell temporarily, perhaps to issue a command that isn't available through the shell or to run a program that doesn't appear on the shell lists, you select **Command Prompt** from the list on the **Start Programs** screen. Just click on **Command Prompt** or use the up or down arrow to highlight it, then press Enter. Alternatively, you can press Shift+F9, as indicated in the key definitions line. When you do either, the shell disappears and you see the information shown in Figure 1.6 at the top of your monitor screen.

You can enter whatever commands you want at the command prompt. You could start up a word processor or spreadsheet, change to a different drive or directory, or do whatever you need. When you are ready to return to the shell, just type EXIT; again, you can use uppercase or lowercase letters. The EXIT command returns you to the shell in the same condition as when you left. There is no crisis if you type DOSSHELL instead of EXIT to return to the shell; if DOS can find the DOSSHELL program, it will still return you to the shell.

```
When ready to return to the DOS Shell, type EXIT then press enter.


Microsoft(R) MS-DOS(R) Version 4.00
          (C)Copyright Microsoft Corp 1981-1988

C:\DOS>
```

Figure 1.6. Command Prompt "Type EXIT" Message

Boot the system, if necessary, before starting this checkpoint.
1. If you don't see the shell, enter the command to bring it up.
2. Put the cursor in the menu bar. Try moving it back and forth.
3. Move the cursor to the program list. Move it up and down.
4. Select the **Command Prompt** from the program list.
5. Go back to the shell from the **Command Prompt** screen.
6. Terminate the shell.

---

1. *The correct command is DOSSHELL. If you get a "Bad command or file name" message, make sure the **Shell** diskette is installed. If you have a fixed disk and DOSSHELL doesn't bring up the shell, your system may not be installed properly. Get help from a colleague or contact your dealer.*
2. *Use F10 to move the cursor to the menu bar and use the left and right arrow keys to move it back and forth. If the arrow keys don't work, press NumLock once, then try them again.*
3. *Use F10 to move the cursor to the program list and use the up and down arrow keys to move it up and down.*
4. *Double-click on the **Command Prompt** option or move the highlight to it and press Enter.*
5. *The correct command is EXIT or DOSSHELL.*
6. *Pull down the **Exit** menu and select the **Exit Shell** option, or press F3.*

# Checking Out Shell Items

The main group of items on the **Start Programs** screen is available for selection. You select an item with the keyboard by highlighting it and pressing Enter. With the mouse, double-click on the item. At first you might forget and single-click on the item. When nothing happens, that should remind you to double-click on the item.

You've already learned to use the **Command Prompt** item. In this part of the chapter, you'll see how to access the other three items and return to this screen.

## Accessing the File System

The file system lets you perform basic file and directory management activities. The following chapters cover it in detail, so we'll just look at it briefly here. After you select the **File System** item, you'll see a screen like the one shown in Figure 1.7. Notice that it has many of the same features as the **Start Programs** screen.

The title bar contains the screen name and the current date and time. The menu bar here includes four menus; you'll use the **Exit** menu to return to the **Start Programs** screen. The help key definition is also included; help is specific to the file system if you press F1 from here. The bottom line shows the same key definitions as those shown on the **Start Programs** screen; you can press F10 to activate the menu bar or use Shift+F9 to get to the command prompt. If you reach the command prompt by this method, EXIT returns you to this screen.

## Changing Onscreen Colors

From the **Start Programs** screen, you can change the way the shell is displayed on your monitor, unless you are working with a monochrome monitor. You can use the **Change Colors** item to reset the colors that DOS 4 uses in its displays. You'll have four choices, and the shell lets you view each one. When you select **Change Colors**, you'll see a screen like the one shown in Figure 1.8. Notice that there aren't any menus in the menu bar, but you can still press F1 to get help. The bottom line shows that you can press Enter to change to the currently displayed set of colors or Esc to cancel the operation without changing colors and return to the **Start Programs** screen. The key

```
 08-08-89                    File System                    5:33 pm
  File  Options  Arrange  Exit                            | F1=Help
  Ctrl+letter selects a drive.
  ▭A  ▭B  ▭C  ▭D

 C:\
     Directory Tree                              *.*
                                    ↑
 ✓C:\                              ⌃    ASMTOC   .CHP     1,118   07-17-89  ↑
   └DOS                                 ASMTOC   .CIF       128   07-17-89  ⌃
   └WP                                  ASMTOC   .GEN    12,866   07-17-89
       └MASMBOOK                        AUTOEXEC .400       155   07-24-89
        └EXTRA                          AUTOEXEC .BAK       183   06-21-89
       └DOS4BOOK                        AUTOEXEC .BAT       163   08-02-89
         └RUTH                          AUTOEXEC .BK!       218   07-24-89
          └MOMENT                       AUTOEXEC .SAV       217   07-24-89
    └DC                                 COMMAND  .COM    37,556   10-06-88
     └MASMPICS                          CONFIG   .400       163   07-24-89
    └HSG                                CONFIG   .BK!        98   06-17-89
    └ASM                                CONFIG   .SYS       126   08-02-89
      └PROGS                            DMDRVR   .BIN     7,545   06-25-87
    └VENTURA                            F1-5     .SCR     8,128   07-13-89
    └TYPESET                       ⌄    GROC2                38   07-21-89  ⌄
    └MOUSE                         ↓    GROC3                38   08-04-89  ↓
  F10=Actions   Shift+F9=Command Prompt
```

Figure 1.7. File System Screen

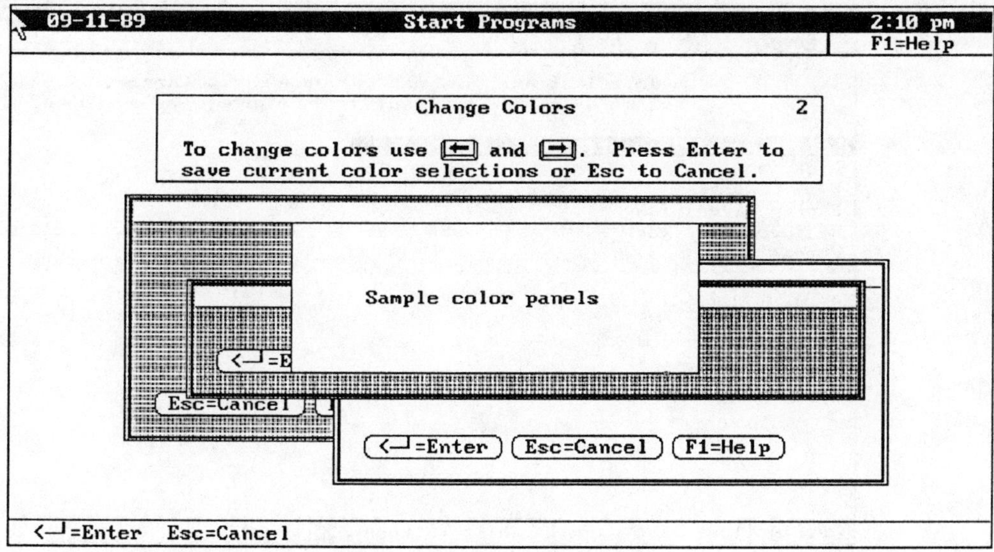


Figure 1.8. Change Colors Screen

definitions in the ovals (called *buttons*) you see in the sample color panels don't work; they are just there to show you the colors.

The numbered box in the upper center of the screen shows you how to see the other color sets. Just click on the arrow icons or press the right or left arrow to page through sets 1 through 4; the displayed set is number 2, but you can't see the colors in the figure. You'll have to try the sets on your own monitor to see their effects.

When you are ready to return to the **Start Programs** screen, select Enter (click on "┘=Enter" in the key definition line or press the Enter key) if you want to change to the currently displayed set of colors. Select **Cancel** to return to the previous colors. Either one returns you to the normal **Start Programs** screen. Notice that you can't get to the command prompt from this screen.

## Accessing the DOS Utilities Screen

When you select the **DOS Utilities** item from the **Start Programs** screen, you'll see a screen that lets you run some basic DOS utility programs, such as setting the time and date, formatting a diskette, and backing up your fixed disk. You'll learn to use these later in this book, as well as to add new utilities to the screen. To see the screen, just select **DOS Utilities** from the **Start Programs** screen. You'll see a screen similar to Figure 1.9. This is actually the **Start Programs** screen with a different list of programs.

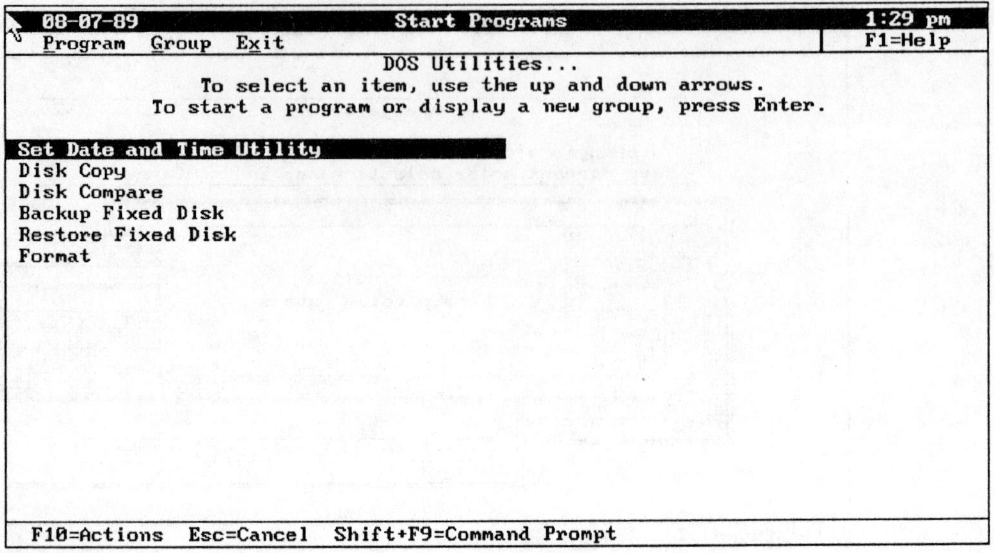



Figure 1.9. DOS Utilities Screen

An additional key is defined on the bottom line; you can select Esc here to return to the basic **Start Programs** screen. This is the only way to get back to the main screen. Using the Exit menu or pressing F3 terminates the entire shell just as they do from the main **Start Programs** screen.

Start at the **Start Programs** screen.
1. If you have a color monitor, examine the available color options. Choose the option you like best.
2. Examine the **File System** screen.
3. Return to the **Start Programs** screen.
4. Examine the **DOS Utilities** group.
5. Return to the main group.

1. *Select the **Change Colors** option. (If you are using a mouse, don't forget to double-click on the option.) Use the arrows to check out the possible color combinations. Select Enter to choose one or **Cancel** to return to the original combination.*
2. *Select the **File System** option.*
3. *Use the **Exit** menu or F3.*
4. *Select the **DOS Utilities** option.*
5. *Select **Cancel**.*

# Using Help

You can get online help from every shell screen by pressing F1 or clicking on the key definition with the mouse. The help you get depends on what option or item is highlighted on the screen; this is called *context-sensitive* help. Figure 1.10 shows the result of asking for help when the **Command Prompt** item is highlighted.

The DOS 4 shell provides information in a *dialog box*, which often asks for additional information as well. Notice the choices in ovals at the bottom of the box; these buttons tell you what to do next. You can select a button by pressing the indicated key or clicking on the oval.

When you select **Cancel**, the dialog box is removed from the screen and you can continue with your work. When you select **Help** from within the **Help** dialog box, you'll get a dialog box containing information about using the online help system. Figure 1.11 shows the resulting dialog box. When you select **Cancel** from this box, you'll return to the previous box

When you select **Index,** you see an alphabetical index of topics from which you can select for further help. It includes such topics as **Keyboard Instructions, File System Instructions**, and **Selecting Instructions**. You get the same index no matter where you selected **Help** from.

When you select **Keys** in the **Help** dialog box, you see a listing of special keys and their effect in the shell. For example, the **Keys** dialog box shows that F1 gets help, F3 exits the shell, and that you can use F11 by pressing Alt+F1, in case your keyboard has only ten function keys.

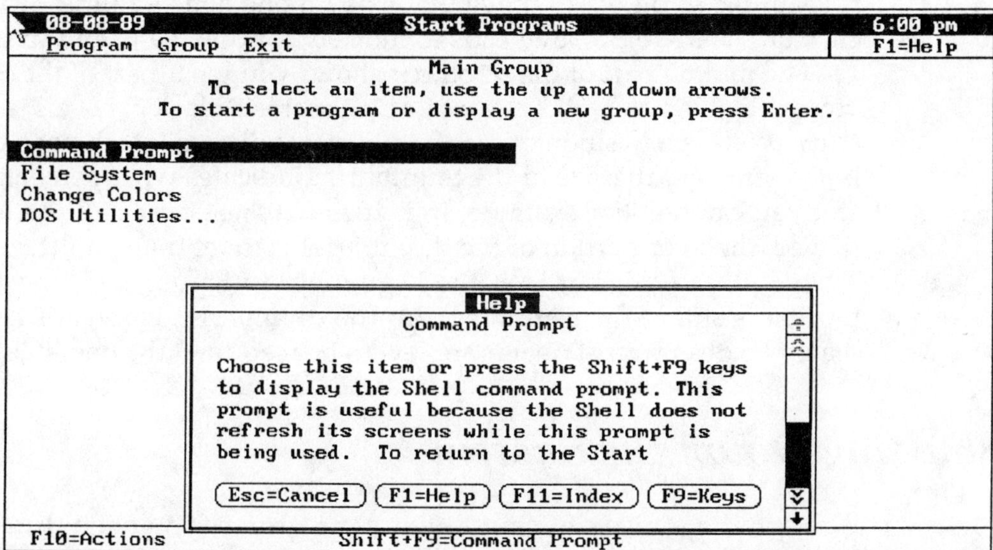


Figure 1.10. Help Dialog Box

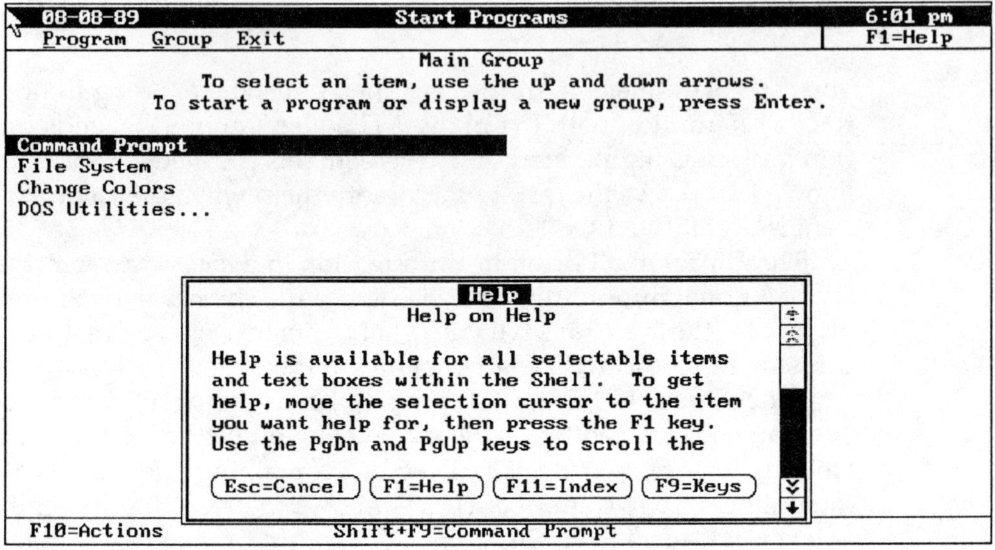


Figure 1.11. Help on Help

The **Help** dialog box is quite small, so it often doesn't show all the information you need. On the right edge of the box is a *scroll bar* that lets you move through the material in the box. With the keyboard, you can use the up and down arrow keys to move up or down one line at a time. The PgDn and PgUp keys move through the text one page at a time (a page is the size of the dialog box). With the mouse, you can click on the up and down arrows in the scroll bar to move up or down one line at a time. You can also click on the double arrowheads to move up or down a page at a time.

The middle part of the scroll bar shows you what part of the whole text you are looking at. Notice the white block set in a black bar. This is called the *thumbprint*. The position of the thumbprint indicates which page of the text is showing and the size of the thumbprint indicates what percentage of the text you can see. For example, in Figure 1.10, just over half the text is displayed; the light portion of the thumbprint is more than half the entire bar. The displayed portion is at the beginning. In Figure 1.11, the displayed portion is still at the beginning, but the thumbprint is much smaller. This dialog box has a great deal more text to be read than the one in Figure 1.10.

## Shutting Down the System

When you are ready to shut down your system, you should follow your dealer's guidelines. Some people like to shut the system down at night. Others turn it off whenever they will be gone for more than a few hours. Others may leave the computer on most of the time, but turn the monitor off to protect its screen. Everyone has to be able to turn the machine completely off in case of emergency.

The first step is to make sure no programs are running. Get to the command prompt if you want to make sure. Some systems have a special program to park the fixed drive in a safe position; if yours does, run it at the command prompt. Then turn off the computer and its accessories. Remove and store any diskettes that you use for booting or for storing data. That's all there is to it.

Start at the **Start Programs** screen.
1. Display help information for the **Change Colors** option.
2. Scroll through the help information by lines and by pages.
3. Examine the **Help Index** information.
4. Examine the **Keys** listing.
5. Return to the **Start Programs** screen.
6. Shut down the system.

1. *Highlight* **Change Colors**, *then select* **Help** *or press F1.*
2. *Click on the up and down arrows and double arrowheads, or press the up and down arrow keys and PgUp and PgDn.*
3. *Click on the* **Index** *button or press F11 (Alt+F1).*
4. *Click on the* **Keys** *button or press F9.*
5. *Select* **Cancel** *until the* **Help** *dialog box disappears.*
6. *Turn off the computer and its accessories.*

## Summary

In this chapter, you have learned to boot DOS 4 and shut it down. While DOS is up, you can move between the shell and the command interface. You can select items and use menus and buttons in the shell. You can get online help whenever you need it.

In later chapters, you'll learn to use all the shell features as well as many DOS commands.

# *Exercises*

These exercises help you review and practice many of the techniques you have learned in this chapter.

| **What You Should Do** | **How the Computer Responds** |
|---|---|
| 1. Shut down your system, if necessary. | 1. Shuts down. |
| 2. Boot DOS. | 2. Starts up hardware and displays initial messages. Then starts up DOS. Displays either command prompt screen (with DOS copyright message) or **Start Programs** screen, depending on whether shell is started automatically. |
| 3. Start up the shell, if necessary. | 3. Displays **Start Programs** screen. |
| 4. Select **Help**. | 4. Displays **Help** dialog box for whatever item is highlighted on **Start Programs** screen (probably **Command Prompt**). |
| 5. Select **Keys**. | 5. Displays **Key Assignments Help** text. |
| 6. Read all the information about keys, scrolling as necessary. | 6. Displays complete text as you scroll through it. |
| 7. Return to the **Start Programs** screen. | 7. Removes **Help** dialog box. |
| 8. Select **Change colors**. | 8. Displays **Change Colors** screen showing the current color settings. |
| 9. Examine the different color schemes. | 9. Displays color choices as you requested. |
| 10. Select the colors of your choice. | 10. Returns to **Start Programs** screen using color scheme you select. |
| 11. Select the command prompt without terminating the shell. | 11. Displays command prompt screen with EXIT reminder at top and DOS copyright message before prompt. |
| 12. Return to the shell. | 12. Returns to **Start Programs** screen. |
| 13. Terminate the shell. | 13. Displays command prompt screen (no EXIT or copyright messages). |
| 14. Reboot. | 14. Restarts DOS; displays either command prompt screen or **Start Programs** screen as in Step 2. |
| 15. Shut down the system. | 15. Shuts down. |

## *What If It Doesn't Work?*

1. If DOS won't boot, make sure you have the correct diskette in drive A:. If you want to boot from your hard disk, make sure no diskette is in drive A:. If you have never been able to boot DOS successfully, get help from an expert. Don't continue with this book until you can boot DOS and complete this exercise.

2. If the shell won't start up, make sure you insert the **Shell** diskette in drive A: before you enter the DOSSHELL command. If you don't have a **Shell** diskette, or if DOS boots from your hard disk, you probably have not installed the shell. Either skip all exercise steps concerning the shell or reinstall DOS to include the shell (see Appendix A).

3. If the Change Colors function does not appear or does not work properly, your monitor is probably not equipped for it. Skip all exercise steps that pertain to changing the colors.

# 2

# *Basic File Operations*

One of the main functions of DOS is to give you control over the files stored on your disks. In this chapter, you will learn to use the shell and commands to:

- Display a list of the files on a disk
- Copy files
- Create ASCII text files
- View ASCII text files
- Print information
- Rename files
- Delete files

## *What Is a File?*

DOS stores your data in files. A file might be a letter, a report, a balance sheet, a mailing list, a grocery list, a tax form, or any other collection of information you want to save together on disk. You decide what to put in each file. Each program is also a file.

DOS maintains a directory and File Allocation Table (FAT) on each disk showing all the filenames, their sizes and locations, when they were last changed, and other information.

## Filespecs

Every file must have a unique specifier, called a *filespec*, with up to four parts, as shown in Figure 2.1. The first part is the drivename. The drivename is optional; when you use a drivename, it must be followed by a colon.

The second part of the filespec is the path. It identifies the directory containing the file. If you're working with unsubdivided directories only, you can forget about the path. Paths are covered in Chapter 3.

The third part is the filename. It has from one to eight characters. It is the only required part of the filespec. Most of the filenames you use will look like these examples:

JOHNSFIL
LASTWEEK
INFLIGHT
MEMOS
X
CHAPTER1
OBASKET
TBILLREP

The fourth part is the extension. It has from zero to three characters. The extension usually identifies the file's type, such as LET for letter, DAT for data, or TST for test. Not every file needs an extension. But if one is used, it is separated from the filename with a period.

DOS recognizes certain extensions and may treat them differently. Here are a few of the standard extensions:

BAT    A batch file containing a set of DOS commands
COM    One kind of program
EXE    Another kind of program

DOS has other standard extensions also, such as BAS for BASIC programs. Many of your application programs will also use particular extensions. For

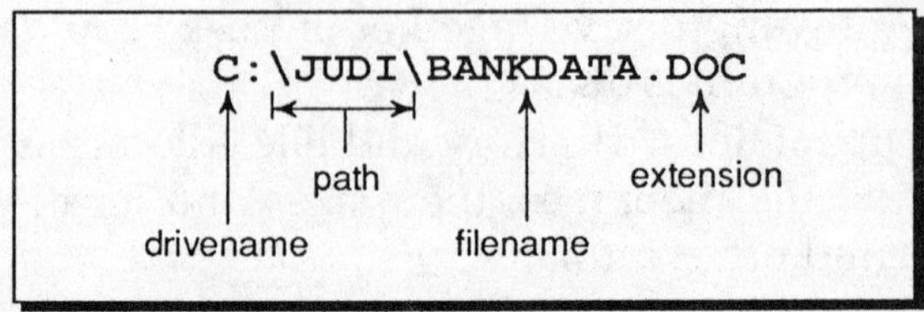


Figure 2.1. Parts of a Filespec

example, you might have an inventory program that will work only on INV files. You might have a mailing label program that creates LAB files.

Many of your files will have no extensions because they aren't needed for any special reasons. For example, document files you create with your word processor might not have extensions.

If you type a filename longer than eight characters or an extension longer than three characters, DOS truncates (chops off) the extra characters. Thus, WEDNESDAYS.MENUS will be read as WEDNESDA.MEN.

You can form the filespec from the following characters:

Letters
Numbers
These symbols: $ % ' - @ { } ~ ! # ( ) & _

You can't use a space, a slash, or any other symbol not shown in the list. Periods, backslashes, and colons cannot be used in names and extensions; they have special meaning in the filespec and cannot be used in other places.

DOS ignores the differences between uppercase and lowercase letters. GREENS.FIL, greens.fil, and Greens.Fil are the same filespec.

The following filespecs are all valid:

FILE#6.DOC
J-GROUP
DON'S.DAT
GR.1

The following filespecs are all invalid for the reasons given:

TEXT/SAV     Slash is not permitted.
M.3.5        Only one period is permitted.
EDS FILE     Space is not permitted.

The combination of filename plus extension must be unique within the directory. For example, if you have a file named BALDLIES, you can't have another file in the same directory named BALDLIES, but you can have BALDLIES.OLD, BALDLIES.1, and BALDLIES.2. You can also have another file named BALDLIES in another directory or on another diskette.

When you are creating a new file, make its name as meaningful as possible. You'll be glad later that you did. Imagine trying to find the file containing last year's income tax figures when your directory contains these filespecs: BC32R.C45, XT10BOB.FGP, MORE.FGP, and WKD. Think how much better these names are: STATAX89, FEDTAX89, BUDGET90, and

BANKBAL. You're limited to an eight-character filename, but you'd be surprised what you can do with eight characters.

## Directory Entries

When you save a file on disk, DOS creates an entry for it in the disk file directory. The entry contains the filename and extension, the size, the date and time the file was last changed, and other information that DOS needs to find the file. Figure 2.2 shows an example of a directory listing. You can see each filename and extension (the periods are not shown), the size in bytes, and the date/time stamp. The date/time stamp shows when the file was last changed, which is not necessarily the same as when the file was created. If you have different versions of a file in different directories, you can use the date/time stamp to find the most recent version.

```
WPT          BAT           22    06-22-89        2:08p
TEMP                     3736    06-19-89        3:45p
WPF11-3      SCR         8128    06-19-89        3:47p
DOS2-1                   1241    07-21-89        6:06p
WPF13-4      SCR         8128    06-19-89        3:52p
APLASPLU     PRS        42371    06-23-89        1:34p
WP{WP}US     SUP         1192    06-29-89        9:29p
       7 File(s)      18495488 bytes  free
```

Figure 2.2. Sample Directory List

This checkpoint requires paper and pencil only.
1. Create a filename (no extension) for the outline of your new novel, which is called *The Gray Psovrath.*
2. Create a filename for your grocery list.
3. Create a filename for your birthday card mailing list.

*1. Some possibilities are OUTLINE, GRAYOUT, and PSOVRATH.*
*2. Some possibilities are GROCLIST and GROCERYS.*
*3. Some possibilities are BDAYCARD, BCARDLIST, and CARDLIST.*

# *The File System Screen*

To view your current directory list on a shell screen, select the **File System** from the **Start Programs** screen. You will see a screen similar to the one shown earlier in Figure 1.7. The title bar shows that this is the **File System** screen. The menu bar shows four menus: **File, Options, Arrange,** and **Exit.** They contain a variety of functions to manipulate files and directories.

Immediately underneath the menu bar is a panel showing your disk drives. Each drive is represented by a picture showing the type of drive: fixed or floppy. When you select a drive in this panel, it becomes the default drive.

The small drawings are *icons*. Not only do they present information graphically, they also cause actions to occur when you click on them. Figure 2.3 shows all the icons that are used in the **File System** screen, their meanings, and their actions.

Underneath the drive panel is a small panel containing the drivename and path of the current drive and directory. In Figure 1.7, the drivename and path are C:\ (the root directory of drive C:). These are the drive and directory that receive all **File System** operations until you change to another drive and/or directory.

The **Directory Tree** panel at the lower left depicts the directory structure of the default drive. All the names shown are directory names; the lines indicate parent-child relationships. The check mark identifies the default directory, whose files are listed in the right-hand panel. You change the default directory by selecting another one.

The right-hand panel is a directory listing of the default directory, shown in alphabetical order. Complete entries are not shown; you can't see the time stamp or the file's attributes. But you can see enough information to select which files you want to work with—to copy, move, delete, and so forth.

| | | |
|---|---|---|
| Diskette Drive | Select associated drive as default |
| Fixed Disk Drive | Select associated drive as default |
| Nonprogram file | Select associated file |
| Program file | Select associated file |
| Page down | Scroll down one page |
| Line down | Scroll down one line |
| Page up | Scroll up one page |
| Line up | Scroll up one line |

Figure 2.3. File System Icons

## Scrolling

Both the **Directory Tree** panel and the directory panel are incomplete. More tree information follows MOUSE (the last directory showing) and more files follow GROC3. You can scroll using the cursor movement keys or by clicking on the scroll bar.

## Selecting Items

To select an item with the keyboard, you must first move the cursor to the desired panel. In screens such as the one shown in Figure 1.7, the cursor shows up as a reverse-video highlight. In the example in Figure 1.7, the highlight is on drive C: in the drive panel. Use the Tab or Backtab key to move the highlight from panel to panel. F10 will also move the highlight back and forth between the menu bar and whatever panel it was in before.

Once the highlight is in the desired panel, use the arrow keys to highlight the item you want to select. What you do next depends on which panel you are in.

In the menu bar, you pull down a menu by highlighting its name and pressing Enter. A shortcut is to type the key letter of the menu name.

In the drive panel, you select a drive by highlighting it and pressing Enter. A shortcut is to press Ctrl plus the letter of the drivename, as in Ctrl+A.

In the **Directory Tree** panel, you select a directory by highlighting it and pressing Enter. It immediately becomes the default directory: both the default directory name and the directory listing change accordingly.

The directory listing panel is different. To select a file in this panel, highlight it and press the *Spacebar*, not Enter. Its icon highlights when it is selected. (If you press Enter, DOS displays the **Open File** dialog box. You'll learn how to use this facility in a later chapter.) To deselect a file, select it again. Each time you press the Spacebar on a highlighted file, its selection status reverses.

Once a file has been selected, you can pull down a menu and select a function to apply to the file. This is how you view, copy, and delete files. You can also select multiple files. Just highlight each one and press the Spacebar. Each icon will highlight. You can select files on different pages in the directory listing. Many functions can be applied to groups of files.

Many keyboard users have trouble at first remembering to press the Spacebar to select or deselect a file. They either press Enter, calling up the **Open File** dialog box, or they simply highlight the desired file but neglect to press the Spacebar. When they pull down a menu, they're surprised that the function they want isn't available.

Another common error is to select multiple files when you intended to select only one. This happens especially when a previously selected file is on another page where you can't see it.

Selecting and deselecting items is much easier if you use a mouse. Simply point to the desired item and click. The highlight moves to that panel and the indicated item is selected.

Boot the system and start the shell, if necessary.
1. Get to the **File System** screen.
2. Pull down the **Exit** menu.
3. Get rid of the **Exit** menu without exiting the file system.
4. Select any directory except the current directory.
5. Select the C:\DOS directory.
6. Select several files.
7. Deselect all selected files.

1. *From the **Start Programs** screen, select the **File System** option.*
2. *Click on the word "Exit" or move the highlight to the menu bar and press the letter "x."*
3. *Click outside the menu or press Esc.*
4. *Click on the desired directory name or move the highlight to the **Directory Tree** panel with Tab, then move it to the desired directory name with the up and down arrows, and press Enter.*
5. *Click on the desired directory name or move the highlight to the **Directory Tree** panel with Tab, move it to the DOS directory name with the up and down arrows, and press Enter.*
6. *Click (once) on each file you want to select or move the highlight to the directory listing with Tab, then move the highlight to each file you want to select, and press the Spacebar. The file is selected when its icon is highlighted.*
7. *Click (once) on each selected file to deselect it or move the highlight to the directory listing with Tab, then move the highlight to each selected file to deselect it, and press the Spacebar. The file is deselected when its icon is not highlighted.*

## Viewing the Directory at the Command Prompt

To view a directory from the command prompt, simply enter the command DIR. Figure 2.4 shows an example of the command and the response. The entries have no icons, but they do show the time stamp. The listing is not

```
A:\>DIR

 Volume in drive A has no label
 Volume Serial Number is 2713-2B04
 Directory of  A:\

ASM6-8              87527 03-21-89   12:49p
ASM6-8   DC2         2914 03-21-89   12:48p
ASM8-3               3193 03-24-89    3:18p
ASM8-3   DC2         1384 03-24-89    3:17p
MASM10-2            46599 12-16-88    2:57p
MASM10-2 DC2        14339 12-16-88    2:56p
MASM4-5              6190 06-24-89    1:36p
MASM4-5  DC2         1509 06-24-89    1:36p
MASM8-5              6924 01-10-89    1:19p
MASM8-5  DC2         1518 01-10-89    1:18p
MASM9-2             25798 12-10-88    6:47p
MASM9-3             34808 12-05-88    3:34p
MASM9-3  DC2         9475 12-05-88    3:33p
XTRAFIGS     <DIR>        07-21-89    6:24p
MOUSE    COM        12122 03-10-87    1:31p
SHUTDOWN EXE         1169 04-05-85   11:32a
       16 File(s)        97280 bytes free

A:\>
```

<hr>

Figure 2.4. DIR Command

interactive. You can't scroll it or select files. It's just an informational report.

Unlike the **File System** screen, the DIR command lists the files in the order they appear in the directory, which is not any particular order. Also included in the report are the volume label (the name of the disk), the volume serial number (the serial number of the disk), the directory name, the number of files in the list, and the amount of space left on the disk.

If the directory is too long to fit on the screen, the first entries scroll off the top, perhaps before you can read them. To prevent that, include /P with the DIR command, as in the following example:

```
DIR /P
```

This parameter, which is called a *switch*, causes DOS to display the directory in pages. Figure 2.5 shows the first page of a paged directory listing. At the bottom of each page, you see the message "Press any key to continue . . . ." When you're ready to see the next page, you can press *almost* any key. Some of the control keys that affect the keyboard but don't send signals directly to the computer—such as Ctrl, Alt, Shift, and CapsLock—won't work.

Another way to handle a long directory is with the /W (wide) switch. This displays the filenames and extensions only, side-by-side, as shown in Figure 2.6. You don't get as much information, but you can see up to 110

```
COMMAND  COM      37556 10-06-88   12:00a
CONFIG   SYS         98 06-17-89    1:59p
AUTOEXEC BAK        183 06-21-89    3:12p
DOS            <DIR>     06-16-89    5:28p
MOUSE    COM      12122 03-10-87    1:31p
WP             <DIR>     06-16-89    5:42p
DC             <DIR>     06-16-89    5:59p
NLQ                  9 05-16-89    9:28a
SHUTDOWN EXE       1169 04-05-85   11:32a
VP       BK!         54 06-16-89    7:04p
HSG            <DIR>     06-16-89    6:41p
ASM            <DIR>     06-16-89    6:44p
VENTURA        <DIR>     06-16-89    7:00p
TYPESET        <DIR>     06-16-89    7:00p
AUTOEXEC BAT        130 07-12-89    3:38p
CONFIG   400         68 06-16-89    7:18p
AUTOEXEC 400        155 06-16-89    7:18p
CONFIG   BK!        132 06-16-89    7:24p
VP       BAT         60 06-16-89    7:28p
MOUSE          <DIR>     06-16-89    7:35p
F1-5     SCR       8128 07-13-89    3:05p
HOT            <DIR>     07-14-89    9:09a
ASMTOC   CHP       1118 07-17-89    5:32p
Press any key to continue . . .
```

Figure 2.5. Sample Paged Directory

files on one 25-line screen. For a directory longer than 110 files you can use
/W and /P together. But you really shouldn't have directories that long.
You'll learn how to keep your directories a reasonable length in Chapter 3.

Start at the command prompt.
1. Display a listing of the current directory.
2. If the top of the directory scrolled off screen, display a paged directory.
3. Display a wide directory.

*1. Enter the command:*

    DIR

*2. Enter:*

    DIR /P

*3. Enter:*

    DIR /W

```
C:\WP>DIR /W

 Volume in drive C is DOS400
 Volume Serial Number is 2713-18E1
 Directory of  C:\WP

.                     ..                  WP{WP}US LEX     WP{WP}US THS     WPHELP   FIL
WPHELP2  FIL     WPINFO   EXE     WPRINT1  ALL     WPSMALL  DRS     WYSE700  WPD
X        EXE     FIXBIOS  COM     GENIUS1  WPD     GENIUSZ  WPD     HRF1Z    FRS
HRF6     FRS     IBMAL0   PRS     IBMAL1   PRS     IBMALT   PRS     IBMPROPR PRS
IBPROII  PRS     KEYS     MRS     MULTISNC WPD     MYDICT   LEX     PAKXP108 PRS
PAKXP109 PRS     STANDARD CRS     STANDARD PRS     WP       DRS     WP       EXE
WP       FIL     WP       MRS     WP{WP}   SET     8514A    WPD     ALTA     WPM
ALTB     WPM     ALTC     WPM     ALTD     WPM     ALTF     WPM     ALTI     WPM
ALTJ     WPM     ALTK     WPM     ALTL     WPM     ALTM     WPM     ALTO     WPM
ALTP     WPM     ALTQ     WPM     ALTR     WPM     ALTS     WPM     ALTT     WPM
ALTW     WPM     ALTX     WPM     ALTY     WPM     ALTZ     WPM     WPF16-3  SCR
BRHR15XL PRS     DOS      STY     EGA512   FRS     EGAITAL  FRS     EGASMC   FRS
EGAUND   FRS     EPFX80   PRS     EPGQ3500 PRS     MASMBOOK         DOS4BOOK
WPT      BAT     TEMP             WPF11-3  SCR     WPF13-4  SCR     APLASPLU PRS
WP{WP}US SUP
        71 File(s)   18423808 bytes free

C:\WP>
```

Figure 2.6. Sample Wide Directory

# Copying Files

You can copy files using the shell or the command prompt. In this section, you'll learn how to make a copy of a file within the same directory, giving it another name. Later on, you'll learn how to copy files to other directories.

## Using the Shell

The Copy function is on the **File** menu, as shown in Figure 2.7. When a menu is pulled down, some of the options might appear gray or dim. Those options are not available at this time. Most of the options on the **File** menu are not available if you pull the menu down without selecting a file first. In Figure 2.7, the **Print** option is not available.

One of the options on the **File** menu is **Copy**. To copy a file, first select the file to be copied on the directory list. In the figure, AUTOEXEC.BAK is selected, as you can see by its highlighted icon. When the desired icon is reversed, pull down the **File** menu and select the **Copy** option. (If it's gray, you didn't select a file before pulling down the menu. Release the menu and try again.)

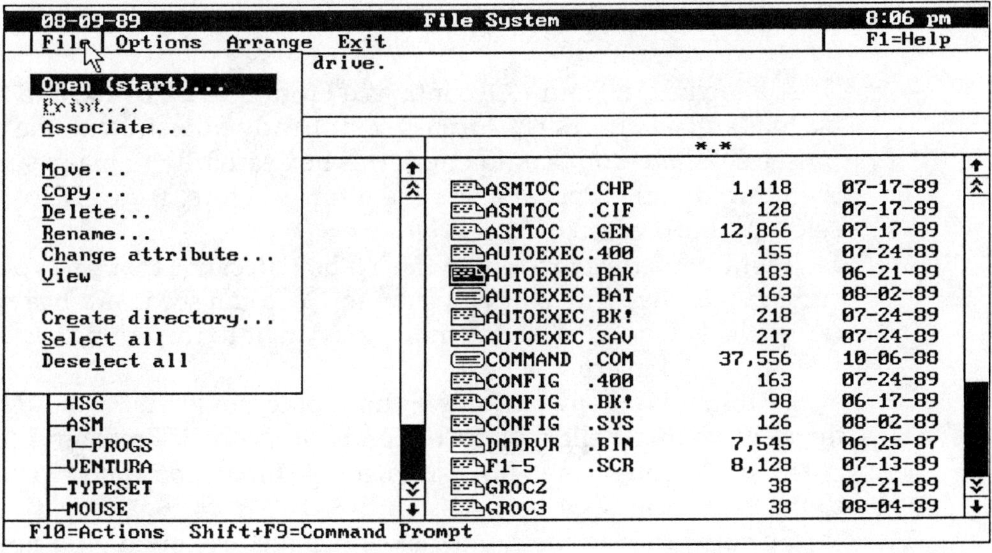

Figure 2.7. File Menu

Notice the three dots after the word "Copy" in the menu. That means DOS needs more information to complete the operation, so DOS gives you a dialog box, as shown in Figure 2.8. The purpose of the dialog box is to collect information. In this case, you must fill in the name of the target file (the file to be created) in order to complete the operation.

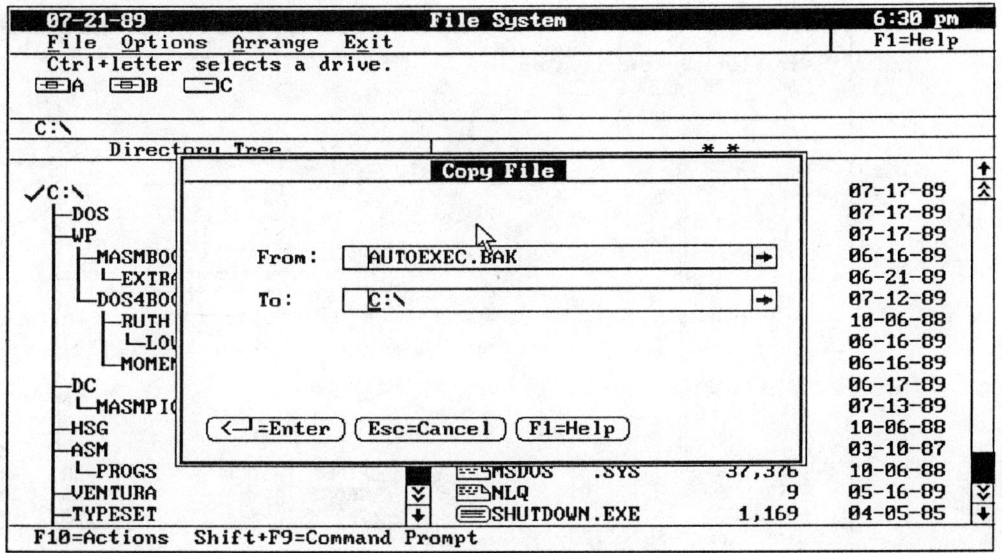

Figure 2.8. Copy File Dialog Box

## Completing Dialog Boxes

The dialog box in Figure 2.8 contains a **From** box, a **To** box, and three action buttons at the bottom. The **From** box is already filled in with the name of the preselected file. You should check this box carefully to make sure that only the desired name appears. (As mentioned before, it's easy to accidentally select multiple files.)

Right now, the cursor is in the **To** box. Because that's a typing box, the cursor takes the form of a typing cursor. You can see it as a heavy underline under the letter "C." You can move the cursor to the **From** box with the Tab key or by clicking on the box.

Within a box, you can move the typing cursor with the left and right arrow keys or by clicking on the ends of the box. Press End to move the cursor to the end of any information already in the box and Home to move it to the beginning.

To copy a file to the same disk and directory, giving it a new name, all you have to do is move the cursor past the default drivename and path (by pressing End), then type the desired new name in the **To** box. If you don't move the cursor first, your typing overtypes the information already in the box, which will cause an error. When the **To** box is correct, select Enter. If you change your mind, select **Cancel** instead of Enter. Figure 2.9 shows the completed dialog box used to make a copy of AUTOEXEC.BAK called C:\AUTOEXEC.OLD. All you have to do is select Enter to make the copy.

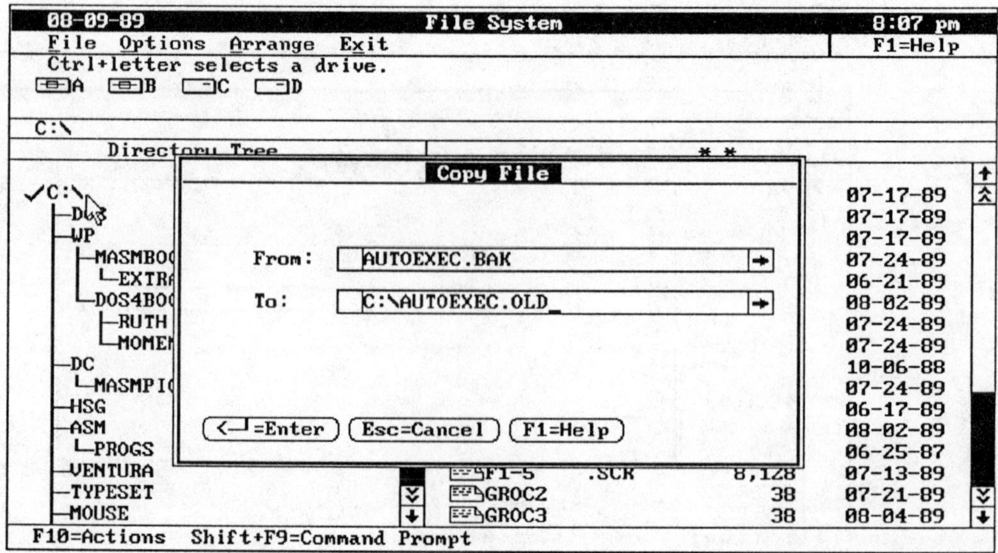


Figure 2.9. Completed Dialog Box

## Overwriting an Existing File

If you enter a filespec that already exists in the target directory, DOS displays the message shown in Figure 2.10. The first line shows the name of the source file. (The message "1 of 1" has meaning when you copy multiple files.) The message doesn't show the target filename that already exists, so you have to remember it.

When you see this message, you have two choices (other than **Help**). You can overwrite the existing file or not. To overwrite it, select item 2, **Replace this file**. To cancel the copy operation for this file, select item 1, **Skip this file and continue**. If you select Enter, the highlighted item takes effect. If you select **Cancel**, the entire copy function is canceled, no matter which item is highlighted.

There are several ways to select an option. You can type the number of the option. You can click on it or move the highlight to it with the arrow keys and select Enter.

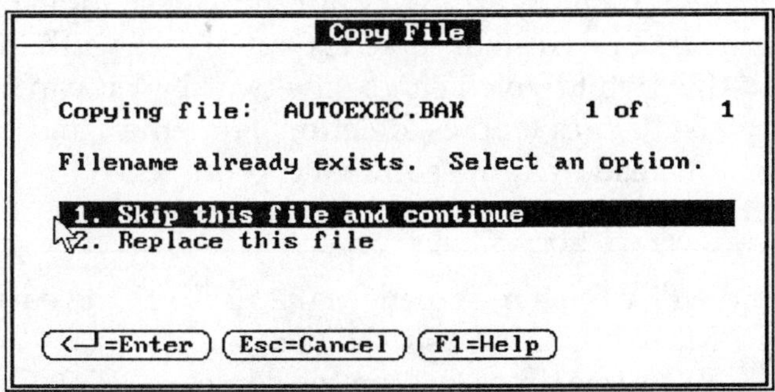


Figure 2.10. Filename Already Exists Message

## Using Commands

The COPY command copies a file. Its format is:

```
COPY source-filespec target-filespec
```

For example, to make a copy of AUTOEXEC.BAK called AUTOEXEC.OLD, you would enter the command shown below. The confirmation message from DOS is also shown.

```
C:\>COPY AUTOEXEC.BAK AUTOEXEC.OLD
   1 File(s) copied
C:\>_
```

The COPY command doesn't warn you about overwrites. If AUTOEXEC.OLD already exists, it is overwritten automatically, with no special messages. If the source file, AUTOEXEC.BAK, doesn't exist, the interaction looks like this:

```
C:\>COPY AUTOEXEC.BAK AUTOEXEC.OLD
File not found - AUTOEXEC.BAK
  0 File(s) copied
C:\>_
```

When you see this message, you have to figure out what you did wrong and try again.

When you create new files at the command prompt and then go back to the **File System** screen, the new files won't show up in the directory listing. When the **File System** first accesses a disk, it reads and stores all the directory and file information from the disk. From then on, it doesn't recognize any changes to the disk or disk directories that it doesn't make itself until it is forced to reread the disk information. (You can force a reread by exiting the **File System**, then restarting it.) But that doesn't mean the changes aren't on the disk. The **File System** screen is out of sync with the real condition of the disk at this point, which can be awkward. You can avoid this situation by making all changes (copies, deletions, renames, and so forth) within the **File System** instead of at the command prompt.

---

Start with the **File System** screen. Make C:\DOS the current directory.
1. Copy COMMAND.COM as COPY1.
2. Copy COPY1 three times, calling the copies COPY2, COPY3, and COPY4.
3. Terminate the shell.
4. At the command prompt, copy COPY1 as COPYA, COPY2 as COPYB, COPY3 as COPYC, and COPY4 as COPYD.

---

1. *Select COMMAND.COM (make sure its icon highlights). Pull down the **File** menu and select the **Copy** option. In the **Copy File** dialog box, press End to move the typing cursor to the end of the **To** box. Add \COPY1 to the path in the **To** box. Select Enter.*
2. *Repeat the procedure in Item 1 for each copy, using the appropriate target filename.*
3. *Press F3 until you see the command prompt.*
4. *Enter these commands:*

```
COPY COPY1 COPYA
```

```
COPY COPY2 COPYB
COPY COPY3 COPYC
COPY COPY4 COPYD
```

## Creating an ASCII File

You can create new files on disk by using the COPY command. The process is awkward, but it's convenient for creating short, simple files. For longer files or more complex files, you'll probably prefer a text editor or word processor.

Figure 2.11 shows a complete example of an interaction that creates a file called GROCLIST. You use this command format:

```
COPY CON target-filespec
```

CON is the DOS name for the keyboard and monitor. When you use CON as a source-filespec, it refers to the keyboard.

After you enter the command, the cursor moves to the beginning of the next line on the screen. You type the first line of your file and press Enter. The cursor moves to the beginning of the next line. You continue typing lines and pressing Enter until you have completed the file. Then you press F6. This types the ^Z symbol you can see in Figure 2.11, which is an end-of-file signal. When you press Enter next, DOS copies the file to the disk and displays the "1 File(s) copied" message.

If you make a typing mistake, backspace and correct it before pressing Enter for that line. Once you have entered a line, there is no way to back up and change it. To make a correction to an earlier line, you would have to

```
C:\>COPY CON GROCLIST
APPLES
PEARS
DOG FOOD
MILK
BREAD
^Z
        1 File(s) copied

C:\>
```

Figure 2.11. Creating a File with COPY CON

start the whole process over again. That's why you should attempt only short, simple files with COPY CON.

Like all COPY commands, this process will overwrite an existing file without warning. As soon as you enter the command, before you start typing lines, the existing file is deleted. Therefore, be sure you get the target-filespec exactly correct before entering a COPY CON command.

COPY CON creates an ASCII text file. That is, every data item in the file is an ASCII code for a letter, number, or symbol. Each line ends with a carriage return symbol followed by a line feed. You'll be able to display and print this file with functions described later in this chapter.

As usual with file operations done at the command prompt, this new file won't show up on the **File System** screen until the **File System** is forced to reread the disk information.

Start at the command prompt. Make sure C:\DOS is the current directory.
1. Create a file called MYDATA containing your name and address on separate lines.
2. Copy MYDATA as MYCOPY.

1. *Enter the command:*

```
COPY CON MYDATA
```

*The cursor will start a new line. Type your name and press Enter. Type your street address and press Enter. Type your city, state, and postal code and press Enter. Press F6 followed by Enter, and DOS will copy your data to disk.*
2. *Enter the command:*

```
COPY MYDATA MYCOPY
```

## Viewing Files

You can display files on your screen through the shell or the command prompt. For the most part, you will limit this function to ASCII text files, which are created by COPY CON, by the nondocument (ASCII) mode of programs such as your word processor, or by a text editor. Examples of non-ASCII files are EXE and COM program files, documents created by a word processor (especially if they are word-wrapped and right-justified), spreadsheets, databases, and graphics.

You can display non-ASCII files using the shell. In regular display mode, garbage (unreadable data) displays on the screen. But you can switch to hex mode, which shows you the contents of each byte as a hexadecimal number. For most DOS users, such a display has no meaning. But many programmers can read and understand the hexadecimal display.

If you try to display a non-ASCII file from the command prompt, garbage will display. The computer will probably beep several times. No harm is done by this, but you won't get any relevant information either.

## Using the Shell

To display a file using the shell, start with the **File System**. Select the desired file, and pull down the **File** menu. The **View** option is available if one (and only one) file is selected. If no files are selected, most of the **File** menu options are gray. In that case, exit the menu and try again. If multiple files are selected, only the **Open** and **View** options are gray. In that case, select **Deselect all** (the last item on the menu). Then try again.

If only one file is selected, the **View** option is available. When you select it, the screen in Figure 2.12 results. The top panel shows general information. The bottom panel shows the file. The key definition line shows options.

If the entire file isn't showing, you can page down and up to see the rest of it. Either press the PgDn and PgUp keys, or click on the PgDn and PgUp icons on the screen. Enter also pages down.

```
 07-21-89                         File System                        6:51 pm
                                                                    F1=Help

                                 File View

      To view a file's content press [PgUp] or [PgDn].

      Viewing file:   C:\GROCLIST


 APPLES
 PEARS
 DOG FOOD
 MILK
 BREAD




 <┘=Enter   Esc=Cancel   F9=Hex/ASCII
```

Figure 2.12. File View Screen

For non-ASCII files, you might want to see the file in hex format, if you know enough to interpret it properly. If you're not a programmer, hex format probably has no meaning to you. Choose the **Hex/ASCII** option to toggle back and forth between hex format and ASCII format. When you're finished viewing the file, select **Cancel** to get back to the regular **File System** screen.

## Using the Command Prompt

To display an ASCII text file using a DOS command, enter the command TYPE followed by the filespec. For example, to view the file named AUTOEXEC.BAT, you would enter TYPE AUTOEXEC.BAT.

If the file won't fit on the screen, it scrolls off the top. You can pause the display by pressing the Pause key (or Ctrl+NumLock if your keyboard doesn't have a Pause key). You can resume it by pressing almost any other key. You can kill the display and get the command prompt back by pressing Ctrl+C or Ctrl+Break. You can't page up and down in the file display in command mode like you can on the **File View** screen. If it scrolls off the top of the screen, its gone. You can TYPE it again if you need to see it. Later on, you'll learn how to display the file one page at a time.

---

Start at the **File System** screen. Make sure C:\DOS is the current directory.
1. View MYDATA.
2. Check your directory for GRAPHICS.PRO or README.TXT. View either one and page through the entire file. (Don't worry about the contents.)
3. Change to the command prompt and view MYDATA.
4. Locate the Pause key on your keyboard.
5. View GRAPHICS.PRO or README.TXT, pausing several times.
6. View GRAPHICS.PRO or README.TXT again, using Ctrl+Break to kill the output.

---

1. *Select MYDATA, making sure no other file is selected. Pull down the **File** menu and select **View**. Select **Cancel** when ready to return to the **File System** screen.*
2. *Press PgDn and PgUp or click on the PgDn and PgUp icons to page through the file.*
3. *Enter the command:*

```
TYPE MYDATA
```

4. *If you have an enhanced keyboard, it's a separate key located in the upper right-hand corner. On other keyboards, you use Ctrl+NumLock for the Pause function.*

*5. Enter:*

    TYPE GRAPHICS.PRO

*or*

    TYPE README.TXT

*Press the Pause key to halt the output; press another key to continue it.*

# Renaming Files

You can change the name of a file by using the rename function, either in the
shell or at the command prompt.

## Using the Shell

To rename a file using the shell, get to the **File System** screen, select the file
in the directory panel, pull down the **File** menu, and select **Rename**. Figure
2.13 shows the dialog box that results.

The current name is shown on the top line. (The "1 of 1" message becomes significant when more than one file has been selected for renaming.)
The typing cursor is in the **New filename** box. All you have to do is type the

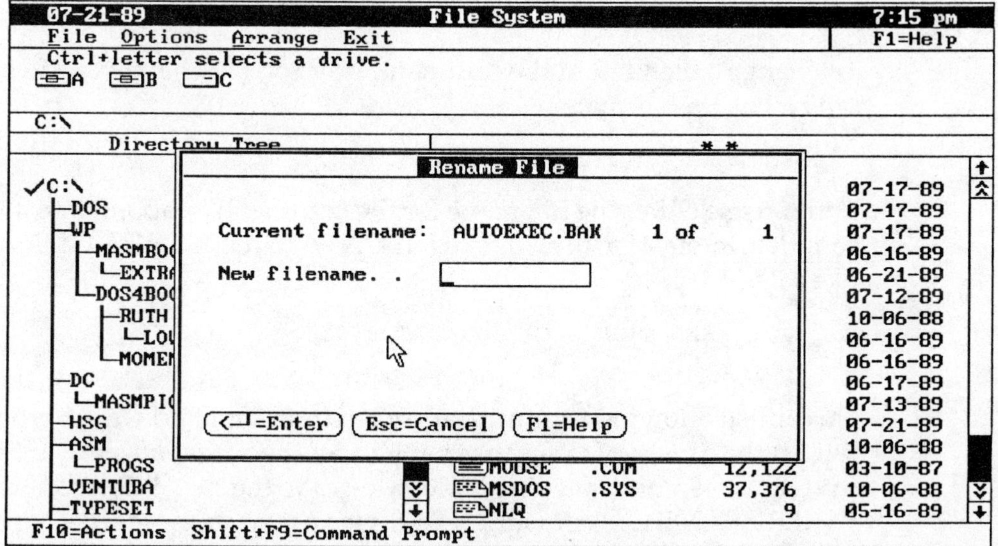

Figure 2.13. Rename File Dialog Box

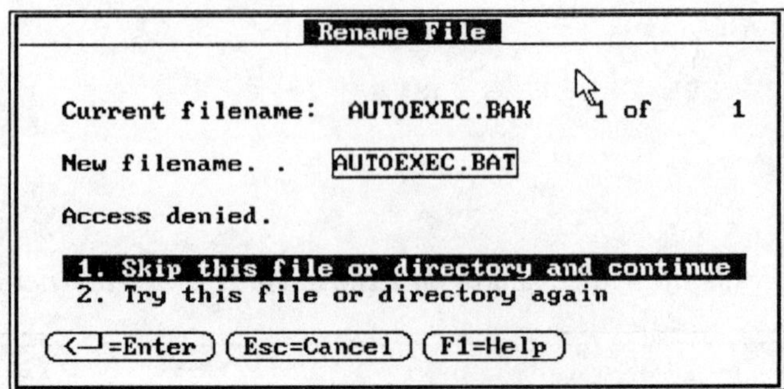


Figure 2.14. Access Denied Message

new filename and extension and select Enter. **Cancel** and **Help** are also available if you need them.

If a file with the new name already exists, an error message and options are added to the dialog box. Figure 2.14 shows the result. If you want to cancel the rename function, select the first option. If you want to enter another new name, select Option 2, **Try this file or directory again**. The dialog box returns to its initial status, as shown in Figure 2.13.

When the rename function works correctly, you see no confirmation message. However, you can see the changed name in the directory panel of the **File System** screen.

## Using the Command Prompt

To change a filename at the command prompt, use the RENAME command, which has this format:

```
REN[AME] current-filespec new-filespec
```

You can use either the full name for the command or abbreviate it to REN. A complete interaction to change JUNEDATA to JUNEDATA.OLD would look like this:

```
C:\>REN JUNEDATA JUNEDATA.OLD
C:\>_
```

No confirmation message appears when the command works properly. You can list the directory to see the changed filespec. It won't show up in the **File System** screen until the **File System** rereads the disk information.

If RENAME doesn't work, you'll see an error message. Perhaps the most common error message is "Duplicate file name or file not found." You'll see this message if the current-filespec doesn't exist, if the new-filespec exists, or both. (The problem is frequently a typo.) If you accidentally omit one or both filespecs, you'll see the message "Required parameter missing."

Start at the **File System** screen. Make sure C:\DOS is the current directory.
1. Rename MYDATA as MYADDR.
2. Rename MYCOPY as MYRENAME.
3. Terminate the shell.
4. Rename COPYA through COPYD as RECOPYA through RECOPYD.

*1. Select MYDATA, pull down the **File** menu, and select **Rename**. In the resulting dialog box, type MYADDR in the **New Filename** box.*
*2. Select MYCOPY, pull down the **File** menu, and select **Rename**. In the resulting dialog box, type MYRENAME in the **New Filename** box.*
*3. Press F3 until the command prompt appears.*
*4. Enter these commands:*

```
REN COPYA RECOPYA
REN COPYB RECOPYB
REN COPYC RECOPYC
REN COPYD RECOPYD
```

# Deleting Files

You can delete a file using the shell or the command prompt. The delete function doesn't really erase the file from the disk. It simply marks the directory entry for reuse. The data is not erased until another file uses the space.

Everyone occasionally deletes the wrong file. Unfortunately, DOS doesn't offer an undelete function. Once deleted, a file is virtually gone, even though the data might still be on the disk. You can buy utility programs that will undelete a file (by reestablishing the original directory entry). If you don't have one of those programs, be very careful when deleting files.

## Using the Shell

The shell takes a cautious approach to deleting files. You must confirm the deletion twice before it takes place. To begin, get to the **File System** screen and select the file to be deleted. Then pull down the **File** menu and select **Delete**. Figure 2.15 shows the dialog box that results.

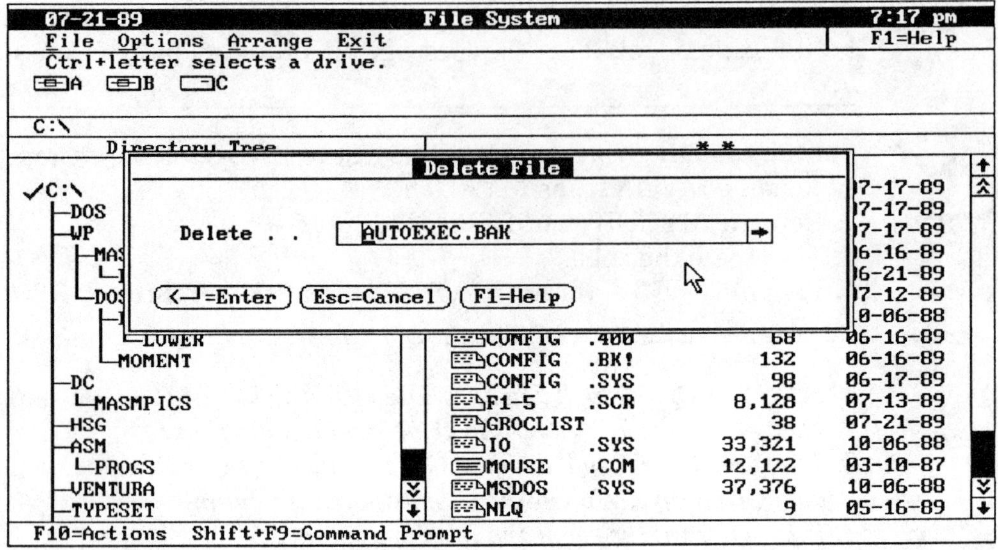

Figure 2.15. Delete File Dialog Box

When you're satisfied that the name is correct, select Enter. **Cancel** and **Help** are also available if you need them. Figure 2.16 shows the message that results when you select Enter.

Here again, check the filespec. If you really want to delete the file, you must specifically select Option 2. If you just press Enter without selecting Option 2, the function is canceled, since Option 1 is the default.

As a reminder, to select an option, you can just type the number of the option. Alternatively, you can click on it or highlight it and press Enter.

When you confirm the deletion, it takes place with no confirmation message. For confirmation, check the directory panel on the **File System** screen.

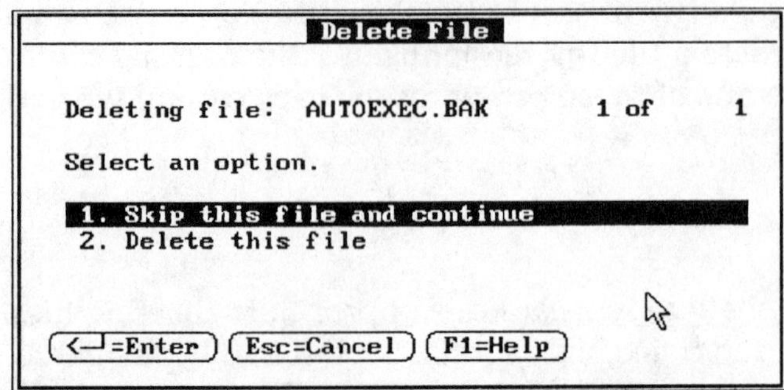

Figure 2.16. Confirm Deletion Message

## Using the Command Prompt

To delete a file from the command prompt, enter the DEL command, which has this format:

```
DEL filespec          (ERASE is a synonym for DEL)
```

A complete interaction to delete a file named DODGERS.ART looks like this:

```
C:\>DEL DODGERS.ART
C:\>_
```

No message appears when the deletion is successful. The "File not found" message means no file named DODGERS.ART is in the current directory.

## Protected Files

A file can be protected from being deleted or changed. You'll learn how to protect and unprotect files in Chapter 5. However, if you try to delete a protected file, you'll see the message "Access denied." Then you must either unprotect the file or change your mind about deleting it. You cannot delete it as long as it is protected.

Start at the **File System** screen. Make sure C:\DOS is the current directory.
1. Delete MYRENAME.
2. Delete COPY1.
3. Terminate the shell.
4. Delete RECOPYA and RECOPYB.

1. *Select MYRENAME, pull down the **File** menu, select **Delete**. Make sure the resulting dialog box shows only MYRENAME as the file to be deleted. Select Enter. In the next dialog box, select Option 2, **Delete this file**.*
2. *Select COPY1, pull down the **File** menu, select **Delete**. Make sure the resulting dialog box shows only COPY1 as the file to be deleted. Select Enter. In the next dialog box, select Option 2, **Delete this file**.*
3. *Use F3.*
4. *Enter these commands:*

```
DEL RECOPYA
DEL RECOPYB
```

# *Working with Multiple Files*

Most of the functions you have learned in this chapter can be performed on multiple files. With the command prompt, you must use a global filespec. In the shell, all you have to do is select as many files as you want to copy, erase, rename, or delete. To see which files are selected, look for highlighted icons. If scrolling is available, you might want to check all pages to make sure you know which files have been selected.

## *Global Filespecs*

A global filespec identifies one or more files by using wildcard characters. A question mark (?) stands for a single wildcard character while an asterisk (*) stands for any number of wildcard characters.

Suppose you want to select all files with the name JUNEDATA and any extension. You could use the filename JUNEDATA.*. This would select JUNEDATA.1, JUNEDATA.2, JUNEDATA.OLD, and JUNEDATA.PD. It also selects JUNEDATA (with a blank extension) since blanks match the wild-card character.

Suppose you want to select only JUNEDATA, JUNEDATA.1, and JUNEDATA.2. You would use the global filename JUNEDATA.?, which matches all the JUNEDATA files that have only one character in the exten-sion; the other two characters must be blank. Of course, since a blank matches a wildcard character, a completely blank extension also matches.

You can use one or more question marks in the middle of a filespec, but asterisks can appear only at the end of the filename or extension. ????DATA.?, JUNE?ATA.?, and JUNE*.1* are all legitimate global filespecs, but *DATA.*1 is not.

You can combine question marks and asterisks in one global filespec as needed. JUNE*.?, ????DATA.*, and ?X*.* are all legitimate filespecs.

Completely global filespecs can be expressed as ????????.??? or *.*. Each selects every filespec.

This checkpoint requires paper and pencil only.
1. Write a filespec to select all files with extension DAT.
2. Write a filespec to select all files whose filenames start with any four characters and end with JUDI.
3. Write a filespec to select all files.

*1. The simplest answer is *.DAT.*
*2. The simplest answer is ????JUDI.*.*
*3. The simplest answer is *.*.*

***Global Filespecs with DIR***   If you include a filespec with the DIR command, only the files that match that filespec are listed. For example, suppose you want to see a listing only of COM files. You could enter this command:

```
DIR *.COM
```

If no files are selected by the filespec, then you will see the "File not found" message.

If you want to find out whether a single file exists in the directory, you can enter a specific filespec. For example, to find out whether JUNEDATA.1 exists in the current directory, you could enter this command:

```
DIR JUNEDATA.1
```

If the file is listed in the response, it exists. If not, you will see the message "File not found."

***Global Filespecs with DEL***   To delete multiple files in one operation, include a global filespec with the DEL command. The following interaction deletes all BAK files in the current directory:

```
C:\>DEL *.BAK
C:\>_
```

You can see that no confirmation message appears. You don't really know the individual names of the files that were deleted, which can be a problem. You know that at least one file was erased because the "File not found" message did not appear. If any selected files were protected, they were not erased. No "Access denied" message is displayed, however. For deleting multiple files, the shell method is safer and more reliable.

To delete all files in a directory, use the *.* filespec. In this case, DOS does ask for confirmation. Here's what the interaction looks like:

```
C:\>DEL *.*
All files in directory will be deleted!
Are you sure (Y/N)?Y
C:\>_
```

Enter an N to cancel the deletion. Enter a Y to confirm it, as shown in the example. Again, you get no confirmation messages. The shell Delete function is safer, if slower.

***Global Filespecs with Other Commands***   You cannot TYPE multiple files, so you cannot use a global filespec with the TYPE command. You can use global filespecs with COPY, but the target must be a device or a directory. You'll learn how to use directories in the next chapter. You can do a global rename but the results can be unexpected. It's safer to rename multiple files with the shell.

## Selecting Multiple Files in the Shell

If you select more than one file, any file operation you choose applies to all the selected files. You can select multiple files by selecting each one individually, or by pulling down the **File** menu and selecting **Select All**. To deselect all selected files, pull down the **File** menu and select **Deselect All**.

One advantage of selecting multiple files in the shell over global filenames with the command prompt is that the filespecs you select don't have to fit a pattern. For example, you can delete JUDI.DAT, RUTH.HLP, and PAULGAME.DOC in one operation.

***Deleting Multiple Files***   When you select **Delete** with multiple files selected, the **Delete File** dialog box lists all the files you have selected. Figure 2.17 shows an example. If the whole list doesn't show in the box, you can scroll through it by moving the typing cursor.

When you select Enter, confirmation options are shown for each file to be deleted. This gives you a chance to change your mind about each file. If you have used the **Select all** feature, you can also eliminate specific files from the group deletion. For example, suppose you want to delete all but MYDATA. You could pull down the **File** menu and select the **Select all** function. Then start the delete operation. For every filename except MYDATA, you would confirm the deletion. When you get to MYDATA, choose the **Skip this file and continue** option. DOS skips MYDATA and shows you the next filename to be deleted.

If you select **Cancel** instead of **Skip this file and continue**, the entire deletion operation is canceled. That is, no more files are deleted.

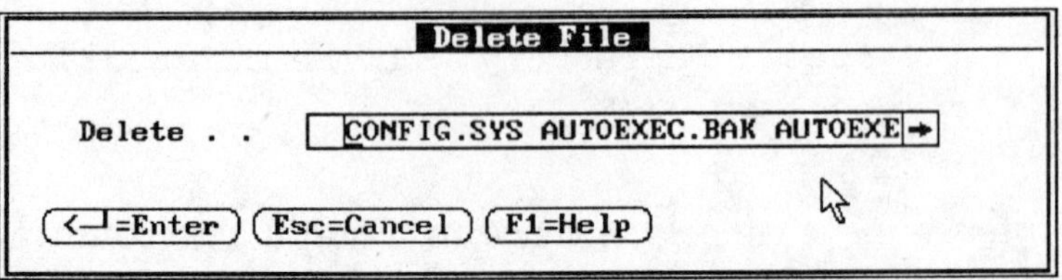


Figure 2.17. Deleting Multiple Files

*Renaming Multiple Files*    When you select the **Rename** option with multiple files selected, a dialog box asks for the new name of each file in turn.

*Other Multiple File Operations*    You can't view multiple files. However, you can copy multiple files; you'll learn how in the next chapter.

Start at the **File System** screen. Make sure C:\DOS is the current directory.
1. Rename COPY2 through COPY4 as RECOPY2 through RECOPY4.
2. Delete RECOPY2 through RECOPY4.

1. *Select COPY2, COPY3, and COPY4, making sure their icons highlight. Pull down the **File** menu and select **Rename**. You will see a dialog box for each selected file. Fill in the **New filename** box and select Enter for each of the files.*
2. *Select RECOPY2, RECOPY3, and RECOPY4, making sure their icons highlight. Pull down the **File** menu and select **Delete**. Check the names in the dialog box; if they are correct, select Enter. Then select Option 2 for each file.*

# Printing Data

DOS offers several ways to print information. You can copy a file to the printer, print the screen, or echo print all your command interactions. There is also a Print function, which you will learn about in a later chapter.

## COPYing to Print

You can use the COPY command to copy an ASCII text file to the printer. All you have to do is use PRN as the target-filespec. To print GROCLIST, for example, you could enter this command:

```
COPY GROCLIST PRN
```

You can use a global filespec for the source-filespec to print more than one file this way, as in:

```
COPY MAIL*.* PRN
```

This would print all files that start with MAIL and have any extension. Copying to PRN works at the command prompt only. If you enter PRN in the **To** box of the **Copy File** dialog box, DOS displays an error message.

## Screen Prints

You can print whatever is showing on the command prompt screen by pressing the PrtSc key, which might need the Shift key too, depending on your keyboard. PrtSc copies a text (nongraphics) screen, such as the command prompt screen, to the printer.

In some cases, you can also copy a graphics screen, such as the DosShell screens, to the printer. First, your printer must have graphics capabilities. Most dot-matrix, inkjet, and laser printers do; most letter-quality (impact) printers don't. Second, you must start up a program called GRAPHICS. You can start it up by entering just the command GRAPHICS, but if it produces unsatisfactory output, then you need to read about the command options in your DOS reference manual. If these conditions are met, you can print graphics screens by pressing the PrtSc key.

## Echo Printing

Echo printing is another form of printing available at the command prompt. Once you turn echo printing on by pressing Ctrl+PrtSc, all lines displayed on the monitor are also printed. Echo printing continues until you turn it off by pressing Ctrl+PrtSc again or by rebooting. It is suspended when you go to the shell, but resumed if you return to the command prompt.

Start at the command prompt. Make sure C:\DOS is the current directory.
1. Make sure your printer is ready.
2. Print MYADDR.
3. Print the screen.
4. Turn on echo printing.
5. View MYADDR on the screen.
6. Turn off echo printing.
7. View MYADDR again.

1. *The power should be on, the cable should be connected tightly at both ends, and paper and ribbon should be installed. If your printer has an online/local feature (sometimes called select/deselect), make sure it's online. Some advanced printers, such as Postscript printers, also need to be placed in DOS mode or a compatibility mode before they can receive data from DOS.*
2. *Enter the command:*

```
COPY MYADDR PRN
```

*(A laser printer might need some preparation time before printing the page, so give it a couple minutes.)*
*3. Press PrtSc or Shift+PrtSc.*
*4. Press Ctrl+PrtSc once. (You won't see any evidence that it is on.)*
*5. Enter the command:*

```
TYPE MYADDR
```

*It should both display and print.*
*6. Press Ctrl+PrtSc once.*
*7. Enter the command:*

```
TYPE MYADDR
```

*It should display only, not print.*

# Summary

In this chapter you have learned how to handle basic file operations with both the shell and the command prompt. You now can create, view, copy, rename, print, and delete files. In the next chapter, you'll learn how to do many of these same operations with directories.

# Exercises

These exercises give you a chance to practice and reinforce the file-handling techniques you have learned in this chapter.

| **What You Should Do** | **How the Computer Responds** |
| --- | --- |
| 1. Start at the **File System** screen. Select the DOS directory. | 1. Displays the **File System** screen with the DOS directory listed. |
| 2. Copy the three files named CHKDSK.COM, COMMAND.COM, and FORMAT.COM as EX1, EX2, and EX3. (You'll have to do three separate copy functions to accomplish this; if you select them all at once, DOS won't let you supply new names.) | 2. For each copy operation you start, displays the **Copy File** dialog box and copies the file as directed. |
| 3. Rename EX1, EX2, and EX3 as SUM1, SUM2, and SUM3. | 3. Displays the **Rename File** dialog box and renames the files as directed. |

4. Delete SUM1, SUM2, and SUM3.

4. Displays the **Delete File** dialog box and deletes the files as directed.

5. View GRAPHICS.PRO or README.TXT.

5. Displays the selected file on a file viewing screen.

6. Terminate the shell.

6. Returns to the command prompt screen.

7. Turn on echo printing.

7. Obeys your command but does not display any acknowledgment.

8. Get a directory listing of all files with extension CPI.

8. Displays and echo prints a listing of all files that match the global filespec.

9. Turn off echo printing.

9. Obeys your command but does not display any acknowledgment.

10. Create an ASCII text file named EXLIST. In it, list your three favorite books.

10. Stores your keystrokes until you enter the line containing ^Z. Then copies the file to disk.

11. Copy EXLIST as COPYLIST.

11. Copies the file as directed.

12. Rename EXLIST as BOOKLIST.

12. Renames the file as directed, but does not acknowledge it.

13. View BOOKLIST.

13. Displays the file on the screen.

14. Print the screen.

14. Prints the current screen.

15. Copy BOOKLIST to the printer.

15. Prints the file as directed.

16. Delete COPYLIST.

16. Deletes the file as directed.

## *What If It Doesn't Work?*

1. If any command results in an "Access denied" message, the target file is write-protected. Ignore it and go on.

2. If the printer won't work, it probably isn't set up correctly. If earlier printing activities you followed in this chapter worked, then check the power and the cable. If you have never succeeded in printing something with DOS, get some expert help.

3. If the file displays but doesn't echo print when it is supposed to, you probably didn't turn echo printing on successfully. Remember to press Ctrl+PrtSc just once.

4. If the Rename function results in the message "Duplicate file name or file not found," you probably had a typo in the command. Check the command and try again.

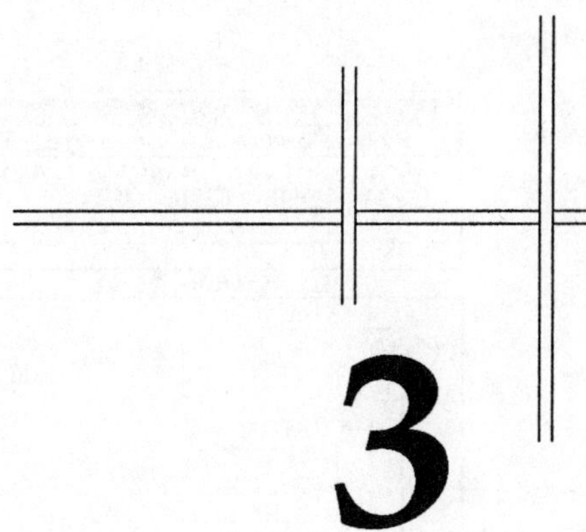

# 3

# Basic Directory Operations

A high-density diskette holds hundreds of files; a fixed disk might hold thousands. Imagine trying to work with a single directory holding that many files. Fortunately, you can divide directories into as many subdirectories as needed to keep them all at manageable sizes. In this chapter, you will learn to:

- Change drives
- Create directories
- Change directories
- Rename directories
- Remove directories
- Access files in other directories
- Access programs in other directories
- Copy files to other directories

## Changing Drives

At any given time, one of your drives is the *default drive*. This is where DOS looks for files and stores new files when you don't specify a drivename in the filespec. Immediately after booting, the boot drive usually becomes the default drive.

You can see the default drive on the **File System** screen shown in Figure 3.1. The default drive and directory are shown just above the **Directory Tree**

```
┌──────────────────────────────────────────────────────────────────────────┐
│ 08-02-89                      File System                      2:29 pm     │
│ File  Options  Arrange  Exit                              │ F1=Help        │
│ Ctrl+letter selects a drive.                                               │
│ ▭A   ▭B   ▭C   ▭D                            ▷                             │
│                                                                            │
│ C:\                                                                        │
│      Directory Tree                              *.*                        │
│                                                                            │
│ ✓C:                      ANSI     .SYS     37,376   10-06-88               │
│   ─DOS                   ASMTOC   .CHP      1,118   07-17-89               │
│   ─DB                    ASMTOC   .CIF        128   07-17-89               │
│     ─CUSTOMER            ASMTOC   .GEN     12,866   07-17-89               │
│       ─DETROIT           AUTOEXEC.BAT        128   07-17-89               │
│       ─TOLEDO            COMMAND  .COM     37,556   10-06-88               │
│       ─OTHER             CONFIG   .SYS        126   08-02-89               │
│     ─INV                 DMDRVR   .BIN      7,545   06-25-87               │
│     ─SALES               F1-5     .SCR      8,128   07-13-89               │
│     ─SUPPLIER            IO       .SYS     33,321   10-06-88               │
│     ─EMPLOYEE            LASER    .BAT         38   07-21-89               │
│   ─WP                    MOUSE    .COM     12,122   03-10-87               │
│   ─CAD                   MSDOS    .SYS     37,376   10-06-88               │
│     ─ARCHITEC            NLQ                   9   05-16-89               │
│       ─TURNER.HOM        SHUTDOWN .EXE      1,169   04-05-85               │
│       ─ACME.OFC          VP       .BAT         60   06-16-89               │
│ F10=Actions   Shift+F9=Command Prompt                                      │
└──────────────────────────────────────────────────────────────────────────┘
```

Figure 3.1. Sample File System Screen

panel. In the example in Figure 3.1, C: is the default drive. You can also see the default drive in the **Directory Tree** panel itself if the top of the tree (the root directory) is showing. On the command prompt screen, the default drive appears in the command prompt.

When you are using the **File System**, changing the default drive changes the information in the **Directory Tree** and directory panels. You might want to do this to find out what is on a drive and to execute file and directory operations on the new drive. With the command prompt, you might want to change to a different drive to access the programs and files on that drive.

## Using the Shell

To change the default drive in the shell, get to the **File System** screen. Then all you have to do is select the desired drive icon. The easiest way is to click on it. If you don't use a mouse, tab to the drive panel. Then you can select the desired drive by pressing Ctrl plus the desired letter, as in Ctrl+A or Ctrl+C. You can also move the highlight to the desired drive icon with the arrow keys and press Enter.

When you change the drive, you'll see that the default drivename and path, the **Directory Tree** panel, and the directory panel all change. DOS might have to take the time to read the disk before it can display the information.

## *Using the Command Prompt*

You can change drives at the command prompt by entering the drivename of the desired drive, being sure to include the colon at the end. Suppose you booted from fixed disk. You can switch to drive A: like this:

```
C:\>A:
A:\>_
```

To switch back to C:, you would do this:

```
A:\>C:
C:\>_
```

If you forget the colon, DOS will look for a program file named A, B, C, or whatever and will likely display the message "Bad command or filename."

You don't have to switch to a drive to access the files on it. You can include the drivename in the filespec. The following command displays the file named CORREGE.DOC from the default directory on drive A: even though drive C: is the default drive:

```
C:\>TYPE A:CORREGE.DOC
```

With some commands, if you specify just a drivename instead of a filespec, all the files in the default directory of that drive are implied. For example, to see a listing of the default directory of drive D:, you could enter this command:

```
C:\>DIR D:
```

To delete all files from the default directory of drive A: you could use this command:

```
C:\>DEL A:
```

# *Tree-Structured Directories*

Figure 3.2 illustrates the type of directory structure possible with DOS. At the top is the root directory, which is automatically placed on every disk when it is formatted for use. The root directory can contain files of its own (listed inside the box) and subdirectories (connected to the box). Each subdirectory can also contain files and subdirectories. The total structure of directories on a disk is called a *directory tree* because the subdirectories branch out from the root directory and themselves branch into subdirectories.

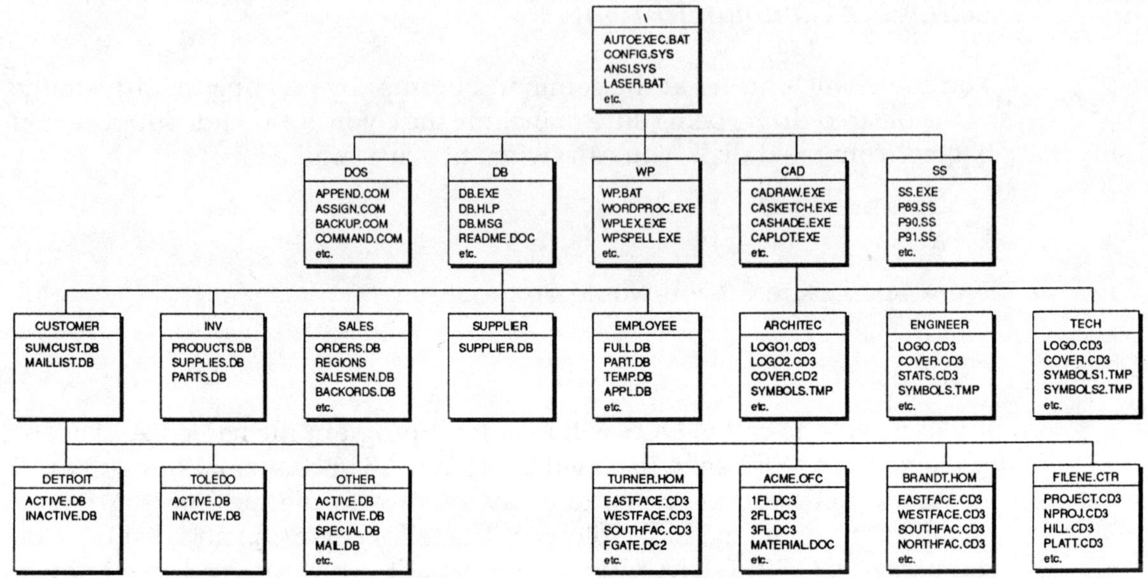


Figure 3.2. Sample Directory Tree

A tree contains several *subtrees*. A subtree is a tree starting at a nonroot directory. For example, the subtree headed by CAD includes ARCHITEC, ENGINEER, TECH, TURNER.HOM, ACME.OFC, BRANDT.HOM, and FILENE.CTR. The relationships among directories are often described in family terms. CAD is the parent of ARCHITEC. ARCHITEC is the child of CAD.

There is no limit to the number of directories or the number of directory levels on a disk except the size of the disk itself. However, you don't want to go down too many levels, as it makes the filespec too long.

Most people set up their tree structures so that each directory contains a meaningful subset of files, much like a separate diskette would. Each major application—database, word processor, spreadsheet, CAD, music sequencer—might have its own directory. You might also have directories for DOS programs, other sets of utilities, and a personal directory for each user of the computer. Under the database directory, you might have a separate directory for each major application of the database—customers, suppliers, inventory, and employees, for example. The same is true for the other application-oriented directories.

It is wise to plan the structure of a fixed disk directory tree in advance, rather than let it grow like Topsy. Once you have created directories and added files and subdirectories to them, it's difficult (but not impossible) to change the structure.

## Paths

A path tells DOS how to find a directory containing a desired file. The path lists all the directories DOS must go through to get to the desired directory. The following filespec contains a path:

```
\CAD\ARCHITEC\TURNER.HOM\SOUTHFAC.CD3
```

The final element in the filespec names the file, in this case SOUTHFAC.CD3. Everything preceding it is the path. The initial backslash (\) is the name of the root directory. Every root directory is automatically named \; you cannot change it. All the other backslashes connect the various elements in the path.

The above path is called an *absolute path* because it starts at the root directory. It will work no matter which directory you are currently in (called the *current* directory). If the desired directory is in the subtree branching out from the current directory, then you can access it with a *relative path*. Suppose that CAD is the current directory. Then you could access SOUTHFAC.CD3with this filespec:

```
ARCHITEC\TURNER.HOM\SOUTHFAC.CD3
```

Notice that the relative path does not start with a backslash. Therefore, DOS starts at the current directory instead of at the root directory.

Two special directory names are a single period (.) and a double period (..). The single period indicates the current directory and the double period indicates its parent. You will see these two directory names in every DIR command listing except for the root directory.

The double period can come in handy in relative paths when you want to reach a directory that's somewhere else in the parent's subtree. For example, suppose you are in ARCHITEC and want to reach a file in ENGINEER. You could use this filespec:

```
..\ENGINEER\LANDCDAM.DC2
```

The initial double period tells DOS to start with the current directory's parent. This is the only time a relative path can go upward in a tree.

If you get a path wrong, you will see this message: "Path not found." Many people get confused about absolute and relative paths at first. But after a while, specifying paths will come naturally.

---

This checkpoint requires paper and pencil only. Use Figure 3.2 and assume that the current directory is \DB\CUSTOMER.
1. Write the filespec to access AUTOEXEC.BAT in the root directory.

2. Write the filespec to access TEMP.DB in the EMPLOYEE directory.
3. Write the filespec to access ACTIVE.DB in the directory TOLEDO.
4. Write the filespec to access FGATE.DC2 in the TURNER.HOM directory.

---

1. *The filespec must start with a backslash:* \AUTOEXEC.BAT.
2. *You could use an absolute path:* \DB\EMPLOYEE\TEMP.DB. *But all you need is a relative path:* ..\EMPLOYEE\TEMP.DB.
3. *The filespec with an absolute path would be:*
     \DB\CUSTOMER\TOLEDO\ACTIVE.DB
   *The filespec with a relative path would be:*
     TOLEDO\ACTIVE.DB
4. *You need an absolute path to reach this file:*
     \CAD\ARCHITEC\TURNER.HOM\FGATE.DC2

# Viewing the Directory Structure

You can view the directory structure on the **File System** screen or with the TREE command.

## Using the Shell

Refer back to Figure 3.1 for an example of the **File System** screen. You can see the directory structure in the left-hand panel, labeled the **Directory Tree** panel. The structure is depicted graphically, with lines indicating parent-child relationships. For example, you can see that SUPPLIER is a child of DB, which in turn is a child of the root directory. If the entire structure doesn't fit in the panel, you can scroll to see the rest of it.

## Using the Command Prompt

The TREE command reports the directory structure, displaying a tree similar to the one in the **Tree** window. Figure 3.3 shows a sample interaction. The format of the command is:

```
TREE [drive][path] [/F]
```

If you don't include a drivename or path, the subtree branching downward

```
C:\CAD>TREE
Volume Serial Number is 2713-9212
Directory PATH listing for Volume HARD WORK
C:.
├───ARCHITEC
│       ├───TURNER.HOM
│       ├───ACME.OFC
│       ├───BRANDT.HOM
│       └───FILENE.CTR
├───ENGINEER
│       ├───ACTIVE
│       ├───1990
│       ├───1989
│       ├───1988
│       └───PROPS
└───TECH

C:\CAD>_
```

Figure 3.3. TREE Command

from the current directory is reported, as in the example in Figure 3.3. If you want to see a different subtree, include the path to the top directory of the tree you want to see. For example, suppose the current directory is ARCHITEC and you want to see the subtree starting at WP. You would enter this command:

```
TREE \WP
```

You can also get a tree for a different drive, as shown in these commands:

```
TREE A:
TREE D:\JUDIF
```

To see the tree for the entire disk, either switch to the root directory before issuing the TREE command or use the name of the root directory (\) as the path, as in this command:

```
TREE \
```

The /F switch causes all files to be listed for each directory in the tree. This is not a complete file entry, as the DIR command provides, just the name of the file. It's one way to find a file when you can't remember which directory you put it in. The beginning of a TREE /F interaction is shown below:

```
C:\NOVEL>TREE /F
```

```
Directory PATH listing for Volume DOS400
Volume Serial Number is 2713-18E1

C:.
    CHAP02
    APPENDA
    OUTLINE
    CHAP02.BK!
    ┌──PRACTICE
    │     NEWFILE.ORG
    │     ANOTHER
    │     NEW2
    │
    └─────TEST
    │         OLD1
    │         OLD2
    │         CRASH.DOC
    └──MOMENT
    │     TIME.FRM
    │     DATE.FRM
```

Notice the name of the directory at the head of the subtree. Rather than show the real name of the directory, DOS uses the . name to indicate that the current directory heads the subtree being shown.

The TREE output might scroll off the screen, especially when you include the /F switch. You can pause it with the Pause key, and then resume by pressing almost any other key. You can print the output by turning Echo Print on (Ctrl+PrtSc) before you enter the TREE command. You can interrupt and kill the output with Ctrl+Break.

# Internal and External Commands

All the commands you have used so far are *internal* commands. That means they are built into the DOS command processor, COMMAND.COM. When you boot DOS, internal commands are loaded into memory, where they stay the entire time DOS runs. Whenever you enter one of the internal commands, the program is immediately available.

TREE is an *external* command. It has its own program file called TREE.COM in the DOS directory. Every time you enter a TREE command, the program must be loaded into memory from TREE.COM. In other words, the program is not saved in memory; if you use it five times in one session, DOS must load it five times.

If the SELECT program installed DOS on your hard disk, DOS can find its own external programs in the C:\DOS directory. In other situations, you might have trouble using external commands such as TREE. If you see the message "Bad command or file name," DOS couldn't find the necessary program file. Chapter 11 explains how to enter a PATH command so DOS can find program files. Appendix A contains information about installing DOS, and Appendix B contains information about working with a diskette-only system. This book assumes from here on that DOS has been set up to find its own files in the C:\DOS directory.

Start with the **File System** screen.
1. Examine the tree structure of the default drive in the **Directory Tree** panel. Scroll if necessary to see the entire structure. Select the **Command Prompt**.
2. Display the tree structure headed by the current directory.
3. If it scrolled off the screen, try again using the Pause key to control it.
4. Display the current tree structure with filenames included. Use the Pause key to control the display.
5. Display the tree structure for the entire disk.
6. Turn on echo printing and display the entire tree structure again.
7. Turn off echo printing.

*1. If you have a mouse, click on the up and down icons to scroll the **Directory Tree** panel. If you don't have a mouse, move the cursor to the **Directory Tree** panel with the Tab key, then press the up and down arrow keys and PgUp and PgDn to scroll.*

*2. Enter the command:*

```
TREE
```

*3. Press Pause to halt the output; press another key to resume it.*

*4. Enter the command:*

```
TREE /F
```

*5. Enter the command:*

```
TREE \
```

*6. Press Ctrl+PrtSc once, then enter the command:*

```
TREE \
```

*7. Press Ctrl+PrtSc once.*

# *Creating Directories*

You can create directories using either the shell or the command prompt. A directory name follows the same rules as a filespec. A directory name must be unique within the parent directory; it cannot duplicate either another directory name or a filespec.

## *Using the Shell*

To create a directory using the shell, get to the **File System** screen and select the intended parent in the **Directory Tree** panel. Then pull down the **File** menu and select **Create directory**. A dialog box asks for the name of the new directory. Fill it in and select Enter. You will see the new directory added to the **Directory Tree** panel.

If the name you entered duplicates either a filespec or another directory name in the same parent, you will see the "Access denied" message added to the dialog box, as shown in Figure 3.4. Select Option 1 if you want to cancel the function, perhaps so that you can select a different parent directory. The **File System** screen will return. Select Option 2 if you want to enter a different name for the new directory. The message will be removed from the dialog box and you can enter another name in the typing box.

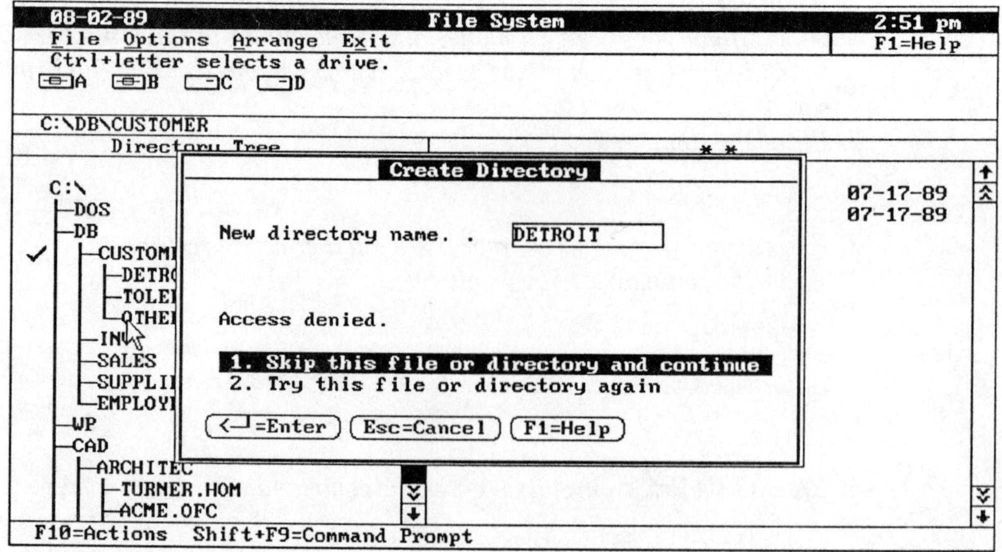



Figure 3.4. Access Denied Message

## Using the Command Prompt

The MKDIR command creates a new directory. Its format is:

```
MKDIR [drive][path]name     (MKDIR can be abbreviated MD)
```

If you omit the drivename and path, the current directory becomes the parent of the new directory. For example, to add ACME.OFC as a child of the current directory, you would enter this command:

```
MD ACME.OFC
```

If you want to add the new directory to some other parent, specify the drivename and/or path of the parent. The following adds a directory to the root:

```
MD \JONATHON
```

The following command adds a directory under \WP\NOVEL:

```
MD \WP\NOVEL\NOTES
```

The following adds a directory under the default directory of drive A:

```
MD A:NOVEL.BAK
```

DOS displays no message when the command succeeds. The message "Directory already exists" means that the new directory name matches an existing name in the intended parent. The message "Unable to create directory" probably means the new directory name matches a filespec in the intended parent. In either case, check the directory structure to pinpoint the problem.

Start at the **File System** screen. Make sure C:\ is the current directory.
1. Create a directory named PRAC1.
2. Under PRAC1, create PRACA and PRACB.
3. Under PRACA, create PRACX and PRACY.
4. Make C:\ the current directory.
5. Terminate the shell.
6. At the command prompt, create a directory under C:\ named PRAC2.

1. *Pull down the **File** menu and select **Create directory**. In the **Create Directory** dialog box, fill in the name PRAC1 and select Enter.*
2. *Make PRAC1 current. Pull down the **File** menu and select **Create directory**. In the **Create Directory** dialog box, fill in the name PRACA and select Enter. Then pull down the **File** menu again, select **Create Directory**, fill in the name PRACB, and select Enter.*

3. *Make PRACA current. Then repeat the above procedure but use the names PRACX and PRACY.*
6. *Enter the command:*

```
MD PRAC2
```

# Changing the Default Directory

Every drive has a default directory. This is where DOS looks for files and stores new files when you don't include a path in the filespec. Immediately after you boot, each drive's root directory becomes its default.

The default directory of the default drive is also the *current directory*. This is where DOS looks if you specify neither the drivename nor the path in a filespec. The current directory would be used in the following command:

```
C:\>TYPE AUTOEXEC.BAT
```

On the **File System** screen, the current directory always shows in the directory panel. To see another directory listing, you must change the current directory by changing the default drive, the default directory, or both. The path of the current directory always appears in the line directly underneath the drive icons and above the **Directory Tree** and directory panels.

In the command prompt screen, the current directory might appear in the command prompt itself, depending on how you installed DOS.

## Using the Shell

To change the default directory of a drive using the **File System**, first make the necessary drive the default drive. Then in the **Directory Tree** panel, select the desired directory. You will see the current directory name change along with the contents of the directory panel. Once you have established the desired default directory for that drive, you can switch to another drive as the default drive. The default directory for a drive remains its default directory even when it isn't the default drive.

## Using the Command Prompt

The CHDIR command establishes the default directory for a drive. Its format is:

```
CHDIR [drive][path]        (CHDIR can be abbreviated CD)
```

If you use the command without a path, it displays the default directory of the indicated drive. To find out what the current directory is, you could enter this command:

```
CD
```

To find out the default directory of drive A:, you could enter this command:

```
CD A:
```

To change the default directory, include the desired path in the command. You can use an absolute or relative path, whichever is more appropriate. An interaction to change the default directory of the current drive to CAD might look like this:

```
C:\WP>CD \CAD
C:\CAD>_
```

In this case, the confirmation is in the command prompt. If your prompt doesn't include the directory path, you can use a CD command with no parameters to find out the current drive. An interaction to change to the root directory of the default drive might look like this:

```
C:\CAD>CD \
C:\>_
```

An interaction to change to the parent directory of the default directory on drive A: might look like this:

```
C:\>CD A:..
C:\>CD A:
A:\DEV
C:\>_
```

The first CD command changed the default directory. Since the change didn't affect the current drive and therefore didn't get confirmed in the command prompt, another CD command was used to confirm the change. The response shows that the default directory on drive A: is now \DEV.

If DOS can't find the directory you request, you'll see this message: "Invalid directory." You might have misspelled it or used the wrong path.

Start with the **File System** screen.
1. Insert a diskette in drive A:. (Don't use a blank diskette for this exercise.)
2. Switch to drive A:.
3. Switch back to drive C:.
4. Make the PRAC1 directory current. (You might have to scroll through the

**Directory Tree** panel to find it.)
5. Terminate the shell.
6. Find out the current directory.
7. Change to the root directory.
8. Change to the \PRAC1 directory.

---

1. *Any nonblank diskette will do.*
2. *Click on the drive A: icon or tab to the drive panel and press Ctrl+A.*
3. *This is similar to Item 2.*
4. *Click on the directory name or move the highlight to it and press Enter.*
6. *If it doesn't show in the command prompt, enter the command:*

```
CD
```

7. *Enter the command:*

```
CD \
```

8. *Enter the command:*

```
CD PRAC1
```

---

# Accessing Files in Other Directories

All the functions you have learned so far, both in the shell and the command prompt, can access other directories by including the drivename and/or the directory name in the filespec. For example, to view a file in another directory on the same drive, you could use a command like this:

```
TYPE \WP\README.DOC
```

To view a file in the default directory of another drive, you could use a command like this:

```
TYPE A:README.DOC
```

This command accesses the default directory on drive A: because no path is specified.

You can also include both the drive and the directory. The following command accesses the \JUDIF directory on drive D:.

```
TYPE D:\JUDIF\ATTACK.TXT
```

All the above examples have shown commands. You can also access other drives and other directories in the shell by including the drivename and/or the directory name wherever you can type a filespec. You'll see some examples of this soon.

You can also prefix a command name with a drivename and/or path to show DOS where to find the program file. For example, suppose the current directory is C:\DOS and you want to run the MOUSE program. The MOUSE.EXE file is located in the C:\DRIVERS directory. You could enter the MOUSE command this way:

```
C:\DOS>\DRIVERS\MOUSE
```

If MOUSE.EXE is on drive B:, you could enter the command this way:

```
C:\DOS>B:MOUSE
```

When you prefix an external command with a drivename or path, the indicated directory affects the program file only. If the command includes other parameters, DOS assumes the current directory for those parameters unless you include drivenames and/or paths for them too. If you enter:

```
C:\DOS>B:TREE
```

DOS would look for the TREE program on drive B:, but would display the tree headed by C:\DOS. To display the tree of drive B:, use the command:

```
C:\DOS>B:TREE B:
```

Later in this book, you'll learn how to set up permanent search paths so that DOS will search as many directories as necessary for programs and data files. Then you won't have to use prefixes like these to access files you want. (If you installed DOS on your hard disk with SELECT, DOS set up a permanent search path for all the DOS external programs, such as TREE. You don't have to worry about accessing these programs.)

# Copying Files from Directory to Directory

You've seen how to copy one file to the same directory, giving it a different name. You can also copy one or more files to other drives and directories.

## Using the Shell

To copy a file to another directory, select the desired file, pull down the **File** menu, and select the **Copy** option. The resulting dialog box includes the current drive and directory as the default in the **To** box. You can edit this to show the drivename and directory you want to use. If you don't supply a new filename, DOS copies the name with the file.

There are several ways to edit text in a typing box. The Home, End, and left and right arrow keys position the cursor. You can overtype a character by positioning the cursor under it and typing the new character. You can insert characters by positioning the cursor and pressing the Ins (insert) key. This turns on insert mode, and the typing cursor changes from an underline to a thin vertical bar between two characters, showing where your typing will be inserted. To get out of insert mode, press Ins again. Whether or not you are in insert mode, pressing Backspace erases the character to the left, while pressing Del erases the current character.

Suppose you want to copy README.DOC from the current directory to the default directory on drive A:. You would overtype the default value in the **To** box with A:. If you want to copy README.DOC to the JUDIF directory on drive D:, you would fill in the **To** box with D:\JUDIF. In both these cases, the copy would be named README.DOC. To copy the file to D:\JUDIF and call it READ.TXT, you would type D:\JUDIF\READ.TXT in the **To** box.

To do a multiple copy, select all the files you want to copy before pulling down the **File** menu. (Remember to click on each desired filespec or use the Spacebar to highlight its icon.) After you select **Copy**, the **From** box in the dialog box shows the names of all the files you selected. If all the names can't be seen in the box, you can scroll through them with the Home, End, and right and left arrow keys or by clicking on the ends of the box. You cannot, however, edit the names.

If you fill in only a drivename in the **To** box, all the files are copied to the default directory on that drive. If you fill in both a drivename and a path, all the files are copied to the designated directory. The files keep their same names in their new locations. You cannot change their names when you do a multiple copy.

DOS displays a dialog box showing each filename as it is copied, along with the message "*n* of *n*" (as in "1 of 17") as a progress report. If any filename already exists in the target directory, the "Filename already exists" message is added to the dialog box. You saw an example of this message in Figure 2.10. You must then choose whether to replace that particular target file. After you make your choice, DOS continues copying files. However, if you select **Cancel**, the remainder of the files are not copied.

## Using the Command Prompt

You can use a global filespec as the source in a COPY command to copy a group of files. The source filespec can include a drivename, path, and/or global filename. (Drives and paths can never be global.) The target filespec can be omitted if you are copying from another directory to the current directory. Otherwise, the target filespec is a drivename and/or path.

Figure 3.5 shows an example of a COPY interaction that copies multiple files. A global filespec is used as the source, and the current directory is implied as the target. DOS lists the name of each file it copies, and reports how many files were copied at the end of the operation.

Suppose you want to copy all files in the default directory of drive A: to the current directory. You could enter the following command:

```
COPY A:
```

Since no source path is given, the default directory of A: is used. Since no filename is given, *.* is assumed. Since no target is specified, the current directory is assumed.

To copy all files starting with CHAP from \WP on the default drive to the current directory, you could enter this command:

```
COPY \WP\CHAP*.*
```

The current drive doesn't need to be involved. To copy all DOC files from D:\JUDIF to the root directory of A:, you could enter this command:

```
COPY D:\JUDIF\*.DOC A:\
```

Suppose you want to copy all the DAT files from the current directory to A:\DATFILES:

```
COPY *.DAT A:\DATFILES
```

Suppose you want to copy all files from A: to C:\WP:

```
COPY A:*.* C:\WP
```

```
C:\WP>COPY A:*.COM
A:COMMAND.COM
A:DISKCOPY.COM
A:FORMAT.COM
A:KEYB.COM
A:SELECT.COM
A:SYS.COM
        6 File(s) copied

C:\WP>_
```

Figure 3.5. Copying Multiple Files with the COPY Command

Start with the **File System** screen. Make C:\DOS the current directory.
1. Copy all files with the CPI extension to C:\PRAC1.
2. Copy all files with the SYS extension to C:\PRAC1.
3. Terminate the shell.
4. At the command prompt, copy all files from PRAC1 to PRAC2.

1. *Select the CPI files. Pull down the **File** menu and select **Copy**. In the **Copy File** dialog box, overtype the target path in the **To** box with C:\PRAC1 and press Enter.*
2. *Select the SYS files and follow the same procedure as in Item 1.*
4. *Enter this command:*

```
COPY \PRAC1 \PRAC2
```

# Disk Full Errors

When copying to a diskette, you can run out of disk space before all the selected files are copied. Even a fixed disk can run out of disk space eventually if you don't clean out the "dead wood" every so often.

Figure 3.6 shows the message that appears in the **Copy File** dialog box when the target disk has no room for the indicated file. If you select Option 1, DOS goes on to the next selected file. Perhaps it is smaller and will fit on the target disk. Alternatively, you can put another diskette in the target drive and select Option 2. DOS will continue copying files to the new diskette. The third alternative is to select **Cancel** and solve the problem another way.

Suppose you want to copy 100 files from your hard disk to diskettes. You know they won't all fit on diskette, but you don't know how many will

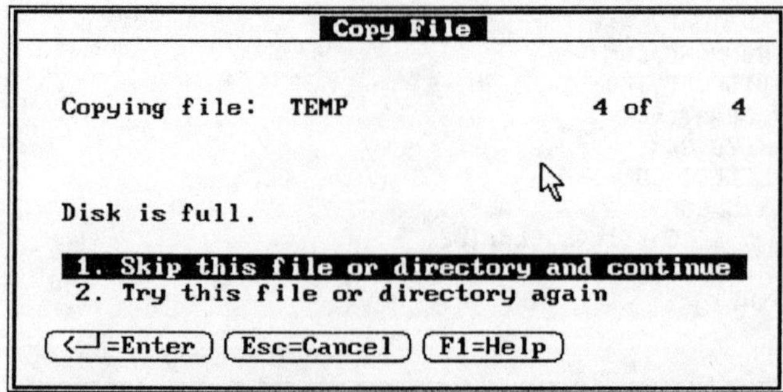


Figure 3.6. Disk Full Message in Dialog Box

```
C:\WP>COPY *.PRS A:
IBMAL0.PRS
IBMAL1.PRS
IBMALT.PRS
IBMPROPR.PRS
IBPROII.PRS
PAKXP108.PRS
PAKXP109.PRS
STANDARD.PRS
BRHR15XL.PRS
EPFX80.PRS
EPGQ3500.PRS
Insufficient disk space
        10 File(s) copied

C:\WP>_
```

Figure 3.7. Disk Full Message with COPY Command

fit on one diskette. Select all 100. Then start the copy function. Each time the "Disk full" message appears, insert another blank diskette in the target drive and select Option 2. When the function terminates, all files will have been copied.

Figure 3.7 shows what happens when a disk full error occurs while performing a COPY at the command prompt. The global filespec selects files in the order they appear in the directory. The last file listed encountered the disk full error and was not copied. The command terminates automatically.

Now you're stuck with a problem. How can you copy the remaining files to the next diskette? The same global filespec would copy the same files all over again. The only solution is to decide which files remain to be copied and copy them using individual COPY commands. Because of this problem, the shell Copy function is vastly preferable to the COPY command when copying multiple files to diskette.

## Moving Files

Moving files from one directory to another is simply a matter of copying them to the new directory and then deleting them from the old. The shell offers a **Move** function; in command mode, you have to enter a COPY command followed by a DEL command.

## Using the Shell

To move files using the shell, select the files, pull down the **File** menu, and select **Move**. On the resulting dialog box, which looks just like a **Copy File** dialog box, fill in the drivename and path (if necessary) of the target directory. You can include a new filename if you wish. You'll see messages if any target files will be overwritten and if any source files are write-protected.

 Start at the **File System** screen. Make \PRAC1 the current directory. Move all the CPI files from \PRAC1 to \PRAC1\PRACA.

*Select all the CPI files. Pull down the **File** menu and select **Move**. In the **Move File** dialog box, edit the **To** box to read C:\PRAC1\PRACA. Select Enter.*

# Renaming Directories

Sometimes you need to rename a directory. You can't really do it very effectively from the command prompt; RENAME gives you an error message if you apply it to a path instead of a filespec. However, you can do it in a very roundabout fashion: Create a new directory with the desired name, copy everything from the old directory to the new directory, delete everything in the old directory, then remove the old directory. But why go through all that? You can easily rename a directory on the **File System** screen.

## Using the Shell

To rename a directory using the shell, select the directory in the **Directory Tree** panel, pull down the **File** menu, and select **Rename**. Then fill in the new name in the **Rename Directory** dialog box. If the new name duplicates an existing filename or subdirectory name in the current directory, you'll see the appropriate error message.

# Removing Directories

When you finish a project, replace an old application with a newer one, or otherwise stop using a directory, you will eventually want to remove that directory from the disk. You can remove a directory in the shell or at the command level. You can never remove the root directory, however.

A directory must be empty before it can be removed. Not only must all files be deleted, all subdirectories must also be removed (except for . and .., which appear in every directory except the root). To remove an entire subtree, you must start at the bottom of the subtree and work up.

## Using the Shell

To remove a directory using the shell, start by selecting the directory on the **Directory Tree** panel. Check the resulting display to make sure the directory contains no files or subdirectories. Then pull down the **File** menu and select **Delete**. The **Delete Directory** dialog box (which looks nearly identical to the **Delete File** dialog box in Figure 2.16) asks you to confirm the delete operation. Select Option 2 to delete the directory. Select Option 1 or **Cancel** to change your mind. After the directory is deleted, DOS switches you automatically to the directory above it in the **Directory Tree** panel.

If the selected directory can't be deleted for some reason—probably because it isn't empty—you will see the "Access denied" message added to the dialog box. You can cancel the operation until you can figure out and fix the problem, then try it again.

## Using the Command Prompt

The RMDIR command removes a directory. Its format is shown below:

```
RMDIR path        (RMDIR can be abbreviated RD)
```

The target directory must be empty. It also must not be the current directory or the root directory. You can use an absolute or relative path depending on the location of the directory. Suppose you want to remove the TURNER.HOM directory, which is a child of the current directory. You could enter this command:

```
RD TURNER.HOM
```

If some other directory is current, you could enter this command:

```
RD \CAD\ARCHITEC\TURNER.HOM
```

If the command is successful, no message is displayed. The message "Invalid path, not directory, or directory not empty" covers a multitude of problems. If DOS can't find the directory you named, it will display this message.

If the directory is not empty—because it contains files or subdirectories—DOS displays the same message. A simple DIR *path* command should tell you which problem you are facing.

If the listing of a directory shows no files or subdirectories, but DOS insists that the directory is not empty, it probably contains *hidden* files. The operating system and some applications hide their working files so that users won't try to access or change them. You'll learn how to deal with hidden files in Chapter 5.

Start at the **File System** screen. Make \PRAC1 the current directory.
1. Rename PRAC1 as PRACTICE.
2. Delete \PRACTICE\PRACB.
3. Delete \PRACTICE\PRACA\PRACX.
4. Terminate the shell.
5. At the command prompt, delete \PRAC2.

*1. Pull down the **File** menu and select **Rename**. In the **Rename Directory** dialog box, fill in PRACTICE as the new name and select Enter.*
*2. Make PRACB current. Delete any files it contains, then pull down the **File** menu and select **Delete**. In the **Delete Directory** dialog box, make sure the directory name is correct, then confirm the deletion.*
*3. Make PRACX current and follow the same procedure as in Item 2.*
*5. Enter the command:*

```
DEL \PRAC2\*.*
```

*then enter the command:*

```
RD \PRAC2
```

## Summary

This chapter has shown you how to work with drives and directories. You now can switch drives and directories, access programs and files in other drives and directories, copy and move files to other directories, rename directories, and remove directories. In the next chapter, you will learn how to handle complete disks.

# *Exercises*

These exercises let you practice the directory maintenance skills you have learned in this chapter.

| **What You Should Do** | **How the Computer Responds** |
| --- | --- |
| 1. Start up the shell, if necessary, and make C:\ the default directory. | 1. Obeys your commands. |
| 2. Create a new directory named \SUMMARY. | 2. Shows the new directory in the tree panel. |
| 3. Copy COMMAND.COM to \SUMMARY. | 3. Copies the file as directed. |
| 4. Rename \SUMMARY as \EXERCISE. | 4. Shows the new directory name in the tree panel. |
| 5. Delete the file in \EXERCISE and remove the directory. | 5. Removes the directory from the tree panel. |
| 6. Terminate the shell. Make C:\ the default directory if necessary. | 6. Displays the appropriate command prompt. |
| 7. Create a new directory named \SUMMARY. | 7. Displays another command prompt. |
| 8. Make \SUMMARY the default directory. | 8. Shows the directory name in the command prompt. |
| 9. Copy COMMAND.COM from the root directory. | 9. Displays "1 File(s) copied." |
| 10. Display the directory contents, then delete the file in \SUMMARY and remove the directory. | 10. Displays another command prompt. |

## *What If It Doesn't Work?*

1. If DOS refuses to make a directory, a duplicate directory name or file-name exists in the parent directory. Use a different directory name.

2. If DOS refuses to delete a directory in the shell, the directory is not empty. Delete all the files in the directory and try again.

3. If DOS refuses to delete a directory at the command prompt, either the directory is not empty or it is the current directory. Delete all the files, switch to a different directory, and try again. (If DOS still refuses to delete the directory, it probably contains hidden files. Don't worry about it now.)

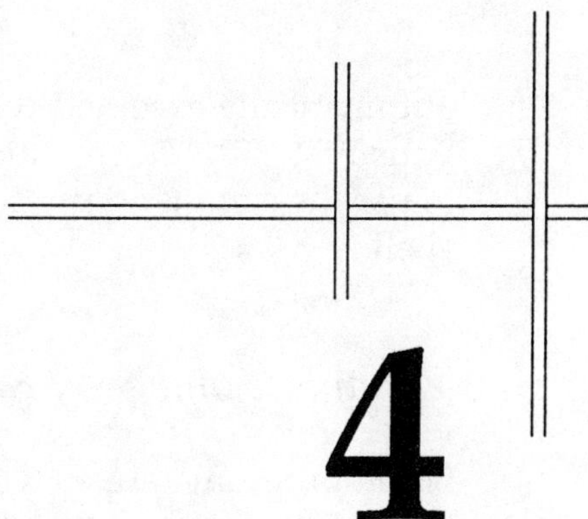

# 4

# *File and Disk Utilities*

Now that you understand how to perform many basic functions using both the shell and the command prompt, you're ready to use more utility programs to manipulate your system.

In this chapter, you will learn to:

- Print files
- Set the system date and time
- Check and change disk labels
- Format disks
- Copy diskettes
- Compare diskettes

## *Printing ASCII Text Files*

In Chapter 3, you learned to use echo printing and COPY to PRN to print ASCII files. You can also print ASCII files without displaying them by using the **Print** option in the shell or the PRINT command. In both cases, you don't have to wait for the file to complete printing to continue with your work. The file will print in the *background*, letting you use the shell and command prompt for other work; this is called working in the *foreground*.

The print function must be initialized before you can use it in the shell. The initialization command may be included as one of the commands that is automatically executed when you boot the system. If not, you'll have to use your first PRINT command at the command prompt. We'll show you how to use the command prompt first. Then you'll see how to print files from the shell.

## Terminate and Stay Resident (TSR) Programs

Some programs are a hybrid of internal and external approaches and are called *Terminate and Stay Resident (TSR)*. A TSR program is external the first time you call it, but once loaded it stays in memory and acts as an internal program.

The PRINT program is a hybrid of an external program and a TSR. Portions of the program stay resident after the program is loaded the first time. Since PRINT is mostly an external program, the PRINT.COM file must be available on disk whenever you want to use it. However, the initialization information stays in the memory-resident portion. That's why you only need to initialize it once after booting.

## Using the Command Prompt

The PRINT command causes a file to be printed. The first time you use it after booting, PRINT also initializes the print function. Figure 4.1 shows a complete interaction that initializes the print function and prints one file.

The basic format for the PRINT command is:

```
PRINT [filespec]
```

If you use PRINT without a filespec, it just initializes the print function (without actually printing anything). You can include a path with the filespec, if necessary. For example, to print AUTOEXEC.BAT in the root direc-

```
C:\>PRINT GROCLIST
Name of list device [PRN]:
Resident part of PRINT installed


   C:\GROCLIST is currently being printed


C:\>
```

tory while you are in the \DOS directory, you would enter this command:

```
PRINT \AUTOEXEC.BAT
```

If you are using the PRINT command for the first time since booting, the display will look much like the one shown in Figure 4.1. When the "Name of list device" message appears, the program pauses. DOS wants to know the name of the device on which to print. If you press Enter, as we did in the example, DOS prints the file on the device called PRN, which is your primary, or only, printer. To select a different device, type the appropriate name before pressing Enter. Figure 4.2 shows the DOS device names. Type the one that describes your printer.

For the remainder of the session, until you boot again, all PRINT commands are directed to the device you selected with the first PRINT command. You can avoid the "Name of list device" interaction by including your default print device in the command, like this:

```
PRINT [/D:device] [filespec]
```

You specify the device to be used following the /D switch. DOS knows immediately which device to use and doesn't bother to ask. The command PRINT /D:PRN initializes the print device without printing a file. The command PRINT /D:PRN AUTOEXEC.BAT initializes the print device and prints the named file on it.

If you specify a file to be printed, the next message you see tells you the file is being printed, assuming that DOS can find the file. You'll hear the printer start functioning. While the file is printing, you can continue using DOS. This gives the print operation a distinct advantage over other methods of printing files under DOS.

| | |
|---|---|
| AUX | Alternate name for COM1 |
| COM1 | First serial port |
| COM2 | Second serial port |
| COM3 | Third serial port |
| COM4 | Fourth serial port |
| CON | Console (keyboard input and monitor output) |
| LPT1 | First parallel port |
| LPT2 | Second parallel port |
| LPT3 | Third parallel port |
| NUL | Nowhere |
| PRN | Synonym for LPT1 |

Figure 4.2. DOS Device Names

The second time you enter a PRINT command, and all subsequent times until you reboot, you will see only the "Filespec is currently being printed" message. Once you have initialized the print function and identified the print device, you can't change the device without rebooting. Specifying the /D switch in a later command results in an error message.

## Global Filespecs with PRINT

If you include a global filespec with the PRINT command, up to 10 files can be specified for printing with this single command. A list of the selected files will be shown on the screen, as in this interaction:

```
C:\>PRINT *.DOC
   C:\FB.DOC is currently being printed
   C:\FC.DOC is in queue
   C:\FD.DOC is in queue
   C:\BACKUP.DOC is in queue
   C:\GRILL.DOC is in queue
   C:\ROGERS.DOC is in queue

C:\>_
```

The print queue is a list of up to 10 files waiting to be printed. You can keep issuing PRINT commands until the queue is full; you'll see a message when it won't hold any more files. Then you must wait until there is room in the queue before issuing any more PRINT commands. DOS prints one file after another, starting each file on a new page.

## Using the Shell

After the print function has been initialized by the first PRINT command, you can print files from the shell. While you are at the **File System** screen, select one or more files to be printed from the directory listing panel, then pull down the **File** menu and select **Print**. (If the **Print** option is gray, the print function has not yet been initialized, or no files have been selected.)

After you select the **Print** option, a confirmation box appears. (It might flash on and off too quickly to read.) Then the **File System** screen reappears so you can continue working.

When you select the **Print** option with multiple files selected, up to 10 files can be placed in the print queue. If all the selected files won't fit in the queue, you'll see a dialog box like the one shown in Figure 4.3. It shows the

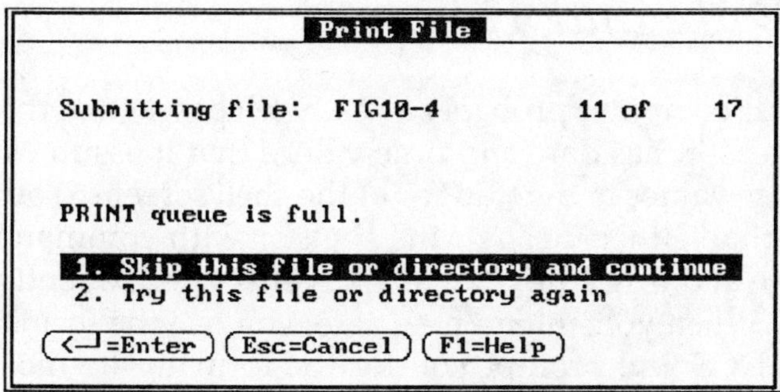


Figure 4.3. Print Queue Full Message

first file that won't fit in the queue. No files following that one are placed in the queue either.

If you want to wait a while to print the remaining files, select **Cancel** immediately; this doesn't cancel printing of the files already submitted, but cancels the request for the later ones. If you select Option 1, you bypass the currently displayed file and are able to choose Option 1 or 2 again for the next file. If you want to keep trying to add a file to the print queue, so that the file will be added as soon as a space becomes available, keep selecting Option 2.

Start at the command prompt. Make \DOS the current directory.
1. Make sure the printer is ready.
2. Print the file named MYADDR.
3. Go to the **File System** screen.
4. Print MYADDR again.

1. *Check that the printer has been turned on, has been cabled correctly, and has paper and ribbon/ink. If the printer can be switched from online (select) to local (deselect), make sure it is online.*
2. *Enter the command:*

```
PRINT MYADDR
```

*If DOS asks for the name of the list device, press Enter to accept the default value.*
4. *Select MYADDR in the directory listing. Pull down the **File** menu and select* ***Print***.

# *System Date and Time*

Your computer probably already keeps track of the current date and time—at least it has date and time values that it assumes are current. You've seen these values in the title bar of the shell screens. You can adjust the date and/or time either through the shell or with commands. Once you change the date and time, the change takes effect permanently.

When you enter a new date, you use the format for the country you are in; DOS will prompt you for the format. The most common format in the U.S. is mm-dd-yy, or month-day-year. Use a value from 1 through 12 for the month, from 1 through 31 for the day, and from 80 through 99 for the year. For dates later than 12-31-1999, you use four digits; this requires the command rather than the shell. The values you specify must indicate a valid date.

When you enter a new time, DOS prompts you with a format as well. The most common one in the U.S. is hh:mm:ss.dd, where hh is hours from 1 through 24, mm is minutes from 0 through 59, and ss is seconds from 0 through 59; dd represents hundredths of a second. You'll never enter hundredths, but you may see it displayed. Most people don't enter seconds either. You can drop elements from the end of the format, as well as any leading or trailing zeros.

DOS displays the date and time in many programs. It also uses them to "stamp" directory entries. When a file is first created and whenever it is changed, the date and time are updated in the directory. As you'll see later, dates and times can be used for sorting and archiving files from directories. It is definitely to your advantage to have the correct system date and time set in your computer.

## *Using the Shell*

The first step in setting the date and time through the shell is to get to the **DOS Utilities** screen. Select **DOS Utilities** from the **Start Program** screen. The resulting screen is really a variation on **Start Programs**; a new set of options from the group **DOS Utilities** is listed. You select items from this screen just as from the other.

The first option is **Set Date and Time**. When you select it, you'll see a dialog box like the one shown in Figure 4.4. Notice that the format for the date is shown. The cursor rests in the **Parameters** box; here is where you type your new date in the format shown. After you select Enter, you'll be prompted to enter a new time. Again, you type it in the **Parameters** box in

**Set Date and Time Utility**

Enter new date ??-??-??

Parameters . . [          ]

( <—┘=Enter )  ( Esc=Cancel )  ( F1=Help )

Figure 4.4. Set Date Dialog Box

the format shown. When you press (or select) Enter, the new time takes effect. You'll see the new values immediately in the title bar. If you leave either value blank, DOS goes to the DATE or TIME command to collect the desired value.

## Using the Commands

At the command prompt, you can set the date and time with the DATE command and TIME command. Here's an interaction in which both are set:

```
C:\DOS>DATE
Current date is 03-17-90
Enter new date: 04-12-90
C:\DOS>TIME
Current time is 14:21:67.32
Enter new time: 15:08
C:\DOS>_
```

DOS displays the value it has for the current date or time, then asks for a new value. To keep the displayed value, just press Enter at that point.

You can specify a wider range of dates at the command prompt than you can with the shell. If you want a date later than 12-31-1999, you can use four digits to represent the year.

Start at the **Start Programs** screen.
1. Change the date and time to any valid values other than the ones that are current.
2. Go to the command prompt.
3. Correct the date.
4. Correct the time.

1. *Select the* **DOS Utilities** *option. From the* **DOS Utilities** *screen, select* **Set Date and Time***. In the date dialog box, type a date in your system's format and press Enter. In the time dialog box, type a time in your system's format and press Enter.*
3. *Enter the command:*

```
DATE
```

*In response to "Enter new date", type today's date in the indicated format and press Enter.*
4. *Enter the command:*

```
TIME
```

*In response to "Enter new time", type the current time in the indicated format and press Enter.*

## Disk Architecture

Data on disks and diskettes is stored in concentric rings called *tracks*. Each diskette has two sides; some early diskettes recorded data on only one side. A fixed disk also has tracks; since it is actually a stack of disks, the fixed disk has several sides, all with tracks. The tracks are divided into *sectors*; with each track having anywhere from 9 to 15 sectors. A fixed disk also has *cylinders*. A cylinder consists of track 1 on all the disk sides, another consists of track 2 on all the disk sides, and so forth. Disks are read by *read-write* heads, which access data in tracks; all tracks in one cylinder can be read at the same position of the heads. While you don't have to remember the details involved in storing data on disk, you will occasionally see messages that specify a track, sector, side, or cylinder. If you encounter a serious problem, make a note of the track, sector, side, or cylinder involved so that you can pass the information along to the person who repairs your system.

Each disk has a boot record, a root directory, and a file allocation table (or FAT) stored in it. The boot record is accessed when you boot from the disk; if the disk does not contain the files necessary for booting, the boot record causes the appropriate error message to be displayed. The root directory includes space for a label that you can specify, and a unique volume serial number supplied by DOS 4 when the disk is formatted. Space for these items is reserved starting in track 0 of the disk.

# *Volume Labels and Serial Numbers*

Every disk you use in your system has a volume serial number, assigned automatically by DOS 4 when it prepares the disk for use. These numbers are unique to each diskette; you can't change them. You see the volume serial number whenever you get a directory or tree listing of your disk at the command prompt.

A disk can also have a volume label, which you provide and can change at will. You see the label, if it exists, whenever you use DIR or TREE to get a listing of your disk. In this section, you'll learn about the labels, how to view them, how to change them, and how to add them.

## *Viewing a Disk's Volume Information*

As you've observed, you see a disk's volume label and volume serial number whenever you use DIR or TREE. You can also get the information without the directory listing; however, you still have to be at the command prompt. The shell doesn't include the commands to see and manipulate the volume information. The VOL command produces the results. Here's the format of the VOL command:

```
VOL [drive]
```

Figure 4.5 shows an interaction that checks the volume information on a labeled fixed disk and an unlabeled diskette. Notice how the messages differ. You can't make changes with the VOL command; it is used to provide information only.

```
C:\DOS>VOL

  Volume in drive C is DOS 4 PART
  Volume Serial Number is 109F-2F23

C:\DOS>VOL A:

  Volume in drive A has no label
  Volume Serial Number is 106E-11D8

D:\DOS>_
```

Figure 4.5. Checking Volume Information

## Changing a Disk Label

Sometimes you want to change a disk label or add one to an unlabeled disk. Keeping the label current with the contents of the diskette is a good idea. The LABEL command lets you do that. Here is its format:

```
LABEL [drive][volume label]
```

For instance, if you want to change the label on drive A: to WINTERCATLG, you would enter:

```
C:\DOS>LABEL A:WINTERCATLG
```

To add a label to the currently unlabeled diskette in drive B:, you could enter:

```
C:\DOS>LABEL B:FORTY YEARS
```

Don't put a space between the drivename and the volume label because DOS will treat the label as another (invalid) parameter. If you omit the volume label (or put a space after the drivename), DOS asks for the label:

```
C:\DOS>LABEL A:
Volume in drive A is INV BACKUP
Volume Serial Number is 106E-11D8
Volume label (11 characters, ENTER for none)?_
```

Now you can type the new volume label. If you press Enter without typing a label, LABEL asks if you want to delete the label:

```
Delete current volume label (Y/N)?_
```

If you respond N, the current label is not changed.

A volume label may contain letters, numbers, and spaces, but many special DOS symbols—such as * and ?—are prohibited. If you enter more than 11 characters, only the first 11 are used. If you get a message that some characters are invalid, revise your label to get rid of the invalid symbols.

Start at the command prompt.
1. Check the label on your fixed disk.
2. Change the label on any diskette in drive A:.
3. Delete the label on the diskette in drive A: and confirm the deletion.

*1. Enter the command:*

```
VOL
```

2. *Place any diskette in drive A:. Enter the command:*

```
LABEL A:text
```

*making sure no space follows the colon.*

3. *Enter the command:*

```
LABEL A:
```

*In response to the "Volume label" prompt, press Enter. In response to "Delete current volume label", enter Y. Then enter the command:*

```
VOL A:
```

*to confirm the deletion.*

# Formatting Disks

When a disk is formatted, DOS checks the disk to make sure it can reliably store data. DOS sets up space for information about files, called the File Allocation Table (FAT). It includes information about how the disk is laid out, how much data it can store, and how it can be accessed. In essence, formatting prepares a disk so that DOS can use it with your system.

Every new diskette you acquire must be formatted before you can use it. Old disks that are ready to be reused can also be formatted. Formatting destroys any former data or layout of a disk, so it offers a measure of security by removing old data completely. A fixed disk is formatted only when you are setting it up. DOS has special safeguards built in to help prevent you from accidentally reformatting your fixed disk and thus destroying data inadvertently. We'll focus on formatting diskettes in this section, since that's the formatting operation you'll perform most often.

By default, the FORMAT program always prepares a diskette for the drive it's in. Thus, if the disk is in a 5.25", double-density drive, FORMAT prepares the diskette in double-density (360K) format. If the disk is in a 3.5", 1.44MB drive, FORMAT prepares the diskette in 1.44MB format. You can override the default format to some extent.

The FORMAT program allows you to use several switches. In this section we'll cover three switches that will meet most of your needs. Here's the basic format:

```
FORMAT drive [/V:label] [/S] [/F:size]
```

Since this is an external command, the FORMAT.COM file must be available. Note that the drivename operand is required; since FORMAT destroys existing data, DOS makes you specify which drive to use and provides no default here. If no switches are used, FORMAT formats the designated diskette according to the type of drive it's in.

The /S (system) switch tells it to make the diskette bootable. The /V (volume) switch lets you include the label in the command instead of having to respond to a message during the process. The /F (format) switch lets you format a disk for a lower density.

You can use the switches either at the command prompt or through the shell. We'll cover the command first, then you'll see how to enter the information through the shell.

## Using Commands

To format a diskette without using any options, you can enter the command specifying only the drivename, as in:

```
FORMAT A:
```

DOS prompts you to insert the diskette to be formatted in the specified drive. FORMAT never begins its work without giving you a chance to install the desired diskette first. That's a safety measure to prevent accidental destruction of existing files on a disk. The message looks like this:

```
Insert new diskette for drive d
and strike ENTER when ready_
```

After you press Enter, you'll see this message:

```
n percent of disk formatted
```

You will hear the drive heads working and see the number (indicated by $n$ above) change in the message from 0 to 100, indicating the percentage of the disk that has been formatted so far. It can take quite a while (several minutes) to format a large-capacity diskette, so be patient. When the operation is completed, this message overlays the percentage message:

```
Format complete
Volume label (11 characters, ENTER for none)?_
```

After you type a label or press Enter, you'll see some more messages:

```
xxxxxxxx  bytes total disk space
yyyyyyyy  bytes in bad sectors
zzzzzzzz  bytes available on disk
```

```
aaaa   bytes in each allocation unit
bbbb   allocation units available on disk

Volume Serial Number is cccc-dddd
```

These lines give the status of the disk. The number of bytes on the disk and the bytes available will be the same in the simple command we're using here, unless bad sectors are identified. The "bad sectors" line will be displayed only if some damaged areas were found. Bad sectors don't make the disk unusable. DOS simply marks those sectors off in the File Allocation Table so they don't get used for data. However, if your format message shows a high percentage of bad sectors, you might consider throwing the diskette away (or getting your money back if it's a new diskette).

The Volume Serial Number will be the unique number DOS has assigned to that diskette. The allocation unit size and quantity differ for different-size diskettes. Space is allocated to a file one allocation unit at a time. If the allocation unit size is 512 bytes, then a one-byte file actually takes up 512 bytes on the disk since that is the smallest amount of space that can be allocated to one file.

The FORMAT program then asks you:

```
Format another (Y/N)?_
```

If you want to format another diskette in exactly the same way, enter the letter Y and the FORMAT program will be repeated. If you don't want to format another diskette, or if you want to do it differently, enter the letter N and the system prompt will be displayed.

*Specifying a Volume Label*   DOS allocates space for a volume label on the disk, asking you to enter a value during the formatting process. Since labels help in identifying disks (not only when you list a directory, but also when you accidentally try to reformat your hard disk), you should provide a label for each diskette you format. You can change labels later, if necessary, by using the LABEL command.

To have DOS create the volume label before it prompts you to do so, include the /V:*label* switch in the FORMAT command. The label name can have up to 11 characters, including spaces. If you use spaces in a label included in the command, enclose the label in double quotation marks. Otherwise, DOS thinks it has a strange parameter following the space. Other file naming rules apply when you use the LABEL command.

Figure 4.6 shows a complete interaction that creates a diskette with the volume label PRACTICE 01. Notice that DOS doesn't have to ask for the label name, since it is included in the command. If you omit this switch, you

```
C:\DOS>FORMAT A: /V:"PRACTICE 01"
Insert new diskette for drive A:
and press ENTER when ready...

Format complete


  1213952 bytes total disk space
  1213952 bytes available on disk

     512 bytes in each allocation unit
    2371 allocation units available on disk

Volume Serial Number is 1056-17D4

Format another (Y/N)?N
C:\DOS>DIR A:

 Volume in drive A is PRACTICE 01
 Volume Serial Number is 1056-17D4
 Directory of  A:\

File not found

C:\DOS>_
```

Figure 4.6. Formatting a Disk with a Volume Label

have to enter a label (or press Enter to omit it specifically) during the formatting process.

*Formatting a Bootable Diskette*    FORMAT can make a disk bootable if you wish. Not all your disks need to be bootable, especially if you'll generally boot from a fixed disk. But it doesn't hurt to make a disk bootable; it just takes up some extra space on the diskette.

You can boot with any diskette that contains the DOS system files. These are COMMAND.COM plus three hidden program files that are stored on the diskette; these hidden files don't show up when you get a directory with DIR, but you'll see them in the shell listing panel. DOS uses them for its internal processing, but you never need to access them yourself. To cause FORMAT to copy the system files onto the diskette, you use the /S switch, as in:

```
C:\DOS>FORMAT B: /V:BOOKCHAP /S
```

Figure 4.7 shows what the entire interaction looks like. You can see the "System transferred" message. Notice also that the messages show how much space is taken up by the system files. We included a directory of the newly

```
C:\DOS>FORMAT A: /V:BOOKCHAPS /S
Format complete
System transferred

   1213952 bytes total disk space
    109056 bytes used by system
   1104896 bytes available on disk

       512 bytes in each allocation unit
      2158 allocation units available on disk

Volume Serial Number is 2340-10DF

Format another (Y/N)?N
C:\DOS>A:
A:\>DIR

 Volume in drive A is BOOKCHAPS
 Volume Serial Number is 2340-10DF
 Directory of  A:\

COMMAND  COM      37556 10-06-88  12:00a
        1 File(s)     1104896 bytes free

A:\>
```

Figure 4.7. Formatting a Bootable Diskette

formatted diskette so you can see that the COMMAND.COM file shows up in the directory.

***Specifying the Diskette Size***   The FORMAT command's /F switch lets you prepare diskettes for lower-capacity drives. You can never prepare a diskette for higher capacity than the drive you are using. And you shouldn't force a diskette to be used for a higher capacity than it was manufactured and tested for. You can format a 720K disk in a 1.44MB drive, or format a 360K disk in a 1.2MB drive. You might want to do this to prepare a diskette to send to a colleague who has a different type of drive. Be warned that the results are not always reliable.

You can include the /F:*size* switch to prepare a disk of lower density than the drive is capable of. Figure 4.8 shows the valid sizes you can specify. The diskette must fit in the drive you are using, of course.

***Formatting a Fixed Disk***   Normally, you won't format a fixed disk unless you get a new one or have major repairs done on your old disk. Formatting destroys all the old data on the disk. Since a format operation can be so disastrous, DOS makes you confirm a request to format a fixed disk and

| 5.25-inch | 360 | 360K | 360KB |
| | 1200 | 1200K | 1200KB |
| | 1.2 | 1.2M | 1.2MB |
| | | | |
| 3.5-inch | 720 | 720K | 720KB |
| | 1440 | 1440K | 1440KB |
| | 1.44 | 1.44M | 1.44MB |

Figure 4.8. Format Size Options

asks you to enter the volume label like a password. You may have to cancel the FORMAT command, use VOL to find out the volume label, then try FORMAT again. However, the process makes you stop and think, thus minimizing inadvertent formatting of the fixed disk. Once the format process starts, it works exactly as on a diskette, except, of course, that it takes a great deal longer. If you reformat drive C:, you will probably want to use the /S switch to make it bootable.

## FORMAT Error Messages

You may get various error messages when you use FORMAT, depending on the conditions that DOS identifies. Here are a few of them:

```
Attempted write-protect violation
Format failure
```

You'll get this message if you try to format a write-protected diskette. If you really want to format the diskette, remove the write protection and try again. Otherwise, format a different diskette.

```
Invalid media or Track 0 bad - disk unusable
Format failure
```

This message covers several situations. It usually means just what it says—that track 0 of the disk is bad—in which case DOS can't write the root directory and File Allocation Table on the diskette. This diskette can never be used with DOS. It might be that you put the wrong type of diskette in the drive. If you only have one diskette drive, however, you'll probably not have incompatible diskette types lying around. In most cases, you can just discard the diskette or return it to the dealer.

```
Parameters not compatible
Format terminated
```

This message could mean you specified some little-known switches that don't work with the ones we've covered. But it usually means you tried to format a diskette with a larger capacity than the drive can handle. Check the drive and diskette when you get this error. If it's a 360K (double density) drive and you used /F:1.2M, you'll get the message above. Put the diskette in a high-density drive or format it for the drive it's in.

```
Disk unsuitable for system use
```

This problem occurs only when you have specified the /S switch. The tracks to receive the system files are bad. DOS will format this diskette, but it can't put the system files on it.

## Formatting through the Shell

To format through the shell, you must first get to the **DOS Utilities** screen. Once there, select **Format**. You'll see the dialog box shown in Figure 4.9. The **Parameters** box includes drive A: as the default; most formats are done in drive A:. You can change this if you want. For example, if your B: drive is a different type, you might want to format in it frequently. You can also add any FORMAT command switches you want to use in the **Parameters** box, just as you would if you typed the complete command. When you select

```
08-07-89                    Start Programs                     3:50 pm
 Program   Group   Exit                                      F1=Help
                            DOS Utilities...
               To select an item, use the up and down arrows.
            To start a program or display a new group, press Enter.


Set Date and Time Utility
Disk Copy
Disk Compare
Backup Fixed Disk
Restore Fixed Disk
Format

                               ┌─────── Format Utility ───────┐
                               │                              │
                               │      Enter drive to format.  │
                               │                              │
                               │   Parameters . .  [a:      ⮕]│
                               │                              │
                               │  ( ⏎ =Enter ) ( Esc=Cancel ) ( F1=Help ) │
                               └──────────────────────────────┘

 F10=Actions   Esc=Cancel   Shift+F9=Command Prompt
```

Figure 4.9. Format Utility Dialog Box

Enter, the shell screen disappears and you see a screen much like the command prompt screen. You'll see any messages here and make responses through the keyboard, just as when working directly with the FORMAT command. For example, if you didn't include the /V switch in the **Parameters** box, you'll have to type your label on this screen.

When the command is finished, you enter Y to format another in the same way, or N to finish. Once you type N and press Enter, you'll see a message telling you to press any key. Then you'll be automatically returned to the **DOS Utilities** screen so that you can continue with other work. It isn't necessary to type EXIT or DOSSHELL to return.

Have a blank or reusable diskette ready. It must be compatible with the capabilities of drive A:. Any data currently on the diskette will be destroyed. Start at the command prompt.

1. Format the diskette in drive A:, using the standard format of the drive.
2. Format the diskette again. This time make it bootable and give it the label DUOTECH INC.
3. Check the directory of the diskette. You should see the label and an entry for COMMAND.COM.
4. Go to the shell and format the diskette again. Make it bootable.
5. If you have two diskette drives, format a diskette in drive B:, using any parameters you wish.

*1. Place the diskette in drive A: and enter the command:*

```
FORMAT A:
```

*Press Enter in response to the first two prompts. In response to "Format another", enter N.*

*2. Enter the command:*

```
FORMAT A: /S /V:"DUOTECH INC"
```

*and respond to prompts as you did in Item 1.*

*3. Enter the command:*

```
DIR A:
```

*4. Select **DOS Utilities** followed by **Format**. Add /S to the **Parameters** box.*

*5. Select the **Format** option again. Replace the default parameters with B: and any other parameters you want.*

# Copying Diskettes

You have already learned to copy files with the Copy function. You can copy all files on a diskette with COPY *.* or by selecting them all before selecting **Copy** from the File menu.

DOS has another way of copying a diskette as well. The Diskcopy function copies a diskette as an entity; it doesn't even look at the file directory. It copies tracks, not files; every piece of data is copied to the same sector and track on the target diskette that it occupies on the source. This function is often very useful, although it is not really a substitute for the Copy function. You can use the Diskcopy function from the command prompt or from the DOS Utilities screen.

When you use the Diskcopy function, DOS requires two diskettes of the same size and type. The source diskette contains the information you want copied to the target diskette. The target can be blank or can contain old, expendable data. It can be formatted in advance, but it need not be. The Diskcopy function destroys whatever is on the target diskette. After the Diskcopy function has been completed, the two diskettes should be identical except for volume serial numbers.

Many DOS users write-protect the source diskette before starting a diskcopy operation. This protects you from mixing up the diskettes and blanking out the data you meant to save.

## Using Commands

Just as with the Format function, you can enter all parameters for the Diskcopy function at the command prompt or in a dialog box. We'll examine the DISKCOPY command first, then you'll see how to use the function through the shell. Here's the format of the DISKCOPY command:

```
DISKCOPY [source-drive] [target-drive]
```

DISKCOPY is an external command, so it may be preceded by a drivename and path if necessary. The drivenames you specify depend on your drive setup. If you have two drives that can handle the same-format diskette, then use both drives; it's much faster than a one-drive copy. If you have only one drive that can handle the diskette that you want to copy, then you must do a one-drive copy. In a one-drive copy, you must insert first the source diskette, then the target diskette into the drive. You might have to switch the diskettes several times to complete the copy. DOS tells you when to insert each diskette.

If you don't specify any drivenames, DOS assumes you want to do a one-drive copy on the default drive. If you specify only one drivename, DOS does a two-drive copy, using the default drive as the target. If you specify two drivenames, DOS does a one-drive copy if the drives match, or a two-drive copy if they are different.

Suppose you have two 720K drives and want to copy a diskette from one to the other. You would enter this command:

```
C:\>DISKCOPY B: A:
```

Suppose you have only one diskette drive and want to copy a diskette. You could enter this command:

```
C:\>DISKCOPY A: A:
```

Suppose you have one 3.5" drive (B:) and one 5.25" drive (A:). To copy a 3.5" diskette, you could use this command:

```
C:\>DISKCOPY B: B:
```

Suppose drive A: is a high-density drive and drive B: is a double-density drive. You could DISKCOPY a double-density diskette using both drives because the high-density drive can read a double-density diskette. Be sure to copy from A: to B:, since the high-density drive might not write a double-density diskette reliably. You couldn't DISKCOPY a high-density diskette using both drives because the double-density drive can neither read nor write a high-density diskette. You'd have to copy your high-density diskettes with the slower, single-drive DISKCOPY.

After you've entered the appropriate DISKCOPY command, you'll see messages prompting you to insert the source and target diskettes. In a one-drive diskcopy, you may have to do this several times. Figure 4.10 shows a complete interaction using two disk drives. Just respond to the prompts until you see the "Format another diskette" message. Type Y to repeat it or N to restore the command prompt. If you type Y, you'll be prompted to insert new source and target diskettes in the same drive(s) as before.

## Diskcopy Function Messages

The Diskcopy function works with diskettes only. It cannot be used to copy a diskette to your fixed disk, to back up a fixed drive, or to copy any of the simulated drives, such as a RAM drive. This message

```
Invalid drive specification
Specified drive does not exist,
or is non-removable
```

```
C:\DOS>DISKCOPY A: B:

Insert SOURCE diskette in drive A:

Insert TARGET diskette in drive B:

Press any key to continue ...

Copying 40 tracks
9 Sectors/Track, 2 Side(s)

Formatting while copying

Volume Serial Number is 17C7-2FZ3


Copy another diskette (Y/N)?N

C:\DOS>_
```

Figure 4.10. DISKCOPY Interaction

means you've specified a simulated drive, a fixed drive, or a nonexistent drive.

During a Diskcopy function, DOS may discover bad sectors on the source or target diskette. Diskcopy does a track-by-track copy, ignoring the information in the directory or File Allocation Table, so it doesn't know that bad sectors have already been identified. In fact, it copies the directory and File Allocation Table from the source to the target along with everything else. This message

```
Unrecoverable read error on drive A
Side x, track xx
Target diskette may be unusable
```

might not represent a real problem. The bad sectors may have been blocked out when the source diskette was formatted and so contain no data anyway, in which case the target diskette is an exact copy of the source diskette and no problem exists (except for some wasted sectors on the target diskette). However, if the bad sectors have developed after the diskette was formatted, then you have a problem that must be solved some other way. You can determine whether any bad sectors have been blocked out in the File Allocation Table with CHKDSK. You can copy the files from the diskette with COPY. If some files won't copy, you can use RECOVER to rescue them. These commands are covered in later chapters.

If you see this message

```
Copy process ended
```

then you know Diskcopy was unable to read the source diskette due to bad sectors, lack of formatting, or other problems. This diskette cannot be used as a source diskette. If it contains the only copy of valuable data, you may need to get help from an expert.

When the bad sector is on the target diskette, you'll see this message:

```
Unrecoverable write error on drive B
Side x, track xx
Target diskette may be unusable
```

You might see this message instead:

```
TARGET diskette bad or incompatible
Copy process ended
```

This copy cannot be used; in fact, it wasn't even made. Try again, using a different target diskette. You can probably still use the damaged diskette, if you must, by reformatting it (which sets aside the bad sectors) and using it for operations other than Diskcopy.

**N**ote | Many prerecorded diskettes are copy-protected to protect the creator's copyright. Read the user's manual accompanying any software you buy to find out if, and how, you can back it up. If you use the DISKCOPY command and get negative messages, the disk is probably copy-protected.

## Using the Shell

To copy a complete diskette through the shell, you must first get to the **DOS Utilities** screen. Once there, select **Disk Copy**. You'll see the dialog box shown in Figure 4.11. In the **Drives** box, you type the names of the source and target drives; be sure to include the colon after each. The effect is the same as in the DISKCOPY command, so be sure both drives can handle the same type of diskette. Then select Enter to start the Diskcopy operation.

When you select Enter, the **DOS Utilities** screen disappears and you see a screen much like the command screen, just as with the Format utility. The messages are the same as when you use the DISKCOPY command at the command prompt. After the command is finished, you enter Y to copy another disk in the same way, or N to finish. Once you type N and press Enter, you'll see a message telling you to press any key. You'll automatically be

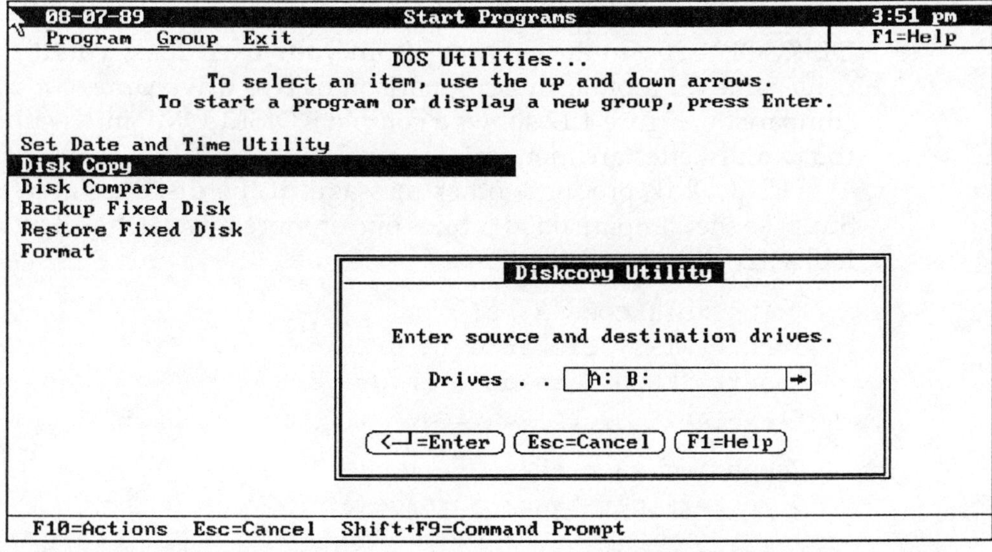


Figure 4.11. Diskcopy Utility Dialog Box

returned to the **DOS Utilities** screen so that you can continue with further work. It isn't necessary to type EXIT or DOSSHELL to return to this screen.

# Checking Your Copy

No computer copying operation is 100-percent reliable. Slight variations in electricity, read/write head tolerances, and the like can produce occasional errors. DOS gives you the opportunity to double-check a copied diskette with the Diskcomp function, which compares two diskettes. Differences, if any, are reported on the monitor. You may want to use the Diskcomp function after using the Diskcopy function, especially with disks containing crucial data. You can use the DISKCOMP program either at the command prompt or through the **DOS Utilities** screen. DISKCOMP is valid only to compare diskettes that were copied by DISKCOPY and that have not been changed since. The only allowable difference is in the volume serial number of the diskette.

## Using the Command

The format of the DISKCOMP command is:

```
DISKCOMP [source-drive] [target-drive]
```

The source and target drives have the same restrictions that apply for DISKCOPY. If you are working from your fixed disk, you'll specify one drivename for a one-drive comparison or two drivenames for a two-drive comparison. Figure 4.12 shows a complete DISKCOMP interaction in which the two diskettes are identical.

DISKCOMP produces other messages if the diskettes aren't identical. Suppose the comparison identifies one or more mismatches. The interaction looks like this:

```
C:\DOS>DISKCOMP A: B:
Insert FIRST diskette in drive A:
Insert SECOND diskette in drive B:
Press any key to continue...

Comparing 40 tracks
9 sectors per track, 2 side(s)

Compare error on
side 1, track 7
C:\DOS>_
```

As you can see from the last message, the two diskettes are not identical. If they are very different, the message will repeat again and again, indicating different sides and tracks, accompanied by a beep for each appearance of the message. You can interrupt the process with Ctrl+Break.

```
C:\DOS>DISKCOMP A: B:

Insert FIRST diskette in drive A:

Insert SECOND diskette in drive B:

Press any key to continue ...

Comparing 40 tracks
9 sectors per track, 2 side(s)


Compare OK

Compare another diskette (Y/N)?N

C:\DOS>_
```

Figure 4.12. DISKCOMP with Identical Diskettes

## Using the Shell

To compare copied diskettes through the shell, you must first get to the **DOS Utilities** screen. Once there, select **Disk Compare**. You'll see a dialog box much like the one for **Diskcopy**, shown in Figure 4.11. In the **Drives** box, you type one drivename for a one-drive comparison or two drivenames for a two-drive comparison. Then select Enter to start the process.

When you select Enter, the **DOS Utilities** screen disappears and you continue much as with the DISKCOPY operation. The messages are the same as when you enter DISKCOMP at the command prompt. After the command is finished, you enter Y to compare another disk in the same way or N to end the DISKCOMP operation. Once you type N and press Enter, you'll see a message telling you to press any key. You'll automatically be returned to the **DOS Utilities** screen so that you can continue with further work. It isn't necessary to type either EXIT or DOSSHELL to return to this screen.

For this checkpoint, you'll need a source diskette and a target diskette of the same type. You can use the diskette you formatted earlier as the target if you want. Use any diskette containing data as the source. Start at the **DOS Utilities** screen.

1. Just in case you get the diskettes mixed up, write-protect your source diskette. This will prevent DOS from writing on it if you accidentally insert it as the target diskette.
2. Use the shell to copy the entire source diskette to the target diskette.
3. Use the shell to compare the two diskettes.
4. Check the labels and volume serial numbers of both diskettes. The diskettes should have identical labels but different volume serial numbers.
5. If you want, try using the command prompt to copy and compare the two diskettes.

---

1. *For a 3.5" diskette, slide the write-protect tab to open the hole. For a 5.25" diskette, place a piece of tape over the write-protect notch.*
2. *Place the source diskette in drive A:. For a two-drive copy, place the target diskette in drive B:. Select **Disk Copy**. For a one-drive copy, edit the **Drives** box to read A: A: or B: B:. Press Enter to start the copy. Obey all prompts to insert diskettes and to press any key. Watch the messages that appear for any indications of problems. In response to the "Copy another diskette" prompt, press N. You'll have to press another key when you're prompted to get back to the **DOS Utilities** screen.*

3. Select **Disk Compare**. For a one-drive comparison, edit the **Parameters** box to read A: A: or B: B:. Press Enter to start the comparison. Obey all prompts to insert diskettes and press any key. Watch the messages that appear for any indications of problems. In response to "Compare another diskette," press N. You'll be prompted to press another key to get back to the **DOS Utilities** screen.

4. Go to the command prompt. Enter the command:

```
VOL A:
```

to see the label and volume serial number for one diskette. If you did a two-drive disk copy, enter

```
VOL B:
```

to display the information for the other diskette. If you did a one-drive disk copy, insert the other diskette in drive A: and again enter:

```
VOL A:
```

5. For a one-drive disk copy, enter these commands:

```
DISKCOPY A: A:
DISKCOMP A: A:
```

For a two-drive disk copy, enter these commands:

```
DISKCOPY A: B:
DISKCOMP A: B:
```

## Summary

This chapter has covered some utilities that you'll find helpful in many DOS sessions. You've learned the Print, Date, and Time functions. In addition, you have learned how to format a disk, check and change its volume information, copy it, and check the copy. In Chapter 5, you will learn more file and directory functions.

## Exercises

These exercises give you a chance to practice the disk management skills you have learned in this chapter.

| **What You Should Do** | **How the Computer Responds** |
|---|---|
| 1. Reboot and get to the command prompt. | 1. Restarts DOS and displays the appropriate command prompt. |
| 2. Print C:\AUTOEXEC.BAT, initializing the Print function in the process. | 2. If you didn't include the /D switch with the command, prompts you for the name of the list device. Then prints the specified file. |
| 3. Set the date and time to January 1, 2001, at midnight. | 3. If you didn't include the date or time in the appropriate command, displays the current one and asks for the new one. |
| 4. Format a new or reusable diskette in drive A:. Label it SUMMARY EX. | 4. Prompts you to insert a new diskette in drive A:, then formats it. If you didn't include the /V switch in the FORMAT command, asks for the volume label. Displays diskette statistics and volume serial number. |
| 5. Check the diskette label and volume serial number. | 5. Displays the diskette's label and volume serial number. |
| 6. Delete the diskette label. | 6. Displays the label and asks for a new one. In response to the Enter key, asks if you want to delete the current label. Deletes the label when you enter Y. |
| 7. Select any diskette that fits drive A: and copy it to the diskette you just formatted. | 7. Tells you when to insert each diskette. Performs the copy, then asks if you want to copy another. |
| 8. Compare the copy with the original. | 8. Tells you when to insert each diskette. Displays compare errors or the message "Compare OK." Asks if you want to compare another. |
| 9. Start up the shell. | 9. Displays the **Start Programs** screen. |
| 10. Print C:\AUTOEXEC.BAT again. | 10. Prints the file. |
| 11. Restore the correct date and time. | 11. Displays the **Date and Time Utility** dialog box—first for the date, then for the time. Corrects the system date and time according to your entries. Prompts you to press a key to continue. |

12. Reformat the practice diskette in drive A:.

12. Displays the **Format Utility** dialog box. Displays a screen similar to the command prompt screen to show FORMAT command messages and to collect your responses. Returns to **DOS Utilities** screen after you respond to final prompt.

13. Copy another diskette to the practice diskette.

13. Displays the **Diskcopy Utility** dialog box. Displays a screen similar to the command prompt screen to show DISKCOPY command messages and to collect your responses. Returns to **DOS Utilities** screen after you respond to final prompt.

14. Compare the copy with the original.

14. Displays the **Diskcomp Utility** dialog box. Displays a screen similar to the command prompt screen to show DISKCOMP command messages and to collect your responses. Returns to **DOS Utilities** screen when finished.

## What If It Doesn't Work?

1. If the PRINT command doesn't cause a file to be printed, check your printer. If it was working earlier, check the cable, the power, and the paper supply. If your printer has never worked with DOS, get help from an expert.

2. If the Format function results in error messages about the target diskette, try a different diskette. Diskettes with bad sectors in track 0 cannot be formatted.

3. If the Diskcopy function results in error messages about bad tracks on the target diskette, try a different target diskette.

4. If the Diskcomp function results in error messages, redo the disk copy and try the comparison again. No comparison errors should be found immediately after a disk copy.

5. If the **Print** option on the **File** menu is gray, either a file isn't selected or the Print function isn't initialized. Try again.

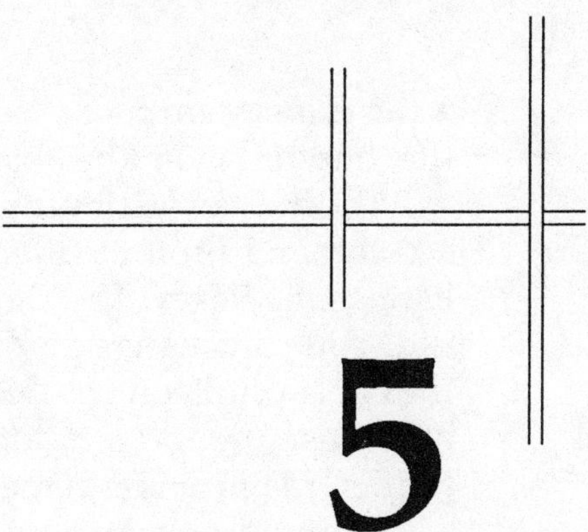

# 5

# *File and Directory Management*

In this chapter, you'll learn more techniques for managing directories and files through the shell. You'll also learn equivalent commands, where they exist. Specifically, you'll learn to:

- Define and change file attributes using the shell and the command prompt
- Rearrange directory displays in the shell
- Display additional file information in the shell
- Change confirmation and selection options in the shell
- Run programs from within the shell
- Associate extensions with programs to be run from within the shell

## *File Attributes*

Every file can have up to four special attributes that affect how it is handled by DOS functions. You can check the status of all four attributes in the shell. You can change three of them from within the shell. And you can change two of them with the ATTRIB command. This section overviews the attributes and shows you how to handle them.

### *What They Are*

The system attribute identifies a system file; this attribute is set by the program that creates the file and does not correspond with the SYS extension. If a file is a system file, a letter **s** will appear when you check the file's attribute, but you won't be able to change it.

The hidden attribute identifies a hidden file, one that does not appear in a command prompt directory listing. Hidden files always appear in shell listings, however. The character **h** indicates that a file has the hidden attribute. You can change any file to hidden within the shell, but you won't see the effect until you use DIR at the command prompt. You can view, copy, or otherwise process a hidden file from the shell, but you can't delete it, so a hidden file provides a measure of protection as well.

The read-only attribute doesn't affect whether a file appears in the directory, but it affects what you can do with the file. You can't modify or delete a read-only file. This attribute (indicated by **R** or **r**) protects the file against accidental or casual changes or deletions. Anyone who knows how to change an attribute, of course, could remove this attribute and have full access to the file.

The archive attribute indicates that the file has been changed at some point. DOS turns this attribute on automatically when you create or modify a file; when you copy a file, the archive attribute is turned on for the new copy. When this attribute is turned on (indicated by **A** or **a**), the file will be backed up if you use the DOS BACKUP command to archive your files. Some other DOS commands also select files for processing based on the archive attribute. You'll learn more about the effects of this attribute later, but you change it just as you do the read-only attribute.


## Full File Information in the Shell

When a file is selected, you can see a panel of information about the file and its surroundings. From the **File System** screen, select the **Options** menu. This menu contains three options:

> **Display options**
> **File options**
> **Show information**

The **Show information** option results in specific information, like that shown in Figure 5.1. In this case, C:\DOS\IO.SYS was selected.

The **Show Information** dialog box has four sections. The first section, headed **File**, names the current file and shows the status of all four attributes. The name IO.SYS is shown in the figure. This file has three attributes turned on; **r** indicates read-only, **h** indicates hidden, and **s** indicates system. The remaining period indicates that the archive attribute is not on. A file

```
  08-01-89                        File System                       8:46 am
  File   Options   Arrange   Exit                                   F1=Help
  Ctr ┌──────── Show Information ─────────┐
 ▭A   │                                   │
      │  File                             │
 C:\  │    Name  : IO.SYS                 │                    *.*
      │    Attr  : rhs.                   │
      │  Selected      C       A          │
 ✓C:\ │    Number:     1       0      ▭HOT      .BAT      128   07-20-89
  ─D( │    Size  :    22,357         ▭HOT      .SAV      128   07-20-89
   L  │  Directory                   ▭IO       .SYS   22,357   07-24-87
 ─T!  │    Name  : ROOT              ▭KEYBOARD.SYS   19,735   02-09-88
 ─H$  │    Size  :   284,725         ▭LASER    .BAT      128   05-13-89
   L  │    Files :        34         ▭LOADHI   .COM    2,381   03-29-88
 ─TI  │  Disk                        ▭MOUSE    .COM    4,734   06-17-87
 ─U!  │    Name  : DOS 4 PART        ▭MOUSE    .SYS    4,568   06-17-87
 ─RL  │    Size  : 25,600,000        ▭MSDOS    .SYS   30,128   07-24-87
   L  │    Avail : 12,849,152        ▭PARK     .COM       48   04-22-86
 ─M(  │    Files :       782         ▭PRINTER  .SYS   13,559   02-09-88
 ─D(  │    Dirs  :        19         ▭QEMM     .COM    2,129   03-29-88
 ─P(  │                              ▭QEMM     .SYS   26,100   03-29-88
 ─W$  │  ( Esc=Cancel )  ( F1=Help ) ▭RUTHC              128   07-28-89
      └───────────────────────────────┘  ▭RUTHNEW            128   07-28-89
  ─POSTS                    ▼   ▭TOUNIX   .MEM      256   05-26-89
  F10=Actions   Shift+F9=Command Prompt
```

Figure 5.1. Show Information Dialog Box

that has only the archive attribute would show **...a**; a file with no attributes would have four periods in this field.

If more than one file is selected, the one selected or deselected most recently is named in the **Show Information** dialog box. If no file has yet been selected or deselected, the first file in the directory listing is shown. The attributes shown apply to the displayed filename.

The **Selected** section shows the current selected disk (C: here), the number of selected files, and the total size of those files. If two columns are shown in this section, the other column refers to the previously selected disk (A: in this example). This feature is very useful if you are going to copy a number of files to a diskette and you want to make sure the diskette has enough room for them.

First select the source drive and select all the files to be copied. Then change to the target drive and select **Show information**. You will see both drives in the **Selected** section. The number and *total size* of the files selected on the source drive are displayed. But the **Disk** section reflects the current drive, which is the target drive if you've followed the right steps. By comparing **Selected:Size** with **Disk:Avail**, you can see whether the target disk has enough room for the copies.

The **Directory** section gives information about the directory that contains the displayed file. The directory name is given, but other directories in the path are not shown. You can also see the number of files in that directory and the total amount of space they occupy.

The **Disk** section gives information about the currently selected disk on which the displayed file is stored. The name provides the volume label. You can see the total size of the disk partition as well as the amount of available space; it is easier to read the information here than on DIR command output because the shell formats numbers with commas for readability. Here, you can check to see how much space remains on a diskette in preparation for adding files to it. The total number of files and directories in the partition is shown as well.

Start at the **File System** screen. Make C:\ the current directory.
1. Examine the attributes of IO.SYS.
2. Examine the attributes of \DOS\MYADDR.
3. Insert any nonblank diskette in drive A: and examine its information. (Notice that the information for the previous drive is also shown.)

1. *Select IO.SYS, pull down the **Options** menu, and select **Show information**. Select **Cancel** to return to the **File System** screen.*
2. *Make DOS current and select MYADDR. Then follow the same procedure as in Item 1.*
3. *Make the diskette current and follow the same procedure as in Item 1.*

## Changing Attributes in the Shell

The shell has a special option you can use to change attributes of one or more selected files. You can change all attributes in one operation or ask the shell to let you change them individually. First select the files whose attributes you want to change. Then pull down the **File** menu and select **Change attributes**. You'll see a dialog box with two choices, in which you decide whether to change attributes for selected files individually or as a group. If you choose to change attributes as a group, all attributes of the group are initially cleared. Once you respond, you'll see the dialog box shown in Figure 5.2. Notice that only three attributes are listed. You can't change the system attribute.

Any attributes marked with a triangle are currently turned on; others are off. You can reverse the status of any attribute by selecting it. Just click on the attribute by using the mouse, or use the arrow keys to highlight it and press the Spacebar to toggle the attribute. When the attributes you want turned on are marked, select Enter to process the action. If you change your

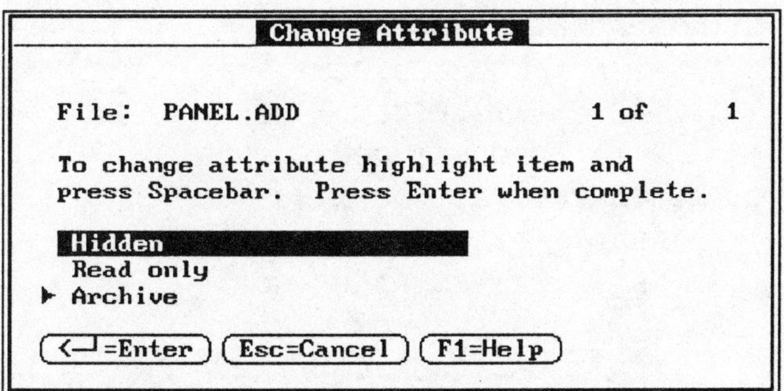


Figure 5.2. Change Attributes Dialog Box

mind, you can select **Cancel** to restore the previous status. Once you have changed the attributes, it's a good idea to check the attributes with **Show information** to make sure they are recorded.

Notice that you can check the status of the various attributes in this dialog box as well as in the **Show Information** dialog box. You don't see the system attribute here, but since you can't do anything with it, that doesn't really matter. If you are using this feature to check attributes, be sure to cancel it when you are finished to prevent inadvertent changes.

Suppose you want to write-protect all EXE files in your current directory without changing any other attributes. First select **Deselect all** to start fresh, then select the files you want to change. When all EXE files are selected, choose **Change attributes** from the **File** menu. When asked if you want to change the attributes individually or as a group, select **individually**. In each following box, turn on the read-only attribute and select Enter. That's all there is to it. (You can't make this change as a group because DOS will automatically turn off all existing attributes.)

## Viewing and Changing Attributes at the Command Prompt

At the command prompt, you can use the ATTRIB command to view and change the read-only and archive attributes. The hidden attribute can be changed only through the shell. Here's the command format:

```
ATTRIB [±R] [±A] filespec [/S]
```

In its simplest form, ATTRIB can be used to display the attributes of the files identified by *filespec*; you can use a single or a global filespec as needed. The /S switch tells DOS to select matching files from the entire subtree. On the following page is an example of displayed file attributes.

```
C:\DOS>ATTRIB *.COM
   A           COMMAND.COM
   A     R     STYLE.COM
   A           FORMAT.COM
C:\DOS>ATTRIB A:\*.COM /S
         R     A:\EXTRA\HSG.COM
   A     R     A:\EXTRA\PS.COM
   A           A:\WS.COM
               A:\TRUE.COM
   A           A:\GLADLY.COM
C:\DOS>_
```

The A indicates that the archive attribute is on for that file; R indicates that the read-only attribute is on. If a letter does not appear, the file doesn't have that attribute.

The rest of the ATTRIB options are used to turn the archive attribute and the read-only attribute on (with a plus sign) or off (with a minus sign). The command ATTRIB +R CHAP*.* gives all files that match the global filespec in the current directory the read-only attribute. The command ATTRIB +A -R \DOS4\CHAP6 turns the archive attribute on and the read-only attribute off for the indicated file.

---

Start at the **File System** screen. Make C:\DOS the current directory.
1. Move MYADDR to the \PRACTICE directory.
2. Make three copies of MYADDR called COPY1, COPY2, and COPY3.
3. Set the MYADDR file to read-only and turn off its archive attribute.
4. Set COPY1 to read-only; set COPY2 and COPY3 to hidden.
5. Terminate the shell. Make \PRACTICE current.
6. View the attributes of all files in the current directory. (Notice that you can't see hidden files, such as COPY2 and COPY3.)
7. Remove the read-only attribute for MYADDR and restore its archive attribute.

---

3. *Select MYADDR. Pull down the* **File** *menu and select* **Change attribute**. *Select Option 1. In the resulting dialog box, highlight* **Read only** *and press the Spacebar to turn on the triangle marker. Move the highlight to* **Archive** *and press the Spacebar to turn off the triangle marker. Then select Enter.*
4. *Select COPY1, COPY2, and COPY3. Pull down the* **File** *menu and select* **Change attribute**. *In the resulting dialog box, select Option 1. Then set the desired attributes in each individual dialog box.*

6. *Enter the command:*

```
ATTRIB *.*
```

7. *Enter the command:*

```
ATTRIB +A -R MYADDR
```

# Rearranging the File System Display

The **File System** display, by default, shows the directory tree for one disk and the file listing for the selected directory. Several options are available for modifying the display to better meet your needs. You can limit the file listing by using a global filename or have it sorted by a feature other than filename. You can have two separate drive or directory listings on the screen. Or you can have a combined listing that includes all files on the current drive.

## File Display and Sequence

By default, the **File System** lists all files in the current directory in the right-hand panel; this is indicated by *.* above the listing panel. And the files are shown in alphabetical order by filename. You can change either of these features. Select the **Options** menu and choose **Display options**. You'll see the dialog box shown in Figure 5.3. The **Name** box shows the current global filename that selects files for display; the default of *.* selects all files, as you have seen. The group of options on the right shows how the displayed files are sorted; the sort option in effect is indicated by the black dot.

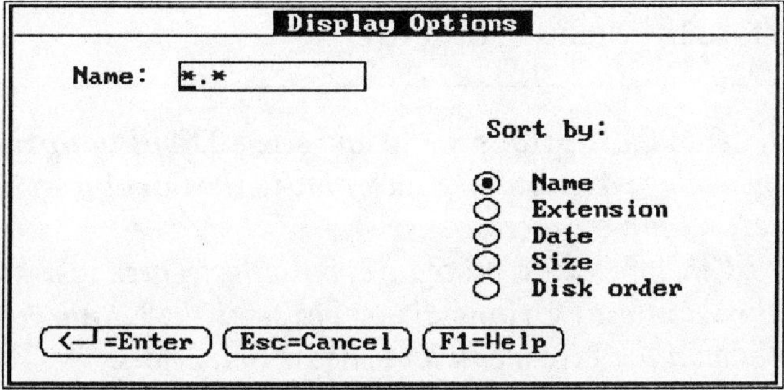


Figure 5.3. Display Options Dialog Box

To change the filenames that are displayed, just type a different global filename. It will appear at the top of the file listing and will control which files are displayed. You can use *.DOC to display all files with extension DOC, T* to display all files with names beginning with T, or whatever else you need. If you want to perform an operation on all EXE files, you might change the global filespec here to *.EXE. When only EXE files are displayed, you can use **Select all** to select all the EXE files for processing rather than having to select them individually from a more extensive file listing.

To change the sort order, select the sequence you want; only one of these sequences can be on at once. Selecting one sort order automatically turns off any others. If you don't want the standard sequence, you can have files sorted by extension, by displayed date (most recent first), or by size (largest first).

If you want the list in the same sequence as it would be if you used the DIR command, select **Disk order**. You can't specify a secondary sort field; if you sort by date, for example, you won't be able to predict the order in which same-size files appear.

If you are using the keyboard, use Tab to get to the **Sort by** options, then the arrow keys to select the option you want. When the sort option you want shows the black dot, select Enter. When you return to the **File System** screen, the files that match your new global filename will be displayed in the sort sequence you chose. When you exit the shell permanently, the default values for sort order and filespec are reset.

Start at the **File System** screen. Make C:\DOS the current directory.
1. Change the sort order to size.
2. Change the sort order to date.
3. Limit the display to COM files.
4. Select all files.
5. Expand the directory listing to include all files. Notice that the COM files are still selected.
6. Restore the default sort order.

---

1. *Pull down the **Options** menu and select **Display options**. In the **Display Options** dialog box, click on **Size** or tab to the **Sort by** section, move the highlight to **Size**, and press Enter.*
2. *Repeat the preceding procedure, but select **Date** instead of **Size**.*
3. *In the **Display Options** dialog box, edit the **Name** box to read *.COM.*
4. *Pull down the **File** menu and choose **Select all**.*
5. *Follow the same procedure as in Item 3 but make the filename *.*.*
6. *Follow the same procedure as in Item 1, but select **Name** instead of **Size**.*

## Modifying the Directory Display

You can cause the **File System** to display two different directories (or different parts of a single directory) or all files on the current drive by using the **Arrange** menu. Its choices are **Single file list** (the default), **Multiple file list** (which means two), and **System file list** (which means all files on the disk). No matter which arrangement you use, the current sort order and filespec apply.

*Displaying Multiple Directories*   When you select **Multiple file list**, the drive, directory, and file information of the shell directory appear in the lower part of the screen, as shown in Figure 5.4. The order is the same in both file lists; if you change the order through **Display options**, both file lists reflect the new sequence.

The new panels in the lower part of the screen are controlled just like the original ones. Select a drive icon to control which drive is displayed in the **Directory Tree** panel. Select a directory to control the files listed in the listing panel. The Tab key lets you move through all the displayed areas.

Even though two directories are shown, only one is active at a time; the line above the upper **Directory Tree** panel shows which directory is currently active. Ordinarily, you can't select files from both directories to be affected by operations on the **File** menu. You'll see later in this chapter how to force the shell to let you select files across directories.

```
 03-07-89                   File System                    11:52 am
  File  Options  Arrange  Exit                             F1=Help
  Ctrl+letter selects a drive.
  [==]A  [==]B  [ ]C

 C:\
          Directory Tree                              *.*
 √A:\                               ↑
                                    ≪    SORT     .4          400   03-06-89
                                         SORT     .EXE      5,882   10-06-88
                                         SORT     .OUT        400   03-06-89
                                    ≫    SORT2    .OUT        400   03-06-89
                                    ↓    TREE     .COM      6,302   10-06-88

  [==]A  [==]B  [ ]C


          Directory Tree                              *.*
 √C:\                               ↑
   ├DOS                             ≪    ANSI     .SYS      1,647   07-24-87
   │ └TEMP                               AUTOEXEC .32         256   05-13-89
   ├TYPESET                              AUTOEXEC .BAK        263   07-31-89
   ├HSG                             ≫    AUTOEXEC .BAT        256   07-31-89
   │ └DOSFIGS                       ↓    AUTOEXEC .SAV        220   07-31-89
  F10=Actions   Shift+F9=Command Prompt
```

Figure 5.4. Multiple File List Display

*Displaying All Files on the Disk*   If you select **System file list** from the **Arrange** menu, the shell will display all the files on the current disk, in the current sort order. Figure 5.5 shows an example. Notice that the left-hand panel now includes information about a file instead of the directory tree. This panel is identical to the **Show Information** dialog box and reflects the same file. The line above the panels shows the complete path of the file identified in the left-hand panel.

The information displayed in the left panel is the same information displayed when you select **Show information** from the **Options** menu. As you select files in the right panel, either with arrow keys or the mouse, the information changes to reflect the most recently selected or deselected file. Notice that the complete path for the displayed filename is shown on the line above the panels.

Your list may show three files named AWARD.LET if you have that file in three different directories. When one of these files is selected, you'll see its immediate directory name in the left panel. The complete path appears on the line above the panels.

Most fixed disks contain hundreds of files. If you use care in naming your files, you can use a global filename (choose **Display options**) to include just the ones you want. If all your correspondence uses the extension LET, you could use *.LET to show only those files from the entire disk in the system file list. You can't limit this list to a certain subtree, however. The entire disk is searched for files that match your global filename.

```
 07-27-89                    File System                    10:37 am
  File  Options  Arrange  Exit                              F1=Help
  Ctrl+letter selects a drive.
  ══A  ══B  ══C

 C:\WS5
                                                   *.*
 File
   Name  : ASCII.PDF       &EXAMPLE.PUB       768    04-03-87    5:21pm
   Attr  : ...a            384K      .PAT      128    08-17-88    5:00pm
 Selected      C     A     386ASM    .EXE  199,728   07-07-88    9:47am
   Number:     0     1     386LINK   .EXE  119,504   07-08-88   12:44am
   Size  :          54     4201      .CPI   17,089   07-24-87   12:00am
 Directory                 5202      .CPI      459   07-24-87   12:00am
   Name  : WS5             ADDRESS            1,536   04-04-89    2:31pm
   Size  :   3,177,616     AIDLET    .BUZ    4,224   06-04-89    2:33pm
   Files :         122     ANSI      .SYS    1,647   07-24-87   12:00am
 Disk                      ANSI      .SYS    1,647   07-24-87   12:00am
   Name  : DOS 4 PART      APPEND    .EXE    5,794   07-24-87   12:00am
   Size  :  25,600,000     APPENDIX  .RVR   11,580   06-01-89    3:09pm
   Avail :  14,888,960     ASCII     .PDF      956   08-18-88    5:00pm
   Files :         698     ASSIGN    .COM    1,530   07-24-87   12:00am
   Dirs  :          16     ASSIGN    .COM    5,753   10-06-88   12:00am

 F10=Actions   Shift+F9=Command Prompt
```

Figure 5.5. System File List Display

When the system file list is displayed, you can select any displayed files to be processed with commands from the **File** menu. This approach lets you process files across directories without any effort. It can get you into trouble, however. Suppose you select six files to be deleted. In the **Delete File** dialog box, you'll see the names of the files to be deleted for confirmation, but you won't see the paths; you'll have to remember which files you chose or assume you were right. It's also easy to select more files than you really wanted. Before starting a multiple file selection for processing, it's a good idea to select **Deselect all** from the **File** menu to start with a clean slate.

Suppose you want to delete all copies of LETHEAD.STY throughout all the directories on your hard disk. You could select **System file list**, then select **Display options** and fill in LETHEAD.STY as the name. The resulting display will list every copy of LETHEAD.STY on the disk. Then, from the **File** menu, first choose **Select all,** followed by **Delete**.

## Selecting across Directories

If you want to select files in several directories for processing together without using the **System file list**, you must turn on a special value reached through the **Options** menu. When you select **File options**, you'll see the dialog box shown in Figure 5.6. You probably won't want to change the first two items, since they add an element of safety. If you don't want to confirm deletions and replacements, however, you can select one or both of these items to turn the feature off.

When you choose **Select across directories**, the shell lets you select files from many directories. If you have two directories displayed, you can select from both; you won't lose a selection when you activate the other listing. You can change your display to another directory, even another drive, and the shell remembers which files were selected.

It's a good idea to choose **Deselect all** before you begin a multiple selection across directories, because it is very easy to get lost. Once you choose an

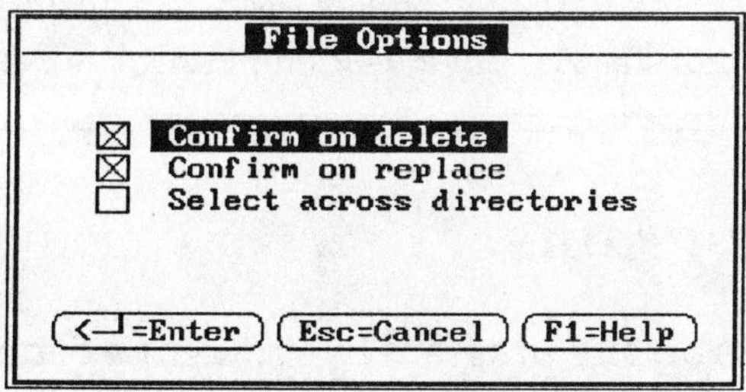


Figure 5.6. File Options Dialog Box

action from the **File** menu, you'll see the selected files in the **From** box in the dialog box, but you won't see the paths there. You must be organized and plan your actions when you select files across directories for processing.

If you have the **System file list** displayed, you can select any files listed, no matter what the status of this feature is. If you have turned on **Select across directories**, however, you'll be able to select from other drives as well.

---

Start at the **File System** screen. Make C:\DOS the default directory.

1. Change the arrangement to display two file lists. Change the lower one to C:\PRACTICE.
2. Select MYADDR and COPY1 in PRACTICE and APPEND.EXE and ASSIGN.COM in DOS. Copy them all to \PRACTICE\PRACA\PRACY.
3. Turn off **Select across directories**.
4. Display all files on the current drive in one list.
5. Page through the directory listing. Notice how the path changes as the highlight moves.
6. Select all versions of COPY1. Watch the information box change as you select each file. Remove their read-only attributes. Then delete the files.
7. Return to the default display.

---

1. *Pull down the **Arrange** menu and select **Multiple file list**. In the lower Directory Tree panel, select the PRACTICE directory.*
2. *Pull down the **Options** menu, select **File options**, then choose **Select across directories**. Pull down the **File** menu and select **Deselect all**. Then select the four files and complete the copy operation.*
3. *Pull down the **Options** menu, select **File options**, then choose **Select across directories** to turn this feature off.*
4. *Pull down the **Arrange** menu and select **System file list**.*
6. *Select all copies of COPY1. Pull down the **File** menu and select **Change attribute**. Select **Change all selected files at once**; this clears all the attributes for the files. Select Enter to get back to the **File System** screen. Select all copies of COPY1 again, then complete the delete operation.*
7. *Pull down the **Arrange** menu and select **Single file list**.*

---

## Running Programs

You can run any program by typing the command at the command prompt or by selecting the program from the **File System** screen, then selecting the appropriate option from the **File** menu.

## Using Commands

You have been running programs such as ATTRIB, COPY, and FORMAT at the command prompt already. You can run other programs in the same way; just type the program name, followed by any required parameters and switches. In order for the program file to be executed, it must have the extension COM, EXE, or BAT.

## Through the Shell

You can run any COM, EXE, or BAT file from the **File System** screen by selecting the file, then selecting **Open** from the **File** menu; you'll notice that these files have the program file icon rather than the data file icon in the file listing. Since this is the default action on the **File System** screen, the highlighted file is started if you press Enter from the **File System** screen with no menu pulled down or double-click on a filename. Figure 5.7 shows the dialog box. The program to be run appears as the **Starting program**; if you got here by mistake, you can select **Cancel** to remove the dialog box. We'll cover associated files shortly.

You can type any options to the program in the **Options** box. For example, if you want to sort a file named GROCERY, you would select SORT.EXE then open the file. In the **Options** box you would type < GROCERY; this tells DOS to use the GROCERY file as the input to the SORT program and to send the output to the screen. As soon as you select Enter to start the program, the dialog box and the **File System** screen disappear and you see the interaction screen, just as with the DOS Utilities. You'll see output there, and you may have to enter data there as well.

If you want to use your word processor, you don't have to get to the command prompt first. Just start your word processor from the **File System**

```
┌─────────────────────────────────────────────┐
│                   Open File                   │
│                                               │
│                                               │
│    Starting program:   WS.EXE                 │
│                                               │
│    Associated file :                          │
│                                               │
│    Options. .  [┌──────────────────────────┐→]│
│                                               │
│                                               │
│                                               │
│      (<─┘=Enter) (Esc=Cancel) (F1=Help)       │
└─────────────────────────────────────────────┘
```

Figure 5.7. Open File Dialog Box

screen, and respond to the dialog box, typing any required options. The next screen will show the opening screen of the word processor, which you can use as usual.

When you terminate a program started through the **Open File** dialog box, you see the familiar message telling you to press Enter to return to the shell.

## Associating Files

Normally, you can only open (or run or start) a file that has extension COM, EXE, or BAT, since these are the only files that represent programs. If you want to examine an Excel spreadsheet, you have to first start EXCEL.EXE, then tell it the file you want to use. If you prefer, you can associate particular nonprogram file extensions with a program; Excel spreadsheets generally use extension XLS and Excel charts use XLC, for example. Once an extension is associated with a program file, whenever you select a nonprogram file that has the associated extension, then open it, the associated program file will be started for the selected file.

For example, if you start JANDATA.XLS, the resulting dialog box, of the form shown in Figure 5.7, indicates EXCEL.EXE as the **Starting program** and JANDATA.XLS as the **Associated file**. You still are able to enter any options that you need to run the program.

To specify associations, first select the program file (COM, EXE, or BAT extension) then select **Associate file** on the **File** menu. You'll see a dialog box like the one shown in Figure 5.8. You can type the extensions to be associated with that program in the box. Any particular extension can be associated with only one program file; when you select a file with the associated extension, the shell must know which program to start.

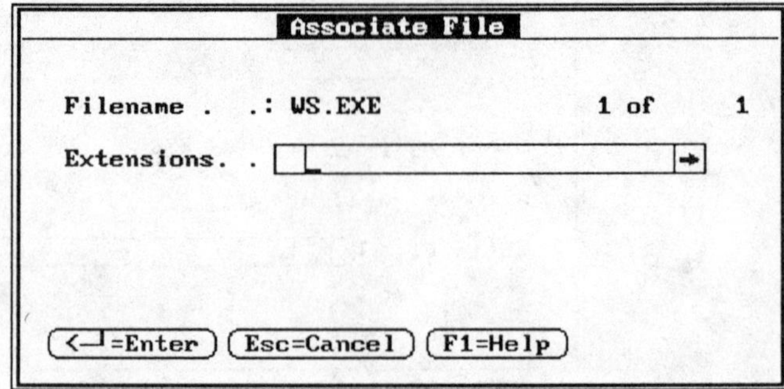


Figure 5.8. Associate File Dialog Box

The shell can handle up to 20 associated extensions. If you associate five extensions with EXCEL.EXE and four with your word processor, you have 11 left. You can divide the 20 in any manner you wish, whether all are associated with the same program or each with a separate one. Don't include the period in the extension entered in the box. If you need more than one extension, use a single space to separate them.

After you select Enter on the **Associate File** dialog box, you'll see another box in which you tell the shell whether or not to prompt you for options when you open the file. The **Open File** dialog box prompts for options; you'll see a similar box when you open an associated file unless you suppress the options.

Start with the **File System** screen. Make C:\DOS current.
1. Run SORT.EXE from the **File System** screen, redirecting input from C:\PRACTICE\MYADDR.
2. If you have installed a word processor on your hard disk, run it from the **File System** screen.
3. Exit the word processor and return to the shell.
4. Rename C:\PRACTICE\MYADDR to MYADDR.LST.
5. Associate the extension LST with C:\DOS\PRINT.COM.
6. Open the file named MYADDR.LST to see the effect.
7. Remove the association from PRINT.COM.
8. If you use a spreadsheet or database program, associate the appropriate extensions with the program name. This will make it easier for you to work with the shell. Practice opening files with associated extensions.

---

*1. Find the SORT.EXE filespec in the directory listing. Double-click on it; highlight it and press Enter; or highlight it, pull down the **File** menu, and select **Open**. Type < C:\PRACTICE\MYADDR in the **Options** box, then select Enter. You will see the sorted output on an interaction screen. Press Enter to return to the File System screen.*

*2. Switch to the directory that contains your word processor files. Find the correct program file and open it as in Item 1. (The program file is the one with the word processor's command name followed by EXE or COM, as in WS.EXE for WordStar or WP.EXE for WordPerfect.) You should get to the opening screen of the word processor.*

*3. Terminate the word processor as you usually do. You will probably see an interaction screen. If a message tells you to press Enter to return to the **File System**, do so. If there is a command prompt, enter DOSSHELL to restart the shell.*

5. *Change to the C:\DOS directory. Select PRINT.COM, pull down the **File** menu, and select **Associate**. In the resulting dialog box, enter LST in the **Extensions** box and select Enter. In the next dialog box, select **Do not prompt for options**.*

6. *Switch to C:\PRACTICE. Double-click on MYADDR.LST; highlight it and press Enter; or highlight it, pull down the **File** menu, and select **Open**. The result should be the equivalent of the command PRINT MYADDR.LST.*

7. *Switch to C:\DOS. Highlight PRINT.COM, pull down the **File** menu, and select **Associate**. In the resulting dialog box, blank out LST in the **Extensions** box.*

8. *Select the program file (such as EXCEL.EXE), pull down the **File** menu, and select **Associate**. In the resulting dialog box, enter extensions appropriate for that application. For example, for EXCEL, you would enter XLS, XLW, XLC, and XLM.*

## Summary

In this chapter, you have seen how to use file attributes, control the information displayed on the **File System** screen, display extra information about files, directories and disks, and set up files so they can be opened from the **File System** screen. In Chapter 6, you'll learn how to tailor the shell for your own uses.

## Exercises

These exercises let you practice the file and directory management techniques you learned in the chapter.

| **What You Should Do** | **How the Computer Responds** |
|---|---|
| 1. Using the File System's **Show Information** option, examine full information for C:\DOS\BOOKLIST. | 1. Displays a **Show Information** panel that shows the file's name, size, etc.—along with information about the directory and drive. |
| 2. Change the attributes for BOOKLIST to hidden and read-only, but not archive. | 2. Displays the **Change Attribute** dialog box showing the file's current attributes. Changes the attributes as you select each item. |

3. Set the arrange type to **System file list** and the display options filespec to MYADDR.*.

3. Displays a list of all the MYADDR files on the entire drive. The left-hand panel becomes an information panel.

4. Use **Select all** to select all the displayed files and **Print** to print them.

4. Prints all the MYADDR files listed in the directory listing.

5. Return to the single file list that shows all files in C:\PRACTICE.

5. Returns to the normal **File System** display. When you change the display options to *.*, displays all filenames.

6. Run TREE.COM from the **File System** screen.

6. Shows the TREE output on an interaction screen. A message at the bottom of the screen tells you to press Enter to return to the **File System**.

7. Associate the LST extension with PRINT.COM.

7. Displays the **Associate File** dialog box in which you can make the association. Records the association when you select Enter.

8. Open C:\PRACTICE\MYADDR.LST from the **File System** screen.

8. Prints MYADDR.LST.

9. Remove the association of LST with PRINT.COM.

9. Displays the **Associate File** dialog box with the current association shown. Records any changes you make to the dialog box when you press Enter.

---

## *What If It Doesn't Work?*

1. If PRINT can't find a file that is clearly shown in the file list, the file is hidden. Unhide it and try again.

2. If the **Print** option is gray, the Print function has not yet been initialized. You must initialize it at the command prompt.

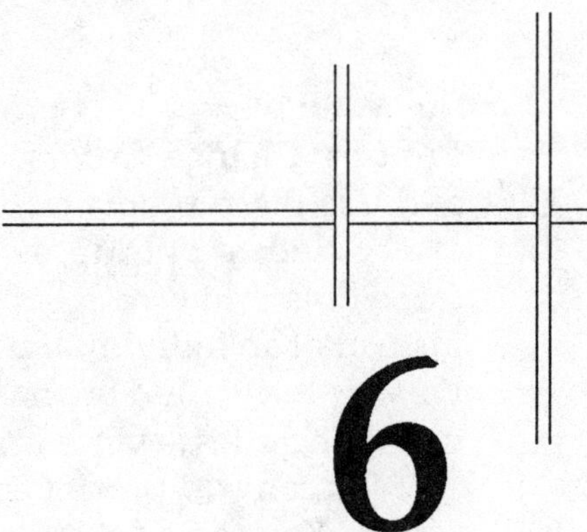

# 6

# *Tailoring the Shell*

When you receive the shell, it is set up to run a few programs; you've already learned to use most of these. In this chapter, you'll learn to add programs and groups to the **Start Programs** menu and to manage these so you can run any programs you want through the shell. Specifically, you'll learn to:

- Add a program to a group
- Change a program definition
- Delete a program
- Copy a program to another group
- Add a group
- Change a group definition
- Delete a group
- Reorder a group
- Define additional dialog boxes for program input
- Define help text for use with new programs and groups

## *Groups and Programs*

The DOS shell is organized in a modular fashion to let you run various programs. That is, the programs are gathered into groups and displayed on screens in menus. For example, the initial **Start Programs** screen displays the **Main** group. This group contains three programs, listed as **Command Prompt, Change Colors,** and **File System**. You've already learned to run and use these programs, which are integral to the shell itself. This screen also includes a group, listed as **DOS Utilities**. The group title ends with three dots to indicate that this item represents another group of programs instead of an individual program. As you know, when you select the group, you next see a list of the items included in the group. The **DOS Utilities** group includes several DOS programs you can run through the shell.

You can add programs to the **Main** group to run them from the opening screen. You can add programs to the **DOS Utilities** group. Or you can add more groups to keep similar kinds of programs together. For example, if you use several different word processors, you might define a group titled **Word Processors**; if you always use the same word processor, you might want to add that program to the **Main** group so that it is immediately available whenever you bring up the shell. If you have several accounting programs, you might define a group titled **Accounting**. Within the group, you can add the appropriate programs.

The **Main** group can contain programs as well as other groups. You can add groups only to the **Main** group, so all other groups can contain only programs. You can add as many groups as you need; each group can contain up to 16 programs.

## The Program Menu

The **Program** menu, shown in Figure 6.1, contains commands to start the currently selected program, to add a new program to the group, to change or delete an existing program from the group, or to copy a program from one group to another.

You already know that you can start a program by selecting it. You get exactly the same effect by highlighting the program title and selecting **Start** from the **Program** menu; this functions as the default option. You'll learn to use the other menu options in this section.

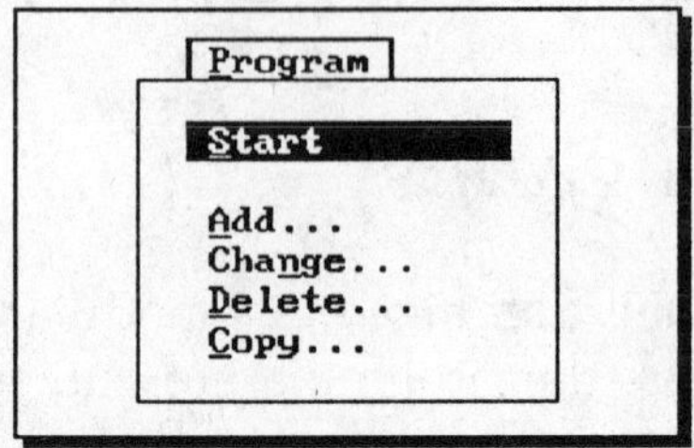


Figure 6.1. Program Menu

## Adding a Program

Suppose you usually use WordStar as your word processor. You start it by typing WS at the command prompt. To use this program from within the shell, you can add it to any already defined group. If you want it available as soon as you start up the shell, add it to the **Main** group. The first step is to pull down the **Program** menu and select **Add**. The shell gives you the dialog box shown in Figure 6.2. After you fill in the required information in the box and select **Save**, the program will appear in the list on the current screen.

*Required Information*   The first two boxes hold required information. In the **Title** box, you must provide a title of up to 40 characters. This value appears on the **Start Programs** screen. In the current example, we'll use Word Processing as the program title.

In the **Commands** box, you enter the command(s) needed to start the program from anywhere in the system; since you don't know from the **Start Programs** screen which directory or drive is current, use an absolute file-spec. If you want to change to a different drive, you can include that command as well. The **Commands** box holds up to 500 characters, which allows extensive commands and long paths. You can use a simple command, such as WS, or a multiple command entry in the form shown below:

```
drive || CD path || command
```

The double bar (||) is produced by pressing F4; it separates commands in the box. The first command changes the default drive to the one that holds the desired program. This is followed by the command separator, then the CD command to switch to the appropriate directory. Following another command separator is the command itself. In our example, we type C:||CD \WS5||WS in the **Commands** box.

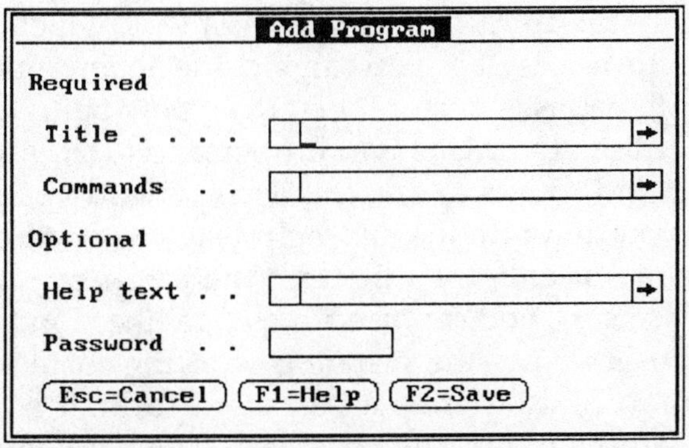

Figure 6.2. Add Program Dialog Box

If you have a set of commands to enter, you might find it easier to define the commands as a batch file (with extension BAT), then run it by its file-name. In this case, use a command like CALL WORDSTAR.BAT in the **Commands** box to start the program. You'll learn more about batch files, which are basically a set of DOS commands, later in this book. Later in this chapter, you'll learn to include more complex commands in the **Commands** box, including providing dialog boxes to request user input.

The **Title** and **Commands** are the only required elements in adding a program. At this point, if you select **Save**, the program is added to the list. When you start the program from the list, the commands are executed, which should cause the program to start.

*Editing in Text Boxes*   Sometimes you'll want to use a value that's too long to fit in the displayed portion of a text box. If you use all 40 allowable characters for a title, the text scrolls horizontally as you type. You can use the arrow keys to move within the text. When a box is selected, you can use the Home key to return the cursor to the beginning of the text or the End key to move the cursor immediately to the end. Use the Insert key to switch between insert and typeover mode. When the cursor appears as a vertical bar, editing is in insert mode; when it appears as an underscore character, editing is in typeover mode. The Delete key erases the character at the cursor; characters to the right slide over to fill the space. The Backspace key erases the character to the left of the cursor, pulling characters from the right to fill the space.

*Optional Information*   You can include Help text for the program if you wish by typing it in the **Help text** box. This text is displayed in a **Help** dialog box if the user selects **Help** (F1) when the title is highlighted on the **Start Programs** screen. The help text is automatically formatted to fit in the dialog box, which looks and works just like help for previously installed programs. You can use up to 478 characters of text, which is about three boxes full in the resulting display. You can include an ampersand (&) if you want to start a new line; this is useful for starting new paragraphs and including a list in help information. Use two ampersands (&&) to insert a blank line. Each ampersand counts as one character toward your limit.

If you don't define any help text, the shell displays a **Help** dialog box that contains only the title from the list. If you don't intend to provide any help for users, you can use a message like "No help provided for this item" so the user knows the system is working correctly.

You can also define a password to limit access to the program if you wish, although this isn't necessary. The password can consist of up to eight standard characters, including spaces; the shell converts all letters to upper-

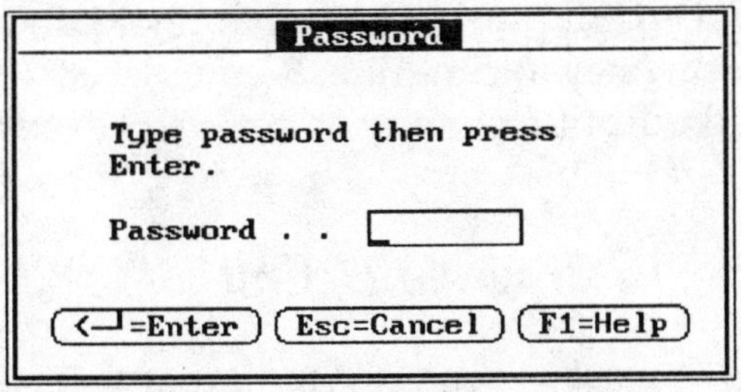

Figure 6.3. The Password Dialog Box

case. If you assign a password, the dialog box shown in Figure 6.3 appears whenever someone tries to start, change, or delete the program from the shell. If you don't type the password correctly, you'll see a **Warning** dialog box containing the message "Password incorrect." When you remove the box, you'll see the **Password** dialog box again, allowing you to reenter the text. Just select **Cancel** if you want to remove the **Password** box.

The password has no effect outside the shell, but it affects whatever you try to do with that program within the shell. Even if you want to remove the password later, you'll have to know it to get at the program.

If necessary, you can view the menu program and discover the password for any program. For programs in the **Main** group, view the file called SHELL.MEU; viewing MEU files makes more sense in hex. Just page through the file until you see the title for which you need to know the password. It will appear just following the title; if the password included any letters, they appear in uppercase.

## Using the Added Program

When you save the added program, its title appears in the program list. If you highlight the title and select **Help**, you should see whatever you entered in the **Help** box. When you select the program directly or start it through the **Program** menu, DOS asks for a password, if any, then executes the commands you typed into the box. You can use the started program just as though you started it from the command prompt.

When you leave the program, you may be returned directly to the shell. Some programs manage to reset some DOS switches and leave you at the command prompt when they terminate. If this happens, you can return to the shell by typing DOSSHELL at the prompt.

If the program ends with a screen display, DOS may return to the shell so quickly that you don't have time to read the display. In that case, end the **Commands** box with a command separator (||) and the special command

PAUSE. PAUSE puts the screen on hold and displays a message telling you to press any key to continue. If you place PAUSE between commands, it lets you read output from one before DOS executes the next.

## Changing a Program Definition

You can change a program definition by selecting **Change a program** from the **Program** menu. You'll have to provide the password if one has been assigned. Then the shell gives you a dialog box just like the **Add Program** dialog box shown earlier in Figure 6.2, but the already defined values appear in the text boxes.

You can click, Tab, or Enter to move between the boxes. Just move the cursor to the position you need and make your changes. Remember to use End to move to the end of the value. When any values you want to change are changed, select **Save** to save the new version and try it out again.

Be sure to remove any text that you don't want to appear; use Delete or Backspace to remove it. This is especially important in the **Password** box; if any extra characters are left from before, you may have trouble figuring out what password you ended up with. To remove a password, use Delete or Spacebar to remove all current characters in the box.

1. Add a program to the **Main** group called **Check the volume information**, which executes the simple command VOL.
2. Try out the program you just added. (The volume information will flash by very quickly.)
3. Change the program definition to pause after displaying the volume information. Also add a few paragraphs of help information.
4. Try out the help system for your revised item.
5. Try out the revised item.
6. Add a new program to the **Main** group called **Change the volume label**, which assigns a new label to the diskette in drive A:. Include some help information and assign a password of XXXX.
7. Insert any formatted diskette in drive A:. Try out the new label program.

1. *Pull down the **Program** menu and select **Add**. In the dialog box, enter "Check the volume information" in the **Title** box. Enter VOL in the **Commands** box. Select **Save** to record the new program, which should then appear in your **Main** group.*

2. Select **Check the volume information**, just as you would select any other item in the group.
3. Highlight **Check the volume information**. Pull down the **Program** menu and select **Change**. Tab to the **Commands** box or click on it to put the cursor in it. Press End to move the cursor to the end of the box. Press F4 to add a command separator ( || ) to the box. Type PAUSE. Then tab to the **Help text** box and type some help text, using && to start a new paragraph. Select **Save** to record the changes you have made in the dialog box.
4. Highlight **Check the volume information** and select **Help**. Select **Cancel** to get back to the **Start Programs** screen.
5. Select **Check the volume information**, just as you did before.
6. Pull down the **Program** menu and select **Add**. In the dialog box, enter "Change the volume label" in the **Title** box; enter LABEL A: in the **Commands** box; enter any text you choose in the **Help text** box; and enter XXXX in the **Password** box. Select **Save** to record the new program.
7. Select **Change the volume label**. In the **Password** dialog box, enter XXXX. Respond to other prompts as necessary.

## Deleting a Program

Deleting a program from a group is as simple as highlighting the program title, then selecting **Delete** from the **Program** menu. If the program is password-protected, you'll have to enter the password. Then you confirm the deletion and it is removed from the list. The program isn't actually deleted from the disk; it is simply removed from the group listing, along with any help text you had defined.

## Copying a Program

You can copy a program to another group if you wish. So far, only two groups are defined—the **Main** group and the **DOS Utilities** group. A group must be defined before you can copy a program into it; you'll see how to define a group shortly.

To copy a program, first highlight the title, then select **Copy** from the **Program** menu. You'll see a message at the top of the screen, as shown in Figure 6.4. This message stays on the screen until you have pressed F2 to complete the copy or F3 to cancel it.

You change to the screen for the destination group in the normal way. If you are currently in the **Main** group, just select the destination group from

> To complete the copy, display the destination group,
> then press F2.  Press F3 to cancel copy.

Figure 6.4. Copy Program Message

the list. On the resulting screen, press F2 and the copied program title appears in the list. If you are in another group, such as the **DOS Utilities** group, press Esc (or select **Cancel**) and you'll be returned to the **Main** group, where you press F2 to complete the copy. If additional groups have been defined, you can move around among them until you display the destination group, then press F2. If you press F3 before F2, the copy is canceled and the currently displayed group is left on the screen.

Start at the **Main** group on the **Start Programs** screen.
1. Copy the **Change the volume label** program to the DOS Utilities group.
2. Try out the program on the **DOS Utilities** screen.
3. Delete the program from the **Main** group.

1. *Highlight **Change the volume label**. Pull down the **Program** menu and select **Copy**. In the **Password** dialog box, enter XXXX. Select **DOS Utilities**. When the **DOS Utilities** screen appears, press F2. The program title should appear on the **DOS Utilities** screen.*
3. *Select **Cancel** to return to the **Main** group. Highlight **Change the volume label**. Pull down the **Program** menu and select **Delete**. In the **Password** dialog box, enter XXXX and then confirm the deletion. The program title should disappear from the screen.*

# Working with Groups

The **Group** menu allows you to create and manipulate groups. Groups can be added only to the **Main** group; most options on the **Group** menu are gray if you select them from within a group other than **Main** or if a group title is not highlighted. In the listing, a group title ends with three dots. You can change or delete groups as needed, but you can't copy them. These operations are performed very much like the corresponding functions for programs. They are available whenever a group is selected. When a program is selected, most group functions are gray, just as program functions may be gray if a group is selected.

One additional function lets you rearrange the order of items in the group's listing. This function is available no matter what is selected, since it affects the entire listing.

## Adding a Group

In order to add a group, you must be at the **Main** group. The resulting dialog box is very similar to the **Add Program** dialog box, except for one field. Figure 6.5 shows the **Add Group** dialog box; a title has already been entered.

The **Title** and **Filename** information are required. The title specifies what appears on the **Start Programs** list. A group title is limited to 37 characters to allow space for the three dots at the end.

The **Filename** box here replaces the **Commands** box of the **Add Program** dialog box. You don't name an existing file here, but you provide the basis for a file that DOS will use to store information about this group. The filename is a standard DOS filename of up to eight characters; the shell automatically appends the extension MEU to the filename. (SHELL.MEU contains the **Main** group information, while DOSUTIL.MEU contains **DOS Utilities** group information.) DOS creates this file to hold information about the programs that you will put in this group later.

The **Help** box is just the same as for programs. You can enter up to 478 characters, including spaces. Use the ampersand (&) anytime you want to force a new line.

You can assign a password, just as with programs, if you wish. If you assign a password to a group, it limits access to the entire group; when the

```
┌─────────────────────────[ Add Group ]─────────────────────────┐
│                                                                │
│  Required                                                      │
│                                                                │
│  Title . . . .     ┌─Accounting Routines──────────┐ →         │
│                    └──────────────────────────────┘           │
│  Filename  . .     ┌──────────────────┐                       │
│                    └──────────────────┘                       │
│  Optional                                                      │
│                                                                │
│  Help text . .   ┌────────────────────────────────────┐ →     │
│                  └────────────────────────────────────┘       │
│  Password  . .   ┌──────────────────┐                         │
│                  └──────────────────┘                         │
│  ( Esc=Cancel )  ( F1=Help )  ( F2=Save )                      │
└────────────────────────────────────────────────────────────────┘
```

Figure 6.5. Add Group Dialog Box

group is selected from the **Main** screen, the **Password** dialog box is presented before the group listing is shown. Once the group listing is displayed, the password won't be required to execute the listed programs; of course, they could have additional password protection if necessary. For example, if you give a password to a group titled **Accounting**, only people who know that password will have access to the programs you add to the **Accounting** group through the shell. The programs in the group can still be manipulated through the command prompt however.

Once the information is entered into the **Add Group** dialog box, select **Save** to save it, just as when adding programs. Then you can try out the group by starting it from the **Main** group screen. At this time, you'll see the message "Group is empty" because you haven't added any programs to it yet. You can add the programs you want directly by using the **Add** option from the Program menu or by using **Copy** to copy programs from another group.

## Managing a Group Definition

You can change a group definition much as you change a program definition. Select **Change** from the **Group** menu and edit the information in the text boxes as needed. Save the information when you're finished and try out the group to see if it works the way you want.

You delete a group just like you delete a program. Select the title on the **Main** group screen, then select **Delete** from the **Group** menu. The shell asks you to confirm the deletion, then removes the group from the screen.

## Rearranging Titles

When you add a program or a group, the shell always places it at the bottom of the current list. You can rearrange the order of titles listed for the current group. Each title must be moved to a new position individually, however. First select the title to be moved. Then pull down the **Group** menu and select **Reorder**. Figure 6.6 shows the message that appears under the group title near the top of the screen. If you've changed your mind about moving the selected item, just select **Cancel**.

Decide where you want the item to appear, then highlight the title at that position and select Enter. The reordered title appears at that position and other titles are adjusted in the list. For example, if you want to move the bottom item so that it is second in the list, highlight the bottom title, select **Reorder**, then highlight the second item in the list and select Enter. If you

To complete the reorder, highlight the new<br>
position, then press Enter.  Press Esc to cancel.

Figure 6.6. Reorder Titles Message

want the first title to be last, highlight the first title, select **Reorder**, then highlight the last title and select Enter. If you want some other titles moved, repeat the process.

Start at the **Main** group on the **Start Programs** screen.

1. Create a new group named **Practice Programs**. Name the file PRACTICE. Provide a brief help message to indicate that help will be provided later.
2. Copy **Check the volume information** to the new group.
3. Add a new program to the group that checks available memory. Call the program **Memory check**. The command is MEM. Follow it with PAUSE so the output can be read.
4. Try out the new program.
5. Copy the new program to the **Main** group.
6. Rearrange the titles in the **Main** group. Put the **File system** at the top. Put all groups at the bottom.
7. If you have a word processor or other program you use frequently, add it to your **Main** group. Try it out and adjust the command until selection of the title puts you right into the program.

1. *Pull down the **Group** menu and select **Add**. Within the dialog box, enter "Practice Programs" in the **Title** box. Enter PRACTICE in the **Filename** box. Enter whatever help you want in the **Help text** box. Then select **Save**.*
2. *Highlight **Check the volume information**, pull down the **Program** menu, and select **Copy**. Then select the **Practice Programs** group. When the **Practice Programs** screen appears, press F2.*
3. *Pull down the **Program** menu and select **Add**. Fill out the dialog box and select **Save**.*
5. *Highlight the title, pull down the **Program** menu, and select **Copy**. Go to the **Main** group screen and press F2.*
6. *Highlight each title you want to move, pull down the **Group** menu, and select **Reorder**. Move the highlight to the desired position and press Enter. You will see the title move.*

> 7. *If your word processing directory is not in your program search path, you need to include a CD command as the first command in the **Commands** box. This will allow you to get to the right directory for your word processor.*

# Tailoring the Dialog Box

Many times, you'll want to display a dialog box for the user to provide input when running a program from within the shell. You can include additional information in the **Commands** box to request the information. You can even tailor the dialog box to provide the appropriate instructions and prompts. For example, suppose you want to use a program that requires you to provide a filespec with the command. Since you'll use the program with many different files, you don't want to include a specific filespec in the command. When the program is started, you want a dialog box to appear so the user can enter the appropriate filespec. You can specify various options and information in the **Commands** box; the limit of 500 characters still stands. You'll learn to do this in the next section.

## Default Dialog Box

To produce a default dialog box, follow the program command with square brackets, with nothing between them. This tells DOS to produce a default dialog box for input and to use that input in the exact position of the square brackets; be sure to leave a space before the set of brackets if the program requires a space between the command name and any other values. If you type RUNOLD [] in the **Commands** box and then start that program, you'll see the dialog box in Figure 6.7.

The dialog box size and text you see are the default; you can specify different text if you wish. When the program is run, whatever text the user types before selecting Enter will appear in the location of the brackets. If the

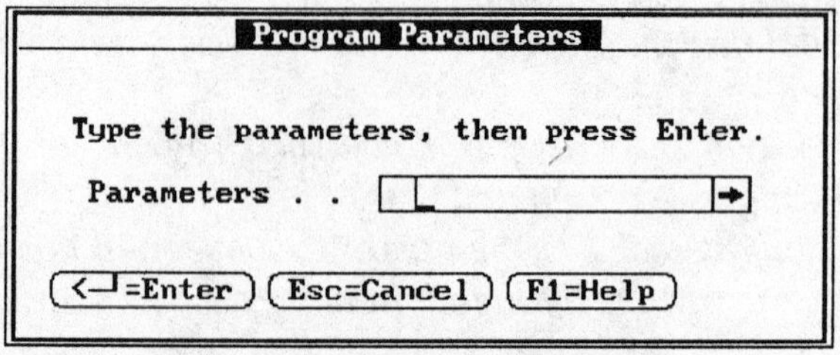

Figure 6.7. Default Dialog Box

user types BATH, the program is submitted as RUNOLD BATH. If the user types B: /S, the program is submitted as RUNOLD B: /S. The user must know what sort of values to type.

## Changing the Text

The square brackets are generally used to include startup options, also called program startup commands. You can specify various options inside the brackets to change the text as well as to have other effects. We'll look at the text options first.

The title of the dialog box appears in the top line; the default title is **Program Parameters.** You can specify a different title (up to 40 characters) with the /T option. If the **Commands** box contains "VOL [/T"Volume Checking"]", that phrase will replace the default title in the resulting dialog box.

The information immediately preceding the text box is called a prompt; the default prompt is **Parameters . .** , as you can see in Figure 6.7. You can specify a different prompt (up to 20 characters) with the /P option. If the **Commands** box contains "VOL [/T"Volume Checking"/P"Drive: "]", both a specific title and a specific prompt will appear in the dialog box. You can use either or both, in any order.

The last character you include in your specific prompt appears immediately to the left of the input box; periods aren't inserted automatically as they are for group names. You may want to be sure to use a space, a period, or a colon at the end of your prompts to allow a little separation. The default prompt includes a space following the last period.

The text above the input box is used for instructions to the user. You can use the /I option to include instructions to the user; be as specific as you want here, but keep in mind you are limited to 40 characters. If the **Commands** box contains "VOL [/T"Volume Checking"/P"Drive: "/I"Enter the drive you want checked"]", the resulting dialog box looks like the one shown in Figure 6.8. Notice that all three text areas are different from those in the default dialog box.

You can use any or all of these three options to tailor the dialog box to meet the needs of the program being run. The rest of the startup options affect other features, rather than text.

## Requesting Additional Input

Each set of square brackets ([ ]) represents a single dialog box. Each dialog box collects information and inserts it into the command at the point the

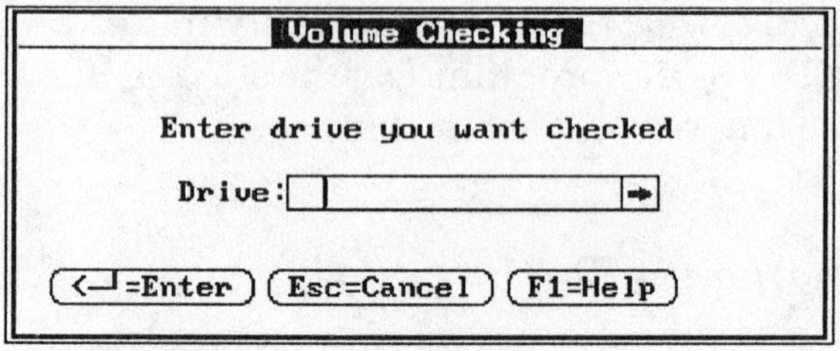

Figure 6.8. Tailored Dialog Box

brackets appear in your definition. If the items should be separated by spaces, be sure to use a space preceding each open bracket.

Suppose you want to use a program that requires two input values. You can include two sets of brackets with program startup commands at the appropriate locations in the command. When you start the program, the shell displays the first box and gets the input, then displays the second box and gets that input. Both input values are appended to the command, which is then executed. Suppose you want to run the DISKCOPY program with two separate input boxes, one for the source diskette drive and one for the target diskette drive. You could use default dialog boxes with this value in the **Commands** box:

```
C:||CD \DOS||DISKCOPY [] []
```

You can include your own text with a command like this:

```
C:||CD \DOS||DISKCOPY [/T"Diskcopy source"/I"Enter the
source drivename"/P"Source drive: "] [/T"Diskcopy
target"/I"Enter the target drivename"/P"Target drive: "]
```

Now two separate dialog boxes will appear, prompting the user effectively. If the user enters A: in the first box and B: in the second, the command is executed as DISKCOPY A: B:. If you neglect to put a space before each left bracket, the command is executed as DISKCOPYA:B: and you'll get an error message from DOS. If this happens, just change the definition to insert the required spaces.

Suppose your word processor can be started with the command name followed by the name of the file to be edited. You can also include an option to override the default mode. For example, you can start WordStar with WS, WS *filespec*, or WS *filespec switch*. Here's how the command might look if you allow for two separate input dialog boxes:

```
WS [/T"WordStar 5"/P"Filespec..."/I"Enter the file name"]
[/T"WordStar  5"/P"Option..."/I"Enter /n for nondocument
or press Enter"]
```

When you start the program, the first dialog box that appears asks for a filespec. After you enter that data, the next box asks you to type /n for the switch or press Enter to bypass it. If you type CHAP2 in the first dialog box and nothing in the second, the program will be executed as WS CHAP2 ; the space at the end doesn't hurt. If you type \UNIXBOOK\CHAP7.DOC in the first dialog box and /N in the second, the program is executed as WS \UNIXBOOK\CHAP7.DOC /N.

You can include additional information in the command line as well. One DOS command is SORT, which often requires extra characters to run correctly. You'll learn to use SORT in detail later on, but it is a good example here. If you want to sort the lines in file GROCERY and store the output in file GROCERY.SRT, you would enter the command, at the command prompt, as SORT < GROCERY > GROCERY.SRT. (The symbol < indicates where the input comes from and > indicates where to send the output.) In the **Commands** box, you could enter the command lines like this:

```
SORT < [/T"Sort a File"/P"Input filespec..."/I"Enter the
file to be sorted"] > [/T"Sort a File"/P"Output
filespec..."/I"Enter the file to hold the sorted output"]
```

When the program is executed, each input value is inserted in the location of the set of square brackets.

Start at the **Main** group.
1. Modify **Check the volume information** to display a default dialog box in which you can enter a drivename if desired.
2. Try out the program and correct it until it works.
3. Modify the program again to place specific values in the dialog box. The title should be "Volume Checking". The information should say "Enter the drive you want checked". The prompt should say "Drive: ".
4. Try out the program again and correct it until the dialog box appears as specified.
5. Add another program to the **Practice Programs** group. Set up the program to specify a source filespec and a target filespec for COPY.
6. Try out your COPY program and correct it until it works.

*1. Highlight **Check the volume information**. Pull down the **Program** menu and select **Change**. Put the cursor in the **Commands** box and press the right arrow key to position it after VOL. If the cursor is an underline, press the Insert key once to turn it into a vertical bar (indicating insert mode). Type a space followed* *by []. The changed command should look like this:*

```
VOL [] || PAUSE
```

*Select **Save** to save the changed program.*

2. *Place any formatted diskette in drive A:. Select **Check the volume informa-tion**. When the dialog box appears, type A: in the **Parameters** box and select Enter. If you don't get the volume information for drive A:, repeat Item 1 to correct the **Commands** box. Keep trying until the program runs correctly.*
3. *Edit the **Commands** box to read:*

```
VOL [/T"Volume Checking"/P"Drive: "/I"Enter the drive you
want checked"] || PAUSE
```

5. *In the **Add Program** dialog box, fill in the **Commands** box to contain something similar to this:*

```
COPY [/T"Copy File"/I"Enter the source filespec"/
P"Source: "] [/T"Copy File"/I"Enter the target filespec"/
P"Target: "] || PAUSE
```

*The spaces before the first dialog box and between the two dialog boxes are re-quired to make the COPY command run correctly.*

---

## Using Default Values

You may want to show a default value in an input box for the user. You would do this if a certain value is more likely to be used. For example, if you have a special program to check and change labels, you might want to use drive A: as the default, since you check most labels on diskettes in that drive.

The /D option lets you specify a default value; include it in the square brackets. Here's how you could add a default value to the volume-checking command:

```
VOL [/T"Volume Checking"/P"Drive: "/I"Enter the drive you
want checked"/D"A:"]
```

The default appears in the box. The user edits it as necessary, just as with the **Copy File** dialog box.

Sometimes you want the default to be removed if the user needs a differ-ent value. You can follow the /D option with /R to cause the default to be removed if the user types anything other than Enter or an arrow key. Here's how you could put a removable default in a command:

```
WS [/T"WordStar 5"/P"Filespec..."/I"Enter the file name"]
```

```
[/T"WordStar  5"/P"Option..."/I"Enter /n for nondocument"/
D"/d"/R]
```

The /R command has no value connected with it; this switch simply makes the default disappear if the user tries to type anything else in the field. It is most useful if you have a default directory appearing in the field. The sequence /D"\WS5\DOSBOOK\"/R causes the specified path to appear in the box, but as soon as the user types anything other than an arrow key, Enter, or End, the default value disappears and the user is in control.

Other default values you can use in the **Commands** box are /# and /@; use these at the end of the string outside the square brackets. The /# option causes the drive from which the shell was started to be used as the default; if no drive is specified in any filespec, this one will be used. The option /@ causes the absolute path to the directory containing the shell programs to be the default; if no path is specified in a filespec, this path will be used. These values won't appear in the dialog boxes, but the effects will be apparent if these defaults are needed.

## Limiting Input Length

You can use the /L option to limit input to a specific length. The value /L"8" could be used to limit an entry to only a filename. The value /L"12" limits the input to a filename and its extension. The input box size in the resulting dialog box is determined by the limitation. An item with /L"15" will have a longer box than one with /L"3", for example. As you've seen, when no length limitation is used, you get the sideways-scrolling input box.

1. Change your **Volume-checking** dialog box (**Main** group) so that it displays a default of drive A:. Try out the dialog box and correct it until it works.
2. Change your **Copy file** dialog box so that it displays C:\PRACTICE as the default value in the target file dialog box. If you type anything at the beginning of the box, the default should disappear. Try out the dialog box and correct it until it works.

1. *The* **Commands** *box should contain this:*

```
VOL [/T"Volume Checking"/P"Drive: "/I"Enter the drive you
want checked"/D"A:"] || PAUSE
```

2. *The **Commands** box should contain this:*

```
COPY [/T"Copy file"/I"Enter the source filespec"/
P"Source: "] [/T"Copy file"/I"Enter the target filespec"/
P"Target: "/D"C:\PRACTICE"/R] ||PAUSE
```

## Additional Program Startup Commands

The shell offers several additional options you can use in creating complex custom commands for your own programs. Figure 6.9 shows a list and a brief description of all the available startup command options. As you learn more about DOS and its command structure, you may want to return here and create more commands for your own use. Many of the options can be combined in various ways to create fairly complex effects. You'll learn many techniques later in the book that can be incorporated into shell dialog boxes.

| | |
|---|---|
| [ ] | Dialog box request; if nothing between brackets, use default form |
| /T"..." | Title for top of dialog box |
| /I"..." | Instructions to appear above input box |
| /P"..." | Prompt for left of input box |
| /D"..." | Default value to appear in input box |
| /R | Remove default if typed over |
| /L"$n$" | Limit input to $n$ characters |
| /M"E" | Limit input to existing files |
| /C"%$n$" | Save variable for next time command is used; then display as default |
| %$n$ | Variable; %1 through %10 |
| /# | Use shell drive as default |
| /@ | Use absolute shell path as default |

Figure 6.9. Program Startup Command Options

# Summary

In this chapter, you've learned to tailor the shell to include your own programs, arranged as you want them. You can now add programs and groups, change them, delete them, copy programs from one group to another, create your own dialog boxes, and rearrange the items in a group. In Chapter 7, you'll learn how to back up and restore your files.

# *Exercises*

These exercises let you practice manipulating programs and groups in the shell.

| **What You Should Do** | **How the Computer Responds** |
| --- | --- |
| 1. Add a new program to the **Main** group called **List directory**, which uses the DIR /P command to display a directory. Include dialog boxes to input the desired drive, path, and/or filename. (Hint: If you use more than one dialog box, no spaces should appear between them.) | 1. Displays the **Add Program** dialog box and records the information you enter there. Adds **List directory** to the **Main** group. |
| 2. Try out your new program and correct it until it works. | 2. Displays each of the dialog boxes you defined and records your input. Then issues a DIR /P command followed by the drive, path, and filespec you entered, if any. Displays the directory listing on an interaction screen. If you included a PAUSE command, waits for you to press a key before returning to the **Start Programs** screen. |
| 3. Create a new group called **Summary exercise**. Give it a password. | 3. Displays the **Add Group** dialog box and records the information you enter there. Creates an MEU file for the group. Adds **Summary exercise...** to the **Main** group. |
| 4. Copy **List directory** to **Summary exercise**. | 4. Displays a message to press F2 to complete the copy. Displays the **Password** dialog box when you select the **Summary exercise** group. Processes the password you enter. Displays the **Summary exercise** group screen, carrying over the "copy" message from the **Main** group screen. After you press F2, replaces "Group is empty" with **List directory**. |

5. Delete all the groups and programs you have created in this chapter (unless you want to keep them):

*Groups:*

Practice Programs
Summary exercise

*Programs*

Check the volume information (Main group, Practice Programs group)
Change the volume label (DOS Utilities group)
Memory check (Main group, Practice Programs group)
Copy file (Practice Programs group)
List Directory (Main group, Summary exercise group)

6. Rearrange the items in the **Main** group and **DOS Utilities** group to suit your needs.

5. Displays the **Password** dialog box for each password-protected item you select. Displays **Delete Item** dialog box for each item you delete. After you confirm each deletion, removes the item from the screen.

6. Each time you select **Reorder**, displays a message to position the highlight and to press Enter. When you do so, moves the title.

## What If It Doesn't Work?

1. Be sure to try out each new program you create and correct its definition until the program works correctly.

2. The spacing around dialog boxes in the **Commands** box can be very important. Consider the spacing you would use if you were entering the command at the command prompt, then use the same spacing before and after the dialog boxes that collect parameters for the command. The brackets and their contents are replaced by whatever value the user types when the dialog box is displayed.

3. Don't forget to include the command separator (obtained by pressing F4) between commands in the **Commands** box.

4. If command output disappears too quickly, add a PAUSE command to the preceding command.

5. If you forget a password, you can view the MEU file for the group. The file is easier to see in hex mode. Page through the file until you find the password you need. (You should recognize it when you see it.)

# 7

# *Backup and Restore*

After you have used your hard disk for a while, it will contain hundreds, or even thousands, of files—both programs and data files. What would be the cost of a hard disk crash that destroys all your files? You can recover your programs if you saved the original diskettes, but what about your data files—your databases, spreadsheets, drawings, reports, and so on? Your hard disk *will* crash eventually. Ignoring the possibility is like not checking the oil in your car. Even if your files aren't destroyed, you might not have access to them for several days while your hard disk is being repaired.

You can protect your investment with a good backup system, whereby you make regular copies on diskette of all files that you create or modify. This helps to protect your files not only from hard disk crashes, but also from accidental erasures, fire, theft, vandalism, and any other method of destroying data. You might want to keep several levels of backup to protect yourself against viruses.

DOS includes facilities to back up and restore files. In this chapter, you will learn to:

- Back up the entire fixed disk
- Back up selected files from the hard disk
- Restore selected files
- Restore the entire fixed disk

# Developing a Backup Plan

The wisest thing you could do for yourself right now is to devise a regular backup system. Decide how often you will back up files, what diskettes you will use, whether you will overlay older backup versions with newer backup versions, how you will label the diskettes, how you will document them, where you will store them, and how long you will keep them. This chapter will help you make those decisions.

Figure 7.1 shows a simple system based on a weekly cycle. Once a week, you back up the entire hard disk. You can omit program files since you still have the originals, but you might find it easier to just include all files with the global filespec *.*. You take the backup diskettes to a safe place, some place away from the computer location so they won't be destroyed in the same disaster that gets the computer and its hard disk. While you're there, you get last week's diskettes, which are now out of date.

On a daily basis, you back up modified files only. You put this diskette away in a safe place. Do you take it to the alternate location? That depends on how rigorous you want to be and how crucial the data is. If you keep the backup diskette near your computer, you stand the chance of losing it in the same disaster that kills the computer. Then you could lose up to six day's worth of revisions.

To restore an individual file, you figure out which backup diskette contains the latest version and restore the file from that diskette. If the hard disk crashes, you can use this approach to restore all the files (after repairs have been made):

1. Get the complete backup set from the alternate location and copy all files to the fixed disk. This will restore everything except the latest versions of files that were modified after the complete backup was made.

| | |
|---|---|
| Once a Week | Back up fixed disk completely. Take the backup diskettes to a storage location away from the computer. Return all last week's backup diskettes for reuse. |
| Daily | Back up modified files only. Put these backup diskettes in a safe place. Save until next week's complete backup operation. |

Figure 7.1. A Simple Weekly Backup Routine

2. Copy the week's modified files to the disk. This adds new files and overwrites modified ones.

The weekly system described here is just one approach to a backup system.
You might want to take a more rigorous approach, perhaps backing up the
entire fixed disk daily and backing up modified files hourly. You might want
to make several copies of the backup diskettes, storing them in various locations. You could keep old complete backups for several weeks in case you
need to fall back to an earlier version of a file, especially with files like spreadsheets and databases, where mistakes might not be apparent immediately.

On the other hand, you might want to be more relaxed, perhaps backing
up the entire disk only once a month and backing up modified files every
few days. That depends on your system security needs. The point is to have
some system and to stick to it.

This checkpoint requires paper and pencil only. You will begin to plan your
backup system.
1. Rate the security needs of your system on a scale of 1 (not very important)
   to 10 (desperately vital).
2. Based on that rating, how often do you think you should back up your
   entire fixed disk? Will you include program files in the backup?
3. How often do you think you should back up modified files?
4. Where will you keep your full-backup diskettes to avoid losing them in
   the same disaster that wipes out your computer? Will you keep your
   modified-files diskettes in the same location, or not worry about losing
   the files on them?

*The answers to this checkpoint depend on your system and applications. Save your
answers. You'll add more details to your plan as you progress through the chapter.*

# *The Archive Attribute and Time/Date Stamps*

Every time you modify a file, DOS records the current date and time in the
directory entry and turns on the archive attribute. In this context, modifying
a file includes creating a new one, changing an existing one, or copying one.
(Copies have their archive attribute turned on, but their date/time stamps
are copied from the original version.) The Backup and Restore facilities can
select files to be backed up or restored based on either their time/date stamps
or their archive attributes.

The time/date stamps help you select all files for backup that were created or modified after a specific date and time—probably the last time you backed up the entire disk. For example, suppose you back up the entire disk on Monday, 9-1-92, at 9:00 in the morning. On Monday night, you want to back up modified files only. You can ask the Backup facility to select all files with a time/date stamp on or after 9-1-92 at 9:01 AM. On Tuesday night, you do the same thing, overwriting Monday night's files. The same files will be backed up again, plus any files you created or modified on Tuesday. The resulting diskette contains all the files you need to bring the hard disk up to date. You repeat this procedure every night until you do the next full backup. At all times you have one set of diskettes that contains the complete collection of modified files for the week.

Another way to approach the daily backup is to select only files that have not yet been backed up. You use the archive attribute to achieve this. When a file is modified (which means it is created, changed, or created by being copied from another file), DOS automatically turns its archive attribute on. When it is selected and copied by the Backup facility, DOS automatically turns its archive attribute off again.

Suppose you back up the entire hard disk on Monday morning. All the archive attributes are automatically turned off. As you modify files on Monday, archive attributes for the modified files are turned on. On Monday night, you select modified files only for backup. Their archive attributes are turned off automatically as they are backed up. Every night, you repeat Monday night's process. Only the files modified since the previous night are selected. You *add* them to the backup diskette, or you create a new diskette each night.

Each of these approaches has its advantages and disadvantages. Using the archive attributes to select only files that were modified that day takes a lot less time because you back up fewer files each day. But you have to store more backup diskettes and you might have to search for a particular file that you want to restore.

If you modify a file more than once during the backup cycle, the archive attribute method gives you multiple versions of the file. It appears on the backup diskette for each day that it was modified. This could be advantageous: You have the ability to fall back on an earlier version to back out of a mistake or to get rid of a virus. On the other hand, it becomes that much harder to find the most recent version of the file to be restored. If you use the time/date method, newer versions overwrite earlier versions. Only the latest version appears on the daily backup diskette.

If you are using a database system to track inventory, sales, or some other aspect of your business, your database probably changes daily. You must give serious thought to whether you want to back up your database using the archive attribute method (where you would end up with a new version of the database every time you back up), or the time/date method (where you would end up with only the latest version).

---

This checkpoint requires paper and pencil only. You will decide which method of daily backups you will use.

Select A or B, depending on which features are more important to you:

A. Less time required to back up files each day; ability to fall back to an earlier version of a file.

B. Fewer backup diskettes required to be stored; only one version of a modified file needs to be available.

---

*If you chose A, then you would probably prefer the archive attribute method of daily backups. If you chose B, you would probably prefer the time/date method. You might want to develop a hybrid version that best meets your needs.*

---

## The BACKUP Command

One way to back up files is through the BACKUP command. You can invoke this command at the command prompt or through the **DOS Utilities** screen in the shell. We'll show you the command and its options first. Then we'll show you how to invoke it via **DOS Utilities**.

BACKUP has many advantages over COPY for making backup copies. It can copy files from an entire tree or subtree, not just from the current or specified directory as is done with COPY. The BACKUP command also can select files according to their archive attributes and time/date stamps. COPY can select files only by name. BACKUP can split a file over two or more diskettes if necessary; COPY quits if it runs out of disk space. (BACKUP is the only DOS facility that lets you copy to diskettes a file larger than the size of a diskette.) The BACKUP command format is shown below:

```
BACKUP source-drive[filespec] target-drive [/F] [/S] [/M]
[/A] [/D:date] [/T:time] [/L:filespec]
```

You must specify both source and target drivenames. You can also specify a path and/or a filespec for the source. The target must be only a drivename; the root directory of the target drive is always used as the target directory. It is erased before it is used, but any subdirectories on the diskette are untouched.

The following two commands have the same effect. They both back up all files in the current directory of drive C: to the root directory of drive A:

```
BACKUP C: A:
BACKUP C:*.* A:
```

The following command backs up all files in the root directory of drive C: to the root directory of drive B:

```
BACKUP C:\ B:
```

This following command backs up all files with extension DAT in the directory C:\INVOICES to the root directory of drive B:

```
BACKUP C:\INVOICES\*.DAT B:
```

Figure 7.2 shows a complete BACKUP interaction. The "Insert" message doesn't appear if the target is a hard disk drive, such as drive D:. A similar message appears if the source is a diskette drive.

Notice that the target diskette is numbered. That's in case it takes more than one target diskette to complete the BACKUP, which often happens when you are backing up an entire subtree or the entire fixed disk. After the BACKUP is finished, write that sequence number on the diskette label along with the date of the backup. If you need to restore the files, the RESTORE

```
C:\PRACTICE\PRACA>BACKUP C: A:

Insert backup diskette 01 in drive A:

WARNING! Files in the target drive
A:\ root directory will be erased
Press any key to continue . . .

*** Backing up files to drive A: ***
Diskette Number: 01

\PRACTICE\PRACA\NEW3
\PRACTICE\PRACA\4201.CPI
\PRACTICE\PRACA\4208.CPI
\PRACTICE\PRACA\5202.CPI
\PRACTICE\PRACA\EGA.CPI
\PRACTICE\PRACA\LCD.CPI

C:\PRACTICE\PRACA>
```

Figure 7.2. BACKUP Interaction

program will ask for the backup diskettes by number. If you have several sets of backup diskettes, you will need the date to know which set to use.

You can also see in the interaction which files were selected for backup by the command. Then entire filespec is shown for each file selected, since BACKUP can select files from more than one directory.

Have available a blank or reusable diskette that fits drive A:. Be sure the diskette is formatted. Warning: Any files in the root directory of the diskette will be destroyed. (Subdirectories will be unharmed.) Start at the command prompt. Make C:\PRACTICE the default directory.
1. Back up all files in the default directory.
2. Check the directory of drive A:. The volume label should be BACKUP 001, and the two files should be BACKUP.001 and CONTROL.001.
3. Now try backing up just the .SYS files in the current directory. Overlay the previous backups. Save your practice backup diskette. You'll use it again in later checkpoints.

*1. Insert the backup diskette in drive A: and enter the command:*

```
BACKUP C: A:
```

*2. Enter the command:*

```
DIR A:
```

*3. Enter the command:*

```
BACKUP C:*.SYS A:
```

## Recommended Switches

Both the /F switch and the /L switch on the BACKUP command can save you time and hassle.

***Formatting Diskettes during Backup***   Suppose you need to back up 30MB of data onto 1.2MB diskettes. You would need at least 25 diskettes. Suppose after filling the 24th diskette, you discover that you have no more formatted diskettes left. You have to abort the command (by pressing Ctrl+Break), format another diskette, and start the entire process over, repeating perhaps an hour's worth of work, depending on the speed of your diskette drive.

You can avoid such inefficiency by always including the /F (format) switch in your BACKUP command. This switch tells DOS to format any unformatted diskette inserted during the backup process. Since the /F switch can prevent lost time, you should include it in all your BACKUP commands.

*Recording a Backup Log*   Backing up a complete fixed disk might take 30 or more diskettes. BACKUP does not simply copy files to the backup diskettes. It organizes them in a special fashion that only BACKUP and RESTORE can handle. All you see in the diskette directory is CONTROL.*nnn* and BACKUP.*nnn*. CONTROL.*nnn* contains the control information--basically, a directory of the files in BACKUP.*nnn*. BACKUP.*nnn* contains all the files. These two files are read-only so that you can't erase them accidentally. In addition, BACKUP changes the volume label of the backup diskette to read BACKUP.*nnn*.

Since you can't display a list of the files backed up on a diskette, how can you find out when a particular file was backed up and what diskette it is on? You can keep your own list, or you can ask BACKUP to keep a log. Figure 7.3 shows an example of a short backup log. You can see the date of the backup on the second line. For each file that was backed up, you can see the number of its backup diskette and its full filespec; in the example, all files were placed on diskette 001.

To tell DOS to create a backup log, specify the /L switch. If you don't include a filespec, the log is named BACKUP.LOG and is placed in the root directory of the source drive, no matter what directories you backed up. You can override the default filespec by including a filespec with the /L switch. If you specify a filename without a path, the current directory is used. You can specify a drivename for the log filespec, but you cannot place it on the target diskette.

```
C:\PRACTICE\PRACA>TYPE C:\BACKUP.LOG

8-21-1989  17:47:54
001  \PRACTICE\PRACA\NEW3
001  \PRACTICE\PRACA\4201.CPI
001  \PRACTICE\PRACA\4208.CPI
001  \PRACTICE\PRACA\5202.CPI
001  \PRACTICE\PRACA\EGA.CPI
001  \PRACTICE\PRACA\LCD.CPI

C:\PRACTICE\PRACA>
```

Figure 7.3. Sample Backup Log

If BACKUP finds a log file of the same name in the same location, it adds to the log file instead of overwriting the file. This helps you keep a running log of which files were backed up when, as well as where they are. You can edit the backup log to erase entries that are no longer valid because you eliminated the backup diskette(s).

When you do a complete hard disk backup, delete the former backup log first and let DOS create a new one. If you are using the archive attribute method of daily backups, let DOS add each day's log to the backup log. All the information you need is then in one backup log. If you are using the time/date method of daily backups, then you should probably keep a separate log of the daily backups and overwrite the log each day. Before doing each daily backup, erase the previous daily backup log.

## Backing Up Subtrees

The /S (subtree) switch includes all directories in the subtree headed by the source directory. The following command causes all files in the root directory of the fixed disk, and all levels of subdirectories beneath it, to be backed up. In other words, all files on drive C: will be backed up.

```
BACKUP C:\ B: /F /L /S
```

The following command causes only the subtree headed by C:\DB to be backed up:

```
BACKUP C:\DB B: /F /L /S
```

Start at the command prompt. Make sure C:\PRACTICE is the current directory. Use the same backup diskette you started in the previous checkpoint.
1. Back up all files in the subtree headed by PRACTICE. Keep a backup log named BACKUP.LOG in the root directory. Just in case the job requires more than one diskette, include the switch to format diskettes as you go.
2. Display the backup log.
3. Now try a partial backup. Back up all files named MYADDR with any extension from the subtree headed by PRACTICE. Overwrite the previous backup diskette. Keep the backup log up to date. Continue to use the /F switch.
4. Check the backup log again. Continue to save this backup diskette for future checkpoints.

*1. Enter the command:*

```
BACKUP C:*.* A: /F /L /S
```

*2. Enter the command:*

```
TYPE \BACKUP.LOG
```

*3. Enter the command:*

```
BACKUP C:MYADDR.* A: /F /L /S
```

*4. Enter the command:*

```
TYPE \BACKUP.LOG
```

## Selecting Files for Backup

There are several ways to select files for backup. You've already seen how you can select them by name by including a global filespec in the command, much as you do in the COPY command. The /D:*date* switch selects all files that were last modified on or after the indicated date. The /T:*time* switch backs up all files that were last modified on or after the indicated time; it is usually used in conjunction with the /D:*date* switch. Suppose you do a complete backup on Monday, August 1, 1992 at 9:00 AM using this command:

```
BACKUP C:\ A: /F /L /S
```

On Monday evening at 7:00, you want to back up all files created or modified since the complete backup. You could use this command:

```
BACKUP C:\ A: /F /L /S /D:8-1-92 /T:9:01
```

This command causes DOS to examine each directory entry in C:\ and all its subdirectories for a date stamp on or after 8-1-92 and a time stamp on or after 9:01 AM. (If you omit the /D:*date* switch, DOS would select all files last modified after 9:00 AM for any date, including those last modified before 8-1-92.)

On Tuesday evening, and each subsequent evening, you use the same command again, placing the previous night's diskette in drive A: so that BACKUP will overwrite the previous files.

The /M (modified) switch selects files for backup based on their archive attribute. To back up all files that have been modified since the last backup operation, you would enter this command:

```
BACKUP C:\ A: /F /L /S /M
```

You would use this command between full backups, saving the resulting diskettes until you do another full backup of the hard disk.

Start at the command prompt. Make sure that C:\PRACTICE is current.

1. Do a full backup of the PRACTICE subtree.
2. Use COPY CON or your ASCII editor to create a new file named BACK1. List some members of your family in this file. Make three copies of BACK1 called BACK2, BACK3, and BACK4.
3. Do a partial backup of the PRACTICE subtree, selecting all files modified since the previous BACKUP command; DOS will back up all files with the archive attribute turned on. You can use the same target diskette as before.
4. Back up all files in the PRACTICE subtree modified after 10:00 yesterday morning. You can use the same target diskette as before. Save the backup diskette for future checkpoints.

1. *Enter the command :*

```
BACKUP C: A: /F /L /S
```

3. *Enter the command:*

```
BACKUP C: A: /F /L /S /M
```

*DOS should select BACK1 through BACK4. No other files will be selected because the complete backup you did in Item 1 turned off all the archive attributes.*

4. *Enter the command:*

```
BACKUP C: A: /F /L /S /D:yesterday's-date /T:10:01
```

*Even though their archive attributes are now off, at least BACK1 through BACK4 should be selected. Other files will be selected if they were modified after 10:00 yesterday morning.*

## Controlling the Archive Attribute

DOS manipulates the archive attribute automatically, but you can also view and change it yourself, using either the **Change attribute** option on the **File** menu or the ATTRIB command (as you saw earlier). By viewing and changing the attributes, you can control which files are selected by the /M switch. You frequently modify files that don't need to be backed up: letters, memos, notes to yourself, to-do lists, and the like. Also, many copies don't need to be backed up. If you turn off their archive attributes before you do your backup operation using the /M switch, they won't be selected for backup, saving both time and diskette space.

You might also want to force a file to be backed up. Suppose you accidentally erased yesterday's backups. You could manually reset the archive attributes of the necessary files, then run the BACKUP command again.

## Using the Shell

You've already learned how to view a file's attributes either in the **Show Information** dialog box or the **Change Attributes** dialog box. Refer back to Figure 5.1 for an example of a **Show Information** dialog box. The example shown there has the attributes **rhs**. Since the fourth position is a dot instead of an **a**, the file's archive attribute is off. Refer back to Figure 5.2 for an example of a **Change Attributes** dialog box. The triangle next to the **Archive** attribute indicates that the attribute is currently on. To turn it off, you would select the **Archive** option. It toggles on or off each time you select it.

## Using the Command Prompt

You have also seen how to use the ATTRIB command to see and change file attributes. ATTRIB without a switch displays the attributes. The following interaction displays the attributes of all files in the current directory.

```
C:\>ATTRIB *.*

        A               C:\AUTOEXEC.BAT
                        C:\CONFIG.SYS
        A               C:\LASER.BAT
             R          C:\COMMAND.COM
             R          C:\MOUSE.COM
        A               C:\NLQ
             R          C:\SHUTDOWN.EXE
        A               C:\VP.BAT
        A               C:\F1-5.SCR
                        C:\ASMTOC.CHP
                        C:\ASMTOC.GEN
                        C:\ASMTOC.CIF
                        C:\DMDRVR.BIN
        A               C:\TEMP
```

The **A** in the first column indicates that the archive attribute is on. These are the files the /M switch will select.

To turn the archive attribute on for one or more files, use the +A switch in the ATTRIB command. The -A switch turns the archive attribute off. The following command turns on the archive attribute for all GEN files in the current directory:

```
ATTRIB *.GEN +A
```

The following command turns off the archive attribute for all LET files in the current directory:

```
ATTRIB *.LET -A
```

## Adding to Backup Files

BACKUP always uses the root directory of each target diskette you give it. It deletes any other files in the root directory. When the backup terminates, the only files in the root directory of the target diskette are CONTROL.*nnn* and BACKUP.*nnn*. If you use the same diskette for the next backup operation, the former backup files will be overwritten by the new ones, unless you use the /A (append) switch. The /A switch causes BACKUP to add the new backup files to the existing CONTROL.*nnn* and BACKUP.*nnn* files.

Suppose you are using the archive attribute backup method. Then you want to save your existing backup files until the next time you do a complete backup. If you want to use the same diskette day after day until it is full, you would use this command for your daily backups:

```
BACKUP C:\ A: /F /L /S /M /A
```

This selects all the newly created or modified files on the entire hard disk and adds them to the backup files already on the target diskette.

If you are using the time/date method of backup, then you want to overwrite the previous day's backup files with the new one. Do not use the /A switch. The appropriate command would be:

```
BACKUP C:\ A: /F /L /S /D:date /T:time
```

## Using the Shell Backup Facility

In the shell, the **DOS Utilities** screen includes a **Backup Fixed Disk** option that yields the dialog box shown in Figure 7.4. All you have to do is modify

```
 09-04-89                    Start Programs                    5:10 pm
  Program  Group  Exit                                         F1=Help
                         DOS Utilities...
               To select an item, use the up and down arrows.
              To start a program or display a new group, press Enter.

 Set Date and Time
 Disk Copy
 Disk Compare
 Backup Fixed Disk
 Restore Fixed Disk
 Format
                               ┌──────────── Backup Utility ────────────┐
                               │                                        │
                               │  Enter source and destination drives.  │
                               │                                        │
                               │  Parameters . .   [c:\*.* a: /s     →]  │
                               │                                        │
                               │  (<─┘=Enter)  (Esc=Cancel)  (F1=Help)   │
                               └────────────────────────────────────────┘

 F10=Actions   Esc=Cancel   Shift+F9=Command Prompt
```

Figure 7.4. Backup Utility Dialog Box

the source, target, and any desired switches in the **Parameters** box; the default values are shown in the example. When you complete the dialog box, the screen clears, you see the BACKUP command messages, and the backup takes place (if no problems are encountered). Then you press any key to return to the DOS Utilities screen.

You probably want to create your own backup options (using the **Add** option from the **Program** menu) on the DOS Utilities screen—one for full backups and one for partial backups. For example, suppose your full backup will always use this set of commands:

```
DEL C:\BACKUP.LOG
BACKUP C:\ A: /F /L /S
```

You might want to create a **DOS Utilities** option titled **Weekly backup** or **Complete backup** or whatever title you prefer. In the **Commands** box, you would enter both commands, using the command separator (F4) between them. Then you can just select the appropriate option whenever you want to do a complete backup.

Suppose you use this command to make a partial backup:

```
BACKUP C:\ A: /F /L: /S /M
```

You might want to create a DOS Utilities option called **Daily backup** or **Back up modified files**. Place the above command in the **Commands** box. Again, this eliminates the need to fill out a dialog box when doing your standard partial backup.

If you use the time/date method of doing partial backups, then you can create a dialog box to collect the desired date and time as part of the procedure. You might prefer to include the date and time in the **Commands** box. This means you have to revise your **Commands** box to change the date and time whenever you do a full backup, but it also means you can do partial backups without going through a dialog box.

1. Determine the command you will use to do a full backup. Will you back up all files on the hard disk? If not, you might need a series of BACKUP commands to back up just the files you want. Will you keep a backup log? What will its name be? Will you delete the previous backup log first? Use these factors to decide the command(s) to use. Don't forget the /F switch.
2. If you want to create a program option on your **DOS Utilities** screen to do a full backup, create the option now. Try out and perfect your new option. You don't have to complete the full backup now. When DOS asks for the first diskette, press Ctrl+Break to cancel the process.
3. Determine the command you will use for partial backups. Will you use the archive-attributes method or the time/date method? Will you append new files to the previous backup diskettes or overwrite the files? Will you add to the backup log or overwrite it?
4. If you wish, add a program to the **DOS Utilities** group for your partial backup command. If you use the time/date method, you'll have to decide whether to use a dialog box to collect the time and date or to build the time and date into the basic function.

1. *For most people, the desired command is:*

```
BACKUP C:\ A: /F /L /S
```

*They might precede it with:*

```
DEL C:\BACKUP.LOG
```

2. *Get to the **DOS Utilities** screen, pull down the **Program** menu, and select **Add**. Fill out the **Add Program** dialog box and select **Save**. The **Commands** box might contain this:*

```
DEL C:\BACKUP.LOG||BACKUP C:\ A: /F /L /S
```

*Next, select the new option and respond to all prompts.*
3. *Most people who use the archive-attribute method will use a command similar to:*

```
BACKUP C:\ A: /F /L /S /M /A
```

*This adds the newly selected files to the previous ones and adds the new log to the existing one. Most people who use the time/date method will use a set of commands similar to these:*

```
DEL C:\DAILY.LOG
BACKUP C:\ A: /F /L:C:\DAILY.LOG /S /D:date /T:time
```

*This creates a new set of backup files and replaces the old log with the new one.*

# Restoring Backup Files

If you have a good backup system, then it is easy to recover from file loss. If your hard disk crashes, you can restore it from your backup diskettes after it is repaired. Even if you edit a file and then decide you don't like the editing, you can restore an earlier version. The only way to retrieve a file from a diskette created by BACKUP is with the RESTORE command. Throughout this discussion of RESTORE, we assume that valid backup copies of the desired files have been made on diskettes by BACKUP.

Suppose you accidentally erase CHAP15 from your fixed disk. You can use this command to restore the file from a diskette to the directory it was backed up from:

```
RESTORE A: CHAP15
```

The first operand specifies the drive containing the backup diskette. CHAP15 specifies the file to be restored. Since no drivename or path are included, DOS looks for a file to restore to the current directory. If a matching file is found in the target directory, it is overlaid. If not, the file is added to the directory.

When BACKUP saves a file, it saves the full path for the file. Therefore, RESTORE knows what directory each backup file belongs to. RESTORE will not restore a file to a different directory than the one it came from. If the backup diskette contains files from C:\NOVEL and you try to restore them to C:\HIST101, you will see "Warning: No files were found to restore."

Figure 7.5 shows a sample RESTORE interaction. First, RESTORE asks for any removable diskettes. Then it reads the diskettes and displays the date of the backup. Read the date; it can warn you if you don't have the latest backup version in the drive. Then the diskette number is displayed, followed by a list of the files that were restored from that diskette.

If you want to restore files to a directory other than the current one, you can include a path with the target filespec. For example, suppose you want

```
C:\PRACTICE\PRACA>RESTORE A: C:

Insert backup diskette 01 in drive A:
Press any key to continue . . .

*** Files were backed up 08-21-1989 ***

*** Restoring files from drive A: ***
Diskette: 01
\PRACTICE\PRACA\NEW3
\PRACTICE\PRACA\4201.CPI
\PRACTICE\PRACA\4208.CPI
\PRACTICE\PRACA\5202.CPI
\PRACTICE\PRACA\EGA.CPI
\PRACTICE\PRACA\LCD.CPI


C:\PRACTICE\PRACA>
```

Figure 7.5. RESTORE Interaction

to restore all DAT files to the C:\GEORGE\CHECKS directory. You could enter this command:

```
C:\>RESTORE A: C:\GEORGE\CHECKS\*.DAT
```

## Restoring from Multiple Versions

If you create your backup diskettes with the /A (append) switch, several versions of a desired file might exist on the backup diskettes. RESTORE finds and restores the first version, then overlays it with the second version, and so on. The final result is the last version of the file that was found on the source diskette, which is the last one you backed up. Figure 7.6 shows a sample interaction. You can see that four versions of FILEA were found on the backup diskette. The last version, which should be the most recent, is the one that remains in the target directory. As you can see, you don't have to worry about getting the most recent version when you create your backup diskettes with the /A switch. It happens automatically when you restore your backup files.

Use the same backup diskette you created in earlier checkpoints. Start at the command prompt. Make sure C:\PRACTICE is the current directory.

1. Make a complete backup of the PRACTICE subtree.
2. Restore all files in the current directory.

3. Delete all files in C:\PRACTICE\PRACA. Check the directory to make sure they're gone.
4. Restore all files in C:\PRACTICE\PRACA from the backup diskette. Check the directory to make sure they have returned. Save the backup diskette for later checkpoints.

---

1. *Enter the command:*

```
BACKUP C: A: /F /L /S
```

2. *Enter the command:*

```
RESTORE A: C:
```

*You should see a list of the files selected for restoration.*

3. *Enter the command:*

```
DEL PRACA\*.*
```

*followed by:*

```
DIR PRACA
```

4. *Enter the command:*

```
RESTORE A: C:PRACA\*.*
```

*followed by:*

```
DIR PRACA
```

```
C:\STYLES>RESTORE A: FILEA

Insert backup diskette 01 in drive A:
Strike any key when ready


*** Files were backed up 08-02-1989 ***

*** Restoring files from drive A: ***
Diskette: 01
\STYLES\FILEA
\STYLES\FILEA
\STYLES\FILEA
\STYLES\FILEA

C:\STYLES>_
```

Figure 7.6. RESTORE with Several Versions of a File

## *Restoring from a Multiple Diskette Set*

If you back up many files or very large files, you'll end up with several backup diskettes numbered 01, 02, and so forth. For example, if you back up 30MB of data onto 1.2MB diskettes, you'll end up with at least 25 backup diskettes.

When you enter a RESTORE command, RESTORE begins by asking you for diskette number 01. It searches that diskette for the desired file(s), then asks for diskette 02, and so on. If you don't override it, RESTORE will search the entire set of diskettes looking for all versions of the backup file(s).

If you want to restore only one file or a small group of files, your backup log tells you which diskette(s) to use. If you haven't put the diskette numbers on the external labels, you can examine the directories to find the desired diskettes. Figure 7.7 shows what the directory of a backup diskette looks like. You can see the 003 in the label and the filespecs. And you can see what date the files were last created or modified.

Suppose you want to restore a file that you know is on diskette 03. When RESTORE asks for diskette 01, insert diskette 03. RESTORE displays this message:

```
Warning! Diskette is out of sequence
Replace diskette or continue if okay
Strike any key when ready_
```

Simply press any key to force RESTORE to accept diskette 03. In the same manner, you could then skip to diskettes 07, 13, 28, and so on.

```
C:\>DIR A:

 Volume in drive A is BACKUP  003
 Directory of  A:\

BACKUP   003      7128   8-02-89   2:30a
CONTROL  003       555   8-02-89   2:30a
        2 File(s)   1205760 bytes free

C:\>_
```

Figure 7.7. Backup Diskette Directory

There is one condition under which RESTORE will not let you skip a diskette. When BACKUP saves files, it crams each diskette as full as possible with data before starting another. It even splits a file over two diskettes if necessary. In fact, a very large file might occupy several diskettes. RESTORE knows when it needs to finish a split file it has partially restored. In that case, it will insist on the next diskette in sequence. If you try to give it another diskette, RESTORE terminates with the message "Not able to restore file."

## Using Global Filespecs with Restore

You can do a global restore, much as you do a global backup. For example, suppose you accidentally enter this command:

```
C:\>DEL *.DAT
```

To restore the DAT files to the current directory, you enter this command:

```
C:\>RESTORE A: *.DAT
```

RESTORE searches the backup diskette(s) on the source drive for all files that match the global filespec, including the specified or implied directory, and restores these files. As usual, later versions overwrite earlier versions.

Figure 7.8 shows a complete interaction using the filespec CHAP*.*. RESTORE lists the files as it finds and restores them.

## Protecting New Versions

RESTORE overlays matching files in the target directory, even if they're read-only. But what if the version on the target drive is a *newer* version, not yet backed up? You've just lost some data. The /P (prompt) switch can help to prevent this. It identifies files with a positive archive attribute and displays:

```
Warning! File CHAP01
was changed after it was backed up
Replace the file (Y/N)?_
```

For read-only files, the /P switch displays this message:

```
Warning! File CHAP01
is a read-only file
Replace the file (Y/N)?_
```

You can decide whether to overwrite each file individually.

```
C:\DOSBOOK>RESTORE A: CHAP*.*

Insert backup diskette 01 in drive A:
Strike any key when ready


*** Files were backed up 08-02-1989 ***

*** Restoring files from drive A: ***
Diskette: 01
\DOSBOOK\CHAP01
\DOSBOOK\CHAP02
\DOSBOOK\CHAP03
\DOSBOOK\CHAP04
\DOSBOOK\CHAP05
\DOSBOOK\CHAP06
\DOSBOOK\CHAP07
\DOSBOOK\CHAP08
\DOSBOOK\CHAP09

C:\DOSBOOK>_
```

Figure 7.8. Restoring with a Global Filespec

**N**ote ‖ The /P switch is a safety valve when doing global restores. You might want to use it in all your RESTORE commands.

## Restoring a Subtree

You can restore files to a single directory or to an entire subtree. The /S switch causes an entire subtree to be restored. DOS will create subdirectories as necessary.

Figure 7.9 shows an example. Before the RESTORE, drive C: has just been formatted and contains only a root directory and the system files. The backup diskette contains 13 files; their filenames indicate which directories they belong in. After the restore, all the necessary subdirectories have been created. The RESTORE command for this particular example is:

```
RESTORE A: C: /S /P
```

## Selecting Files by Archive Attribute and Time/Date Stamp

You can select files to be restored in much the same way you select them for backup. The /M switch causes RESTORE to compare the source and target directories. Any files in the target that have been modified since the last

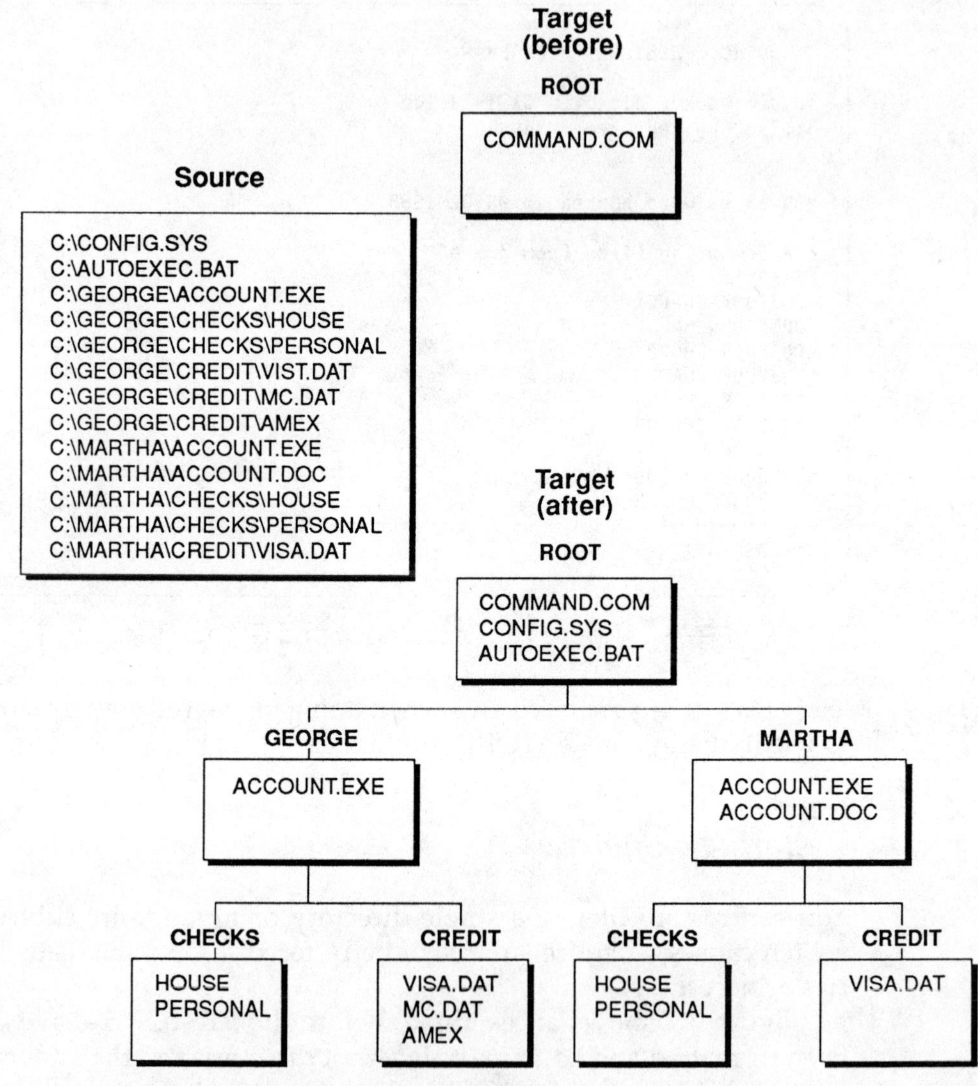


Figure 7.9. Restoring a Subtree

backup (the archive attribute is on) are restored, thus eliminating the modifications. Any missing files are also restored. The intention of the /M switch in RESTORE is to undo modifications. Suppose on Tuesday you modify three files in C:\BAND\NEWS. In addition, you delete two files. Then you realize that all the work you did was wrong and you want to fall back to Monday night's files. You put Monday night's backup diskette in drive A: and enter this command:

```
C:\>RESTORE A: C:\BAND\NEWS\*.* /M /P
```

Notice the differences between the /M switch here and the way it's used with BACKUP. With BACKUP, /M is guided by the source entry. With RESTORE, the switch is guided by the target. RESTORE also selects files that are missing in the target.

The /N switch restores only missing files to the target directory. Suppose, in the previous example, you don't want to restore the modified files, only the deleted ones. Then you could enter this command:

```
RESTORE A: C:\BAND\NEWS\*.* /N
```

The /B:*date*, /A:*date*, /E:*time*, and /L:*time* switches let you select which files to restore based on their date/time stamp in the *target* directory. The /B:*date* switch selects files to be overwritten with a time stamp on or *before* the indicated date. The /E:*time* switch selects files to be overwritten with a time stamp at or *earlier* than the specified time. The /A:*date* switch selects files to be overwritten with a date stamp on or *after* the specified date. The /L:*time* switch selects files to be overwritten with a time stamp at or *later* than the specified time.

No matter which date/time switches you use, missing files are restored. That is, if C:\NOVEL\CHAP15 exists in the source directory, but not in the target directory, it is restored to the target directory.

Again, notice the difference in the ways the date and time switches are used with BACKUP and RESTORE. BACKUP examines the source directory, while RESTORE examines the target. BACKUP selects only files that were modified on or after a specific date and time, while RESTORE can also select files that were modified on or before a specific date and time.

---

Start at the command prompt. Make sure C:\PRACTICE is the current directory. Use the same backup diskette you created in the preceding checkpoint.
1. Restore all SYS files to the subtree headed by the current directory.
2. Restore all files in the current subtree modified after 9:00 AM yesterday.
3. Delete all filenames beginning with BACK from the current directory.
4. Restore all missing files to the current directory.

---

1. *Enter the command:*

```
RESTORE A: C:*.SYS /S
```

*You should see a list of the files selected for restoration.*
2. *Enter the command:*

```
RESTORE A: C: /A:date /L:8:59 /S
```

3. *Enter the command:*

```
DEL BACK*.*
```

4. *Enter the command:*

```
RESTORE A: C: /N
```

*The BACK*.* files should be restored.*

# Restoring the Entire Fixed Disk after a Crash

Now consider how you would restore your entire fixed disk after a crash. It has been repaired, repartitioned with FDISK, and reformatted with the /S switch. It contains only the root directory with the hidden files and COMMAND.COM.

You also have a set of 25 diskettes made last Monday morning, backing up the entire disk. In addition, you have one diskette containing all the daily modified files. To restore all files from the full backup, you would enter this command:

```
RESTORE A: C:\*.* /S
```

To restore all files from the daily backup, you would use exactly the same command.

# Using the Shell to Restore Files

The **DOS Utilities** screen includes a **Restore Fixed Disk** program that yields the dialog box shown in Figure 7.10. The default parameters are shown in the figure. All you have to do is modify the **Parameters** box with the source, target, and switches you want to use. There is no sense in trying to create a more specific restore option because every restore situation is different.

# Other Methods of Backing Up and Restoring

BACKUP and RESTORE are not the only way to back up and restore your fixed disk. You could, for example, work out a system using COPY. This would give you usable files and a readable directory on the backup diskettes. But COPY can't work with multiple directories or multiple target diskettes, and it can select files only by name. DOS also includes a command

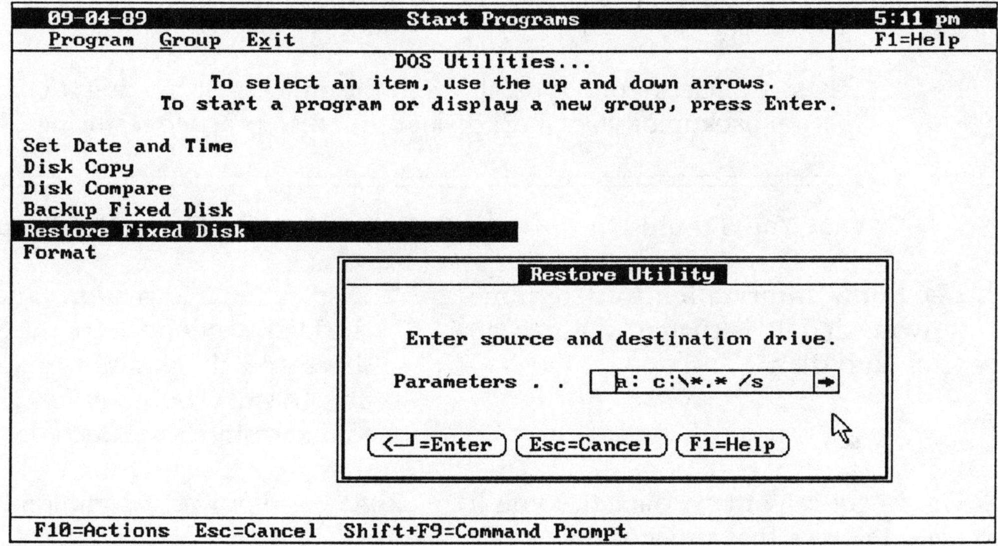



Figure 7.10. Restore Utility Dialog Box

called XCOPY that can select files from an entire subtree based on the archive attribute, but produces usable target files and a readable directory. You might find that you prefer XCOPY to BACKUP and RESTORE. You'll learn about XCOPY in Chapter 9.

Some people find none of the DOS backup commands to be fully satisfying. In fact, you can buy separate backup utilities that have more features and tend to work faster than BACKUP. If you're dissatisfied with COPY, BACKUP and RESTORE, and XCOPY, check with your dealer or your favorite software magazine for more information.

# Summary

This chapter has shown you how to back up and restore your fixed disk by using the BACKUP and RESTORE commands. In the process, you should have begun, at least, to design your own backup system. You'll probably want to adapt it as your system grows.

**N**ote || BACKUP and RESTORE have changed considerably from earlier DOS versions. If you sometimes work with earlier versions of DOS, you'll find that the files created by the new BACKUP are incompatible with earlier RESTORE versions. Don't try to mix them.

## *Exercises*

These exercises guide you through the process of making a complete and partial backup of your hard disk. You'll also practice restoring files.

| **What You Should Do** | **How The Computer Responds** |
|---|---|
| 1. Use **Show Information** to determine how much data is currently stored on your hard disk. | 1. Displays an information panel in which the **Disk** section shows the **Size** of the drive and the amount of space available (**Avail**). (Subtract **Avail** from **Size** to determine how much data is on the disk.) |
| 2. Figure out how many diskettes you'll need to store that much data. You'll probably want to use your highest-capacity diskettes. Make sure you have as many new or reusable diskettes as you need. Warning: BACKUP destroys any files in the root directories of the target diskettes. If a target diskette contains a lot of data in subdirectories, it won't hold much backup data. | 2. Awaits your next command. |
| 3. Back up your entire hard disk. (By now, you should know what command or **DOS Utilities** option to use for this process.) | 3. Prompts you to insert diskettes in the target drive. Formats unformatted diskettes (if you included the /F switch in the command). Deletes all files in the root directories of the target diskettes. Backs up selected files onto target diskettes, assigning a sequential number to each target diskette. Creates a backup log or adds to the existing one if you included the /L switch. |
| 4. Copy C:\COMMAND.COM as C:\NEWCOM.<br>Copy C:\DOS\PRINT.COM as C:\DOS\NEWPRINT.<br>Copy C:\PRACTICE\MYADDR as C:\PRACTICE\NEWADDR. | 4. Makes the copies as you've directed. |

5. Back up all modified files on your hard disk. Use a new diskette or add them to the backup diskettes you made in Step 3.
6. Delete C:\NEWCOM and C:\PRACTICE\NEWADDR.
7. Restore C:\NEWCOM and C:\PRACTICE\NEWADDR from the backup diskette.

5. Selects C:\NEWCOM, C:\DOS\NEWPRINT, and C:\PRACTICE\NEWADDR for backup.
6. Deletes the files as directed.

7. Restores the files as directed.

## *What If It Doesn't Work?*

BACKUP can be unreliable. If you have trouble restoring backed up files during this exercise, you should consider a different backup method. You might want to build your backup system around XCOPY (explained in Chapter 9). Or you might want to buy backup software from another company. There are several good products on the market.

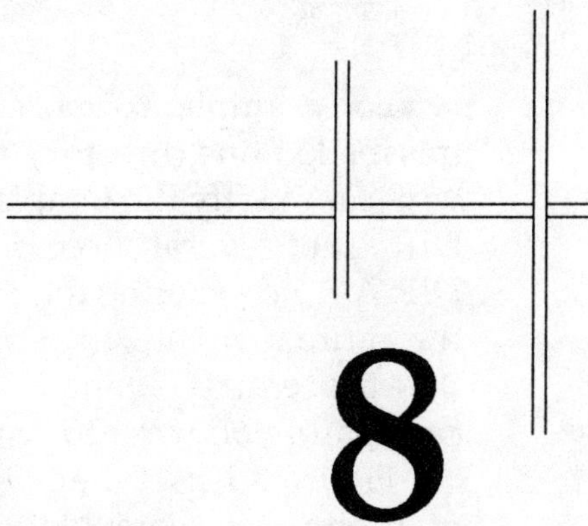

# 8

# *Advanced Command Entry*

DOS provides several features you can use in entering and manipulating commands. These features simplify and speed up the command entry process, and help you avoid errors at the keyboard.

In this chapter, you'll learn to:

- Manipulate the command-line template
- Use function keys to modify the previous command
- Redirect output from the screen to a file or device
- Redirect input to come from a file instead of the keyboard
- Pipe the output of one command to serve as input to another
- Use the MORE filter to page output
- Use the SORT filter to rearrange lines in a file
- Use the FIND filter to locate lines in a file

## *The Command-Line Template*

When you type a command at the DOS prompt, DOS doesn't respond until you press Enter. Once you press Enter, the command, as it appeared when Enter was pressed, is executed. The characters that make up the command are stored in a buffer; you can then use the contents of this buffer as a template in preparing the next command. DOS lets you use various keyboard keys to edit and manipulate characters from the template as you prepare the next command.

For example, suppose you've typed a command with a long path, but misspelled one directory name. Rather than retyping the entire command, you can modify the template. If you want to check the root directories (with DIR A:) of several successive diskettes, you can insert the first diskette, type DIR A:, and examine the result. Replace the diskette and press F3 to retrieve the entire template, then press Enter and examine the result. You can repeat this procedure—using F3 to retrieve the entire template—as long as the command you want to issue is the same.

Figure 8.1 lists the editing keys that manipulate characters in the command-line template. Notice that the first five function keys and a few control keys are used. You may already have used Esc and Ctrl+C to cancel a command being typed.

## *Retrieving Characters*

Suppose the screen contains this interaction:

```
C:\DOS>DIR A:

CHKDSK    COM         17787        10-06-88   12:00a
AUTOEXEC BAT           512         08-12-90    1:18p
        27 File(s)                 489,567 bytes free

C:\DOS>_
```

At this point, the template contains the six characters in the previous DIR command. If you press F3 at the prompt, all six characters are copied to the screen at the DOS prompt. You just press Enter and the command is executed again. Suppose you want to check the directory of drive B: next. You

| | |
|---|---|
| F1 | Retrieve one character from template to line |
| F2*n* | Retrieve up to character *n* from template |
| F3 | Retrieve remaining characters from template |
| F4*n* | Delete up to character *n* from template |
| F5 | Replace template with current line |
| Del | Delete one character from template |
| Ins | Toggle insert mode (keyboard into template) |
| Esc | Cancel current line and don't affect template |
| Ctrl+C | Cancel line, don't change template, display prompt |

Figure 8.1. Command-line Editing Keys

could press F3, then press **Backspace** twice and type B: before pressing Enter, just as though you **had changed** your mind about the command while typing it.

Another option is to use **F1; this key** retrieves a single character at a time. When you press F1 for the **first time,** DOS places the first character (D) on the command line. When **you press F1** three more times, DOS places the next three characters (I, R, **and space)** on the command line. At this point, you can type B: and press **Enter.**

Suppose your screen **looks like this:**

```
C:\DOS>TYPE \TOOLS\REPORTS\MARS.T
   Path not found - \TOOLS\REPORTS\MARS.T

C:\DOS>_
```

The first directory should **have been entered** as POOLS. You can combine the use of F1 and F3 to **make the correction.** Here's the procedure to use:

1. Press F1 six times to place **the first six** characters (TYPE \) on the command line.

2. Type P; the character you type **appears** on the command line, and the cursor in the template advances one character. Now the command line contains TYPE \P and the template is positioned at O.

3. Press F3 to retrieve the rest of the template into the command line. Then press Enter to submit the line.

Now the screen looks like this:

```
C:\DOS>TYPE \TOOLS\REPORTS\MARS.T
   Path not found - \TOOLS\REPORTS\MARS.T

C:\DOS>TYPE \POOLS\REPORTS\MARS.T
   (file listing)

C:\DOS>_
```

Figure 8.2 shows how the template works. Each time F1 is pressed, the next character in the template is copied to the command line. When a keyboard character is typed, it replaces the character in the corresponding position in the template. When F3 is pressed, all remaining characters in the template are copied to the command line.

Sometimes you may want to remove a character from the template; you can do this with the Del key. When the command-line cursor is positioned just before the character you want to omit, the template cursor is poised at

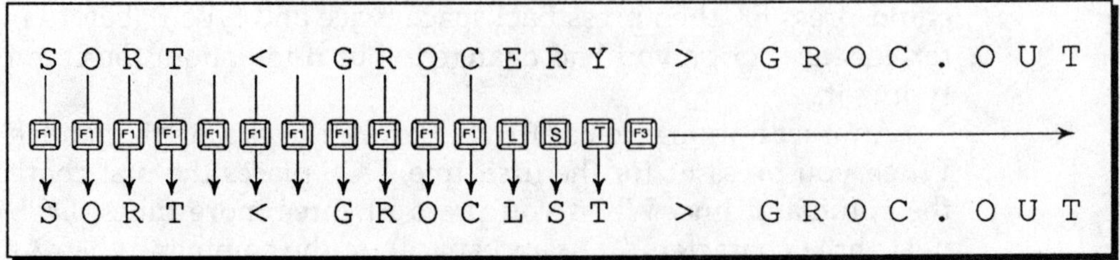


Figure 8.2. Using the Template

the next character. Suppose you accidentally misspell TYPE and the screen looks like this:

```
C:\DOS>TYPEE \POOLS\REPORTS\MARS.T
    Bad command or file name

C:\DOS>_
```

You can press F1 four times to put TYPE on the command line and to position the cursor in the template at the second E. Press Del. The cursor in the template moves ahead one character, to the space, but nothing appears on the command line. Press F3 to add the rest of the characters to the command line.

You can use Del to delete several characters. Suppose the screen looks like this:

```
C:\DOS>TYPPE \PPPOOLS\REPPORTS\MARS.T
    Bad command or file name

C:\DOS>_
```

Press F1 until the first P appears, then press Del to remove the second P. Press F1 again until the next P appears, then press Del twice to remove two extra characters. Press F1 again until the third P appears, then press Del again to remove the extra one. Now press F3 to place the rest of the characters in the command line.

Sometimes you'll want to insert characters rather than delete them. If you type new characters, they will overlay the existing characters in the template. Instead, you can insert characters by pressing the Ins key, then typing the characters to be inserted. They appear in the command line, but the cursor in the template doesn't move. Pressing another editing key—including Del, F1, and F3—turns off insert mode. Since the Ins key acts as a toggle, you can also press Ins again to turn off insert mode. Suppose your screen looks like this:

```
C:\DOS>TYP \POOLS\PORTS\MARS.T
   Bad command or file name

C:\DOS>_
```

You first press F1 three times to put TYP on the command line, then press Ins and type E. The character is placed on the command line but the cursor doesn't move in the template. When you press F1 again, the space is placed on the command line. Continue pressing F1 until the second \ appears. Then press Ins again and type RE. When you press F3, the characters PORTS\MARS.T are added to the command line. When you press Enter, the correct command is executed.

Suppose you used the wrong directory in the path—the directory should have been JACUZZIS instead of POOLS—and DOS gives you the message shown below when you try to execute the command:

```
C:\DOS>TYPE \POOLS\REPORTS\MARS.T
   Path not found - \POOLS\REPORTS\MARS.T

C:\DOS>_
```

To make the correction, you could press F1 six times to use the first six characters (TYPE \). Then press Del five times to move the template cursor to the next backslash; this effectively deletes POOLS from the template. Then press Ins and type JACUZZIS. Finally press F3 to end insertion and place the rest of the template on the command line.

Alternatively, you could press F1 six times, then type JACUZ. When the incorrect characters are replaced, press Ins, type ZIS and press F3. You'll discover that many techniques achieve the same results.

## *Manipulating the Entire Template*

It's easy to erase the template; just press Enter at the DOS prompt and the command-line buffer is empty. If you notice that the editing keys don't seem to work, you probably accidentally erased the buffer. Enter any command to place characters in it again.

Pressing Esc or Ctrl+C when the command line contains characters cancels the current command line without changing the previous contents of the buffer. When you press Esc, DOS places a backslash at the end of the line and moves the cursor to the next line; you don't get a new command prompt. When you press Ctrl+C, you'll see ^C at the end of the line, then you receive a new command prompt. In both cases, however, the template will not be changed. If you press F3, you can check the contents of the template. Then press Esc again to cancel the command and to move the cursor to a new line. Now you can see the entire template and edit it more easily.

If you want to replace the template with the current command line, but don't want to execute the command, press F5. DOS replaces the entire template with the current contents of the command line, places the @ symbol at the end of the line, then moves the cursor to the next line without giving you a new prompt. You can proceed to edit the line as needed before you press Enter to execute it.

 Start at the command prompt. Make the \PRACTICE directory current. Use the command template as much as possible in each of these steps.
1. Enter the command:

```
DIR \DOS
```

2. Repeat the command you entered in Item 1.
3. Enter the command:

```
DIR PRACA
```

4. Enter the command:

```
TREE /F A:
```

5. Enter the command:

```
TREE A:
```

6. Enter the command:

```
TREE /F A:
```

7. Enter the command:

```
DIR PRACTICA\PRACTICY
```

(An error message will result.)
8. Correct the command to:

```
DIR PRACA\PRACY.
```

2. *The fastest way to do this is to press F3 followed by Enter.*
3. *One way to do this is to press F1 four times, then type PRACA and press Enter.*
4. *You'll have to type the command from scratch.*
5. *One way to do this is to press F1 five times, press Del two times, press F3, then press Enter.*

6. *One way to do this is to press F1 five times, press Ins and type /F followed by a space, press F3, then press Enter.*
8. *One way to do this is to press F1 eight times, press Del three times, press F1 six times, then type Y and press Enter.*

## Affecting Multiple Characters

You may find that you must press F1 repeatedly to copy several characters from the template or press Del repeatedly to skip over template characters. The F2 and F4 keys let you simplify the process. When you press either of these keys, you must next type a character.

If you press F2, then a character, all characters in the template from its current cursor position up to, but not including, the first occurrence of that character are copied into the command line. Suppose the screen looks like this:

```
C:\DOS>TYPE JACUZZIS\REPORTS\MARS.T
   Path not found - JACUZZIS\REPORTS\MARS.T

C:\DOS>_
```

You want to insert a backslash before the first directory name. You could press F2 followed by J. The characters "TYPE  " appear on the command line. Press Ins, then type \ and press F3 to copy the rest of the line. If you neglect to press Ins, the slash overlays the J, resulting in \ACUZZIS.

You can skip over characters in the template, deleting them from the command line, by pressing F4 followed by a character. Suppose the screen looks like this:

```
C:\DOS>TYPE JACUZZIS\REPORTS\MARS.T
   Path not found - JACUZZIS\REPORTS\MARS.T

C:\DOS>_
```

You want to remove the first directory in the path. First you press F2 and the letter J, which copies the first five characters to the command line. Then press F4 followed by the letter R; this advances the cursor to the R in the template. When you press F3, the characters REPORTS\MARS.T are copied to the command line. When you press Enter, the modified command line is processed and replaces the former command in the buffer.

Figure 8.3 shows how template modification with F2 and F4 works. Notice that the function key is followed by a character that tells DOS how far to go in the template.

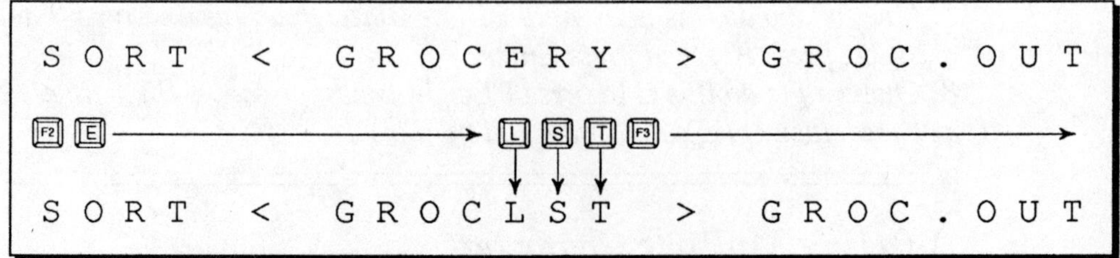


Figure 8.3. Template Manipulation

This checkpoint accomplishes the same results as the previous one. Use as few keystrokes as possible to accomplish each step. Start at the command prompt. Make sure C:\PRACTICE is the current directory.

1. Enter the command:

```
DIR \DOS
```

2. Repeat the command you entered in Item 1.
3. Enter the command:

```
DIR PRACA
```

4. Enter the command:

```
TREE /F A:
```

5. Enter the command:

```
TREE A:
```

6. Enter the command:

```
TREE /F A:
```

7. Enter the command:

```
DIR PRACTICA\PRACTICY
```

(An error message will result.)

8. Correct the command to:

```
DIR PRACA\PRACY
```

---

2. *The fastest way to do this is to press F3 followed by Enter.*
3. *One way to do this is to press F2 followed by \, then type PRACA and press Enter.*

4. *You'll have to type the command from scratch.*
5. *One way to do this is to press F2 followed by /, press F4 followed by A, press F3, then press Enter.*
6. *One way to do this is to press F2 followed by A, press Ins and type /F followed by a space, press F3, then press Enter.*
8. *One way to do this is to press F2 followed by T, press F4 followed by A, press F2 followed by T, then type Y and press Enter.*

# Output Redirection

As you know, DOS uses the screen to display standard output from commands. For instance, when you use DIR or TYPE, the output appears on the screen. You can redirect standard output to a file or a different device instead. In most cases, you'll want to use a file or a print device; PRN and LPT*n* refer to a parallel printer, while COM*n* refers to one of your serial ports. Figure 4.2 contains a list of the valid devices you can specify.

You can use redirection for any output that is normally sent to the screen if the program does not expect a keyboard response. You can't use redirection easily with DATE or TIME, since these commands require you to press Enter at least once to accept a new date or time. Redirection is for data normally sent to the screen; it is not designed for error messages, which are always sent to the screen.

The symbol > indicates output redirection and must be followed by a filespec or a device name. The command DIR \ sends the root directory listing to the screen. The command DIR \ > SAVE.DIR sends the root directory listing to a file named SAVE.DIR. If you name a file that doesn't already exist, DOS creates it. If the file already exists, DOS replaces the contents with the current directory listing. When you use redirection, the output does not appear on the screen; the next characters you see on the screen make up the DOS prompt. If the command can't be executed for some reason, an error message may appear on the screen.

If you want a printed copy of the directory, you can type DIR > PRN, which sends the listing directly to the printer. You can omit colons in all device names used in redirection. You can use spaces around the redirection symbol if you wish, but the spaces are not required.

The command DIR \WS5\UNIX\CH* > UNIXCHPS sends the requested directory listing to the named file (UNIXCHPS). The command TREE /F > \DOCS\TREESTAT.JAN sends the output of the TREE command to the named file. The command VOL>PRN prints the output of the VOL command.

### Appending Redirected Output

If a file already exists when it is named as the target of redirected output, DOS replaces the file's contents with the output. If you use the symbol >>, the output is redirected to the named file but is added to the end of any existing contents. As with simple redirection, DOS creates the file if it doesn't already exist. Although you can use a space before or after the >> symbol if you wish, don't use a space between the two characters; if you do, DOS won't know what you want and you'll get an error message instead.

Suppose you want to keep a continual record of the files in your working directory. Each day when you end your work session you could use the command DIR >> SAVE.DIR. The first time you use this command, DOS creates the SAVE.DIR file. Each additional time you use the command , the directory is added to the end of the file. At the end of the week, SAVE.DIR contains five directories, with the most recent directory at the end.

# Input Redirection

You have learned to use a few commands that expect keyboard input. DATE, TIME, and FORMAT require such a small amount of input that redirection usually isn't useful. Input redirection uses the symbol < to parallel the output redirection symbol. If you've already studied Chapter 6, you saw input redirection used in the SORT command. The command SORT < GROCERY > SORTED.GRO uses the file named GROCERY as redirected input and produces a redirected output file named SORTED.GRO. You'll learn to use SORT in more detail later in this chapter.

# Piping

Piping occurs when DOS takes the output of one program and uses it directly as the input to another program. Generally, standard output that would otherwise go to the screen is piped directly to another program as standard input. Piping uses the vertical bar symbol. If you enter the command DIR | SORT, the sorted directory listing is produced. Instead of being sent to the screen, the DIR output is piped to SORT as input. The DIR | SORT command is equivalent to these:

```
DIR > TEMP.FIL
SORT < TEMP.FIL
DEL TEMP.FIL
```

Piping uses a temporary file on disk, providing it with a temporary name. When the piping process is finished, the temporary file is automatically erased. If the default disk is write-protected or full, piping won't work. You'll see several uses for piping as you continue in this chapter.

# Filters

A filter is a special program that takes input, manipulates it in some way, and produces output that is somehow different from the input. DOS provides three filter programs that you can use: MORE, SORT, and FIND. All can use various forms of redirection and piping.

## Using the MORE Filter

When output is sent to the screen, it may scroll off the top before you get a chance to read it. This can happen with directory listings as well as displayed files. The MORE filter lets you use input redirection or piping to produce paged output to the screen, with the message --More-- appearing on the bottom screen line. Pressing any key continues the display.

The MORE command expects standard input, which is usually supplied from redirection or piping, as shown in Figure 8.4. You can use either technique to achieve the same effect. Notice that the MORE command appears first if you use input redirection and last if you use piping.

You can use MORE to produce easy-to-read screen output. This command is useful whenever the output is longer than one screen. In fact, it doesn't take much more effort to type MORE < *filespec* than to type TYPE *filespec*. If you type TYPE *filespec* and process the command, then want to see the same output paged, just use F3 to recall the command and add | MORE to the command line. MORE creates a temporary file on the default disk, so it must not be write-protected or full; if DOS can't create the temporary file, you'll get an error message when you try to use MORE.

| | |
|---|---|
| **Input Redirection** | `MORE < GROCERY.LST` |
| **Piping** | `TYPE GROCERY.LST \| MORE`<br>`DIR \| MORE` |

Figure 8.4. Using MORE

You can use MORE with just about any program that produces standard output. For example, the command DIR \DOS | MORE creates a paged listing of the files in the DOS subdirectory.

If you type MORE and press Enter, the cursor moves to the next line and waits for you to provide further information; MORE needs some input and expects it to come from the keyboard if no redirection or piping is specified. If this happens to you, just press F6 (just as with COPY CON) and then press Enter to end the input and restore the command prompt.

Start at the command prompt. Make sure C:\PRACTICE is the current directory.

1. Save the current directory listing in a file named SAVIT.
2. Add the listing of the root directory to SAVIT.
3. Display the contents of SAVIT on the screen, broken into pages.
4. Display TREE output, broken into pages, with all filenames included.

*1. Enter the command:*

```
DIR > SAVIT
```

*2. Enter the command:*

```
DIR \ >> SAVIT
```

*3. Enter the command:*

```
MORE < SAVIT
```

*4. Enter the command:*

```
TREE /F | MORE
```

## The SORT Command

The SORT command produces a sorted listing of lines from an ASCII file. SORT expects the input file to be redirected or piped, just as MORE does. The precise sequence of the output depends on the way your DOS was installed and on the COUNTRY.SYS file in effect. In most cases, the ASCII collating sequence is used. In general, that sequence corresponds to alphabetical order. Numbers sort before letters; most symbols sort before numbers. SORT is not case sensitive; that is, it ignores the difference between uppercase and lowercase letters in sequencing the output. By default, the

SORT command sorts starting with the first character in each line. Each character on the line is considered in sequencing the lines. The lines below are in standard U.S.A. sort sequence:

```
$8,799 Maximum Auto Sales
% Down Finance Company
1-2-3
1000 Acres Wilderness Park
782 Bunbury Lane Booksellers
99 Degrees
Anchor Associates
Janesmark 12
Stevenson Carriages
William Tell Overtures
```

If you omit an input source, SORT expects keyboard input and sorts the lines you type. You could produce a sorted listing of items, but you would have to type each item. If you want to sort six items on screen, first use SORT with no options. After you press Enter, the cursor rests at the left edge of the screen. Type the six items, pressing Enter after each. At this point, here's how the screen will look:

```
C:\DOS> SORT
PEACHES
APPLES
PLUMS
PERSIMMON
PEARS
BANANAS

_
```

Press F6 or Ctrl+Z to add the end-of-file mark, then press Enter, just as when creating a file from the keyboard. DOS sorts the input and sends it back to the screen, which now looks like this:

```
C:\DOS> SORT
PEACHES
APPLES
PLUMS
PERSIMMON
PEARS
BANANAS
APPLES
```

```
BANANAS
PEACHES
PEARS
PERSIMMON
PLUMS

C:\DOS>_
```

As you can see, this isn't a very useful application of sorting. Normally, you'll provide the SORT input through redirection or piping. If the list of fruits is in a file called FRUITS, you could sort it to the screen with SORT < FRUITS, using input redirection. You could sort a directory listing with DIR | SORT, piping the DIR output to be used as SORT input. You could sort the FRUITS input file to an output file named FRUITS.ALF with SORT < FRUITS > FRUITS.ALF.

You can use piping for either input or output to the SORT command, or even both. The command DIR C:\ | SORT uses the listing of the root directory on the C drive as input to the sort and sends the output to the screen. The command DIR C:\ | SORT | MORE causes the output to be paged. The command SORT < FRUITS | MORE causes the sorted output of the FRUITS file to be paged to the screen.

## Using SORT Command Switches

The SORT command allows you to use two switches, which are shown in Figure 8.5. The /R option lets you request a reverse alphabetical sort if you prefer. The /+*n* option lets you start the sort at a different position in the line; the rest of the line from the start position is considered in the sort. You can use both switches in either order, but both must immediately follow the word SORT.

*Reverse SORT*  To produce a reverse alphabetical-order sort, use the /R option in the SORT command. This option causes the letters to sort from Z

| /R | Reverse order of sort | SORT /R < GROCERY.LST > GROCERY.BAK |
|---|---|---|
| /+*n* | Start at column *n* | DIR \| SORT /+10 |

Figure 8.5. SORT Command Switches

through A, then the numbers from 9 through 0. The lines below are in reverse sort sequence:

William Tell Overtures
Stevenson Carriages
Janesmark 12
Anchor Associates
99 Degrees
782 Bunbury Lane Booksellers
1000 Acres Wilderness Park
1-2-3
% Down Finance Company
$8,799 Maximum Auto Sales

***Changing the Starting Position*** A default sort starts with the first character in each line. Blanks sort first, so lines beginning with spaces sort first in the output when you start with column 1. You can use the */+n* option to start sorting based on some other position in the line. Wherever you start, the remainder of the line is crucial to the sort sequence. If you use DIR | SORT /+9 > SORTEXT.OUT, the sort starts in the ninth character position. Characters in positions one through eight are ignored; those in positions nine through the end of the line determine the output sequence.

Figure 8.6 shows the standard directory listing format, with columns indicated for each field. +9 or +10 will sort by extension, and +16 or +17 will sort by size. The leading blank won't cause any problems if every line has the blank in the same position.

If you sort by date (+24), you are actually sorting by month; all lines from January (01) precede all lines from February (02), and so forth. The year has no effect unless the rest of the date is identical. If you sort by time (+34), 1:12p precedes 2:12a, no matter what the date is.

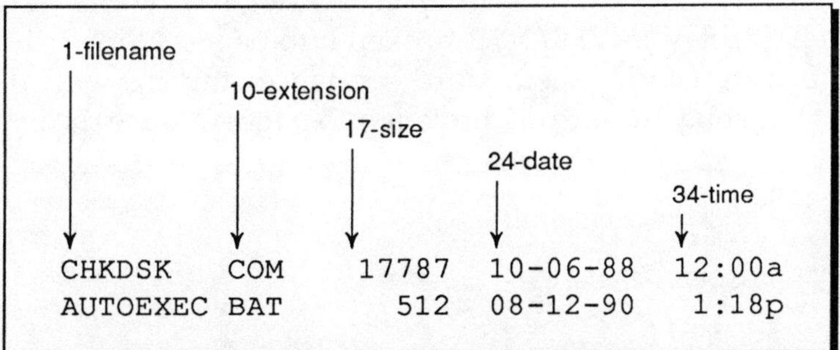


Figure 8.6. Labeled Directory Output

You may have a data file containing lines (or records) in which each line pertains to a particular item. Figure 8.7 shows an example. Such a file can be sorted beginning at the start of any field. The DOS SORT command always considers all remaining characters of the line as the sort field. You can't sort by manufacturer, then by item number within each manufacturer.

```
1-entire line                              37-quanity
  2-item number                              42-cost
        7-item name                               50-manufacturer

H2345  Hammer, claw                    36       8.50 S-C
H4545  Hammer, sledge                  24      14.90 Ben
H4687  Hammer, ball peen               18       8.14 S-C
H9231  Screwdriver, 3 inch             48       1.79 Gen
E1212  Sander, plane                   19      28.50 Mar
E1423  Jigsaw, 4 inch blade            10      27.42 Mar
E2398  Screwdriver, cordless           95      18.80 Mar
S1111  Lathe                            7     148.00 Mar
E4444  Router                           6      20.75 Mar
P1010  Grill, Weber                   117      19.40 Web
P2222  Cooler, small                  280       8.40 Coo
P2224  Cooler, medium                 175      14.20 Coo
P2226  Cooler, large                   86      26.00 Coo
```

Figure 8.7. Data File

Start at the command prompt. Make sure C:\PRACTICE is current.
1. Sort the file BACK1 to the screen. Compare the output to the contents of BACK1.
2. Display a sorted directory of C:\DOS, broken into pages.
3. Sort the SAVIT file in reverse order, saving the result in SAVIT.OUT.
4. Display SAVIT.OUT, broken into pages. Notice the order of the lines.
5. Sort SAVIT in standard sequence starting with the filespec extension; display the output, broken into pages. Notice the order of the sorted lines.

*1. Enter the command:*

```
SORT < BACK1
```

*followed by:*

```
TYPE BACK1
```

2. *Enter the command:*

```
DIR \DOS | SORT | MORE
```

3. *Enter the command:*

```
SORT /R < SAVIT > SAVIT.OUT
```

4. *Enter the command:*

```
MORE < SAVIT.OUT
```

5. *Enter the command:*

```
SORT < SAVIT /+10 | MORE.
```

# FINDing Lines

Still another filter is the FIND command. This command locates lines that contain the string you specify. You might use FIND to locate all the lines in a directory listing that contain "Mar" or to find the lines in a data file that contain "DuoTech". The FIND command format is shown below:

```
FIND [switches] "string" [filespecs]
```

Normally, you specify one or more files to be searched in the FIND command. The command FIND "EXE" SAVIT finds all lines containing EXE in the SAVIT file in the current directory and sends these lines to the screen. The output looks something like this:

```
---------- SAVIT
MAKEDISK    EXE      66890    11-09-89   12:00a
EXE2BIN     EXE       7963    11-09-88    1:12p
```

If you don't include a filespec, FIND expects to use standard input; although this can be from the keyboard, the data is normally redirected or piped from some other program's output. The filespec must be specific; it can't include an ambiguous file name. However, you can name as many separate files as you wish; just use a space to separate filespecs. If more than one file is searched, the output lines are separated according to the file searched. For example, suppose you use the command FIND "Arthur" ROUTE.DOX CLEAR.DOX. The output might look like this:

```
---------- ROUTE.DOX
Arthur P. Washington
Arthur Associates, Inc.
when the senior partner of Arthur Associates shall deem it
```

```
---------- CLEAR.DOX
and Arthur Andersen Co. as the primary auditors.
```

The string to be located must be enclosed in double quotation marks; if the string itself includes double quotation marks, repeat the character. The command FIND "the ""M"" factor" DUOTECH.DOC locates a string containing double quotation marks.

The output can be piped to another program or redirected to another file or device. The command FIND "EXE" SAVIT | MORE pipes the output directly to the MORE command for paging to the screen. The command FIND "EXE" SAVIT > SAVEXE.OUT sends the output to a file. If you want sorted output, you should sort the file before you extract lines with FIND. If you sort the FIND command output, you'll be sorting the filename lines as well. If several files were used, the sorted output wouldn't reflect the file from which lines were extracted.

## FIND Command Switches

The FIND command allows you to use certain switches to affect which lines are located. These switches are shown in Figure 8.8.

The /V option results in the lines that don't contain the specified string. The /C option results in only a count of the lines that are identified. If more than one file was searched, you'll get a specific count for each file, like this:

```
C:\DOS>FIND /C "Arthur" ROUTE.DOX CLEAR.DOX

---------- ROUTE.DOX: 3

---------- CLEAR.DOX: 1

C:\DOS>_
```

The /N option places a relative line number before each identified line. Here's an example:

```
C:\DOS>FIND /N "Arthur" ROUTE.DOX

---------- ROUTE.DOX
[8]Arthur P. Washington
[9]Arthur Associates, Inc.
[18]when the senior partner of Arthur Associates shall
deem it

C:\DOS>_
```

| | |
|---|---|
| /V | Produce lines that don't contain string |
| /C | Produce a count of identified lines |
| /N | Include line number with each identified line |

Figure 8.8. FIND Command Switches

You can combine /N and /V if you wish, in either order, to get line numbers with a listing of lines that don't contain the specified string. The /N switch has no meaning with /C; you'll just get a count of the lines if you use both of these switches.

Start at the command prompt. Make sure C:\PRACTICE is current.
1. Find all lines in SAVIT that contain the characters SYS and send those lines to the screen.
2. Find all lines in SAVIT that contain 89 and page them to the screen.

1. *Enter the command:*

```
FIND "SYS" SAVIT
```

2. *Enter the command:*

```
FIND "89" SAVIT | MORE
```

## Summary

In this chapter, you've learned a great deal about entering commands and manipulating input and output. You'll find all these techniques useful as you continue using DOS in your computer sessions.

## Exercises

These exercises let you practice and perfect your use of the command template, piping and redirection, and the DOS filters.

| **What You Should Do** | **How the Computer Responds** |
| --- | --- |
| 1. Start at the command prompt. Make sure C:\PRACTICE is the current directory. | 1. Awaits your commands. |
| 2. Sort BACK1 and save the result in SUMSORT. | 2. Creates a new file called SUMSORT containing lines sorted in ascending ASCII order. |
| 3. Repeat the preceding command, saving the result in SUMSORT2. | 3. Retrieves characters from the command template as you press F1 through F4. Creates another new file called SUMSORT2 containing lines sorted in ascending ASCII order. |
| 4. Repeat the preceding command, sorting the lines in reverse order into SUMSORT2. | 4. Retrieves characters from the command template as you press F1 through F4. Replaces the previous contents of SUMSORT2 with a set of lines in descending ASCII order. |
| 5. Sort BOOKLIST and add the result to SUMSORT2. | 5. Retrieves characters from the command template as you press F1 through F4. Adds sorted lines from BOOKLIST to SUMSORT2. |
| 6. Find all lines in SAVIT that contain the number "2". Page the output to the screen. | 6. Selects lines from SAVIT. Pipes the output to MORE. Displays the output one page at a time. |

## What If It Doesn't Work?

1. If the SORT command results in the message "Too many parameters", you forgot to put the redirection symbols < and > in the command.

2. If F1 through F4 produce no results, the template is empty. You probably pressed Enter at the command prompt when no command had been typed.

3. If the sorted lines from BOOKLIST overlay SUMSORT2 instead of being added to it, you probably used the > redirection symbol instead of >>.

4. If the FIND command results in the message "Parameter format not correct", you put the quoted string after the filespec. It must precede the filespec.

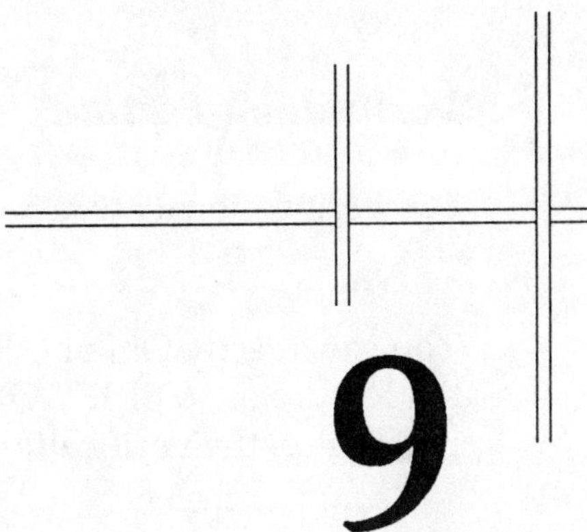

# 9

# *Copying Files*

You have already seen how to do basic file copying with the **Copy** option on the **File** menu and the COPY command. But the COPY command has some options that you have not yet learned. Furthermore, two more commands provide additional copying facilities: XCOPY and REPLACE. In this chapter, you will learn to:

- Verify copies
- Concatenate files
- Select files for copying from an entire subtree
- Select files for copying by their archive attributes
- Select files for copying by their time/date stamps
- Display a yes/no prompt for each selected file
- Copy only missing files
- Select files to replace in an entire subtree

## *Verifying Copies*

You've seen before that copies are not always perfect. If you're concerned about getting perfect copies, then you should *verify* the copy. There are two ways to verify copies. You can turn on the verification feature, which then verifies all files written to the disk until you turn it off again. Or you can use the /V switch with the COPY command, which verifies only this particular copy.

## Verification Feature

The verification feature is controlled by the VERIFY command. Its format is:

```
VERIFY [ON or OFF]
```

You can specify ON or OFF, but not both. The command VERIFY ON turns the feature on. VERIFY OFF turns it off again. If you enter VERIFY with no parameter, the verification status is displayed, as in this interaction:

```
C:\>VERIFY
VERIFY is on

C:\>_
```

When verification is on, every file that is written to disk or modified on the disk is verified. As DOS writes each sector, it checks the new sector against the source. If it finds a mistake, DOS rewrites the sector and checks it again. If DOS is unable to write a sector correctly after several tries, it displays a warning message.

Disk writes take longer when verification is on, but you probably won't notice the extra time, and the results could be worth the slight wait. Especially with program files, a bad copy could mean the entire program doesn't work or, worse, that the program malfunctions without your knowledge.

## Individual Verification

If you don't want to leave the verification feature on all the time, you can apply it to individual copies with the /V switch on the COPY command. For example, to copy and verify SORTER.EXE, you could enter this command:

```
COPY SORTER.EXE A: /V
```

# Concatenation

You can use the COPY command to *concatenate* files. This means you copy two or more files together to create one file. In the COPY command, you can either connect the source filespecs with plus signs (+) or use a global source filespec but a single target filespec.

Files concatenated according to this method must have end-of-file marks. If for any reason you want to concatenate program files or any other files without end-of-file marks, then you must use some special switches. Most of the time, you would have no need to do this. If you need to know how to do concatenation without end-of-file marks, see your DOS reference manual for details.

## Using Plus Signs

If you want to control the exact order of the source files, or if their names don't fit a global pattern, use plus signs to connect them. You may put spaces around the + symbol, but they aren't necessary. Here's an example:

```
C:\>COPY LEFT + RIGHT WHOLE
LEFT
RIGHT
 1 File(s) copied

C:\>_
```

The new WHOLE file contains first LEFT and then RIGHT. The original LEFT and RIGHT are unchanged. You can concatenate as many files as you want this way, as long as the entire command takes less than 127 characters and the destination disk has room for the new file. To concatenate five files, CHAP1 through CHAP5, you could enter:

```
C:\>COPY CHAP1 + CHAP2 + CHAP3 + CHAP4 + CHAP5 REPORT
```

If you don't specify a destination for the concatenated files, DOS uses the first file in the list as the destination. It doesn't create a new target file unless one is specified at the end of the command. When DOS encounters this command

```
COPY OLD.DAT + NEW.DAT
```

it adds the contents of NEW.DAT to the file OLD.DAT. NEW.DAT doesn't change, but OLD.DAT is now different.

The following command copies all five files, in the order shown, into CHAP1. The other files aren't changed.

```
COPY CHAP1 + CHAP2 + CHAP3 + CHAP4 + CHAP5
```

If any source file cannot be found during concatenation, DOS just skips that file and goes on. No warning message is displayed unless DOS can't find *any* source files. When no destination is specified, DOS concatenates into the first source file *that it can find*. Look at this command:

```
COPY FILEALL + FILEA + FILEB + FILEC
```

If FILEALL is missing, but FILEA is present, DOS uses FILEA as the destination file. No warning message is displayed.

## Using Global Filespecs

If you specify a global source and a single destination, all the matching source files are concatenated to create the destination file. The following command concatenates all files in the current directory with extension DAT. The result is called ALL.DAT. The concatenation is made in the order in which DAT files are found in the directory.

```
COPY *.DAT ALL.DAT
```

If the directory already contains an ALL.DAT, it is replaced by the concatenated file. In such a case, you will see the message "Contents of destination lost before copy." What it means is this: ALL.DAT was set up as the destination file. The first DAT file replaced it; the next DAT file was added to that; and so forth. Then DOS found ALL.DAT in the directory as a source file because ALL.DAT matches the source filespec *.DAT. DOS can't use ALL.DAT as both the source and the destination, so it issues the above (somewhat cryptic) message, skips over ALL.DAT as a source file, and goes on to the next source file. No harm has been done, unless you wanted the original ALL.DAT included in the new file. In that case, you should use this command instead:

```
COPY ALL.DAT + *.DAT
```

This concatenates all other DAT files into ALL.DAT (as long as ALL.DAT actually exists). You'll still see the "Contents of destination lost before copy" message, but since ALL.DAT remains as the first part of the concatenation, you can ignore the message.

## Parallel Concatenation

You can also do a parallel concatenation using global identifiers. In a parallel concatenation, files with identical filenames but different extensions are concatenated. The following example shows what happens if you concatenate *.DAT with *.CAT to create *.FAT:

```
LOST.DAT  + LOST.CAT  = LOST.FAT
FOUND.DAT + FOUND.CAT = FOUND.FAT
TRUE.DAT  + TRUE.CAT  = TRUE.FAT
FALSE.DAT + FALSE.CAT = FALSE.FAT
```

The command COPY *.DAT + *.CAT *.FAT accomplishes the parallel concatenation. This is the self only instance where it is appropriate to use a global filespec as a destination in a COPY command.

## *Date and Time Stamps with Copied Files*

When you copy a file without concatenation, the date and time stamps in the directory entry are also copied. That is, the copy does not receive the current date, because you have not modified the file.

Concatenation is different. When you use COPY to create a new file by concatenating two or more files, the new file receives the current date/time stamp. Thus, if you merge BFILE and CFILE into AFILE, the date and time associated with AFILE are updated. If you want to copy a file and force the copy to have a new date and time, you can "pretend" to concatenate it, as in:

```
COPY B:WORDWRAP+
```

This will copy WORDWRAP from drive B: to the current directory; the current date and time are associated with the new copy. You can also use this method to update the date and time of any file, without actually making a copy of it. However, you must add two commas to the end of the command so DOS knows you are not trying to copy the file onto itself. To update HILLTREE's time/date stamp without making any other changes to it, you would enter this command:

```
COPY HILLTREE+,,
```

If you leave out the commas, you will see the message "File cannot be copied onto itself."

If you want to specify a destination and use the current date and time, code the two commas after the plus sign so that DOS doesn't read the destination file as part of the concatenation. The commas signal DOS that there are no more files to concatenate. The following example makes a copy of WORDWRAP called NEWWRAP, which is associated with the current date and time:

```
COPY WORDWRAP+,, NEWWRAP
```

If the two commas are omitted in this command, DOS will try to concatenate NEWWRAP into WORDWRAP, which might not be what you want.

---

Start at the command prompt. Make sure C:\PRACTICE is current.
1. Check whether verification is on or off.
2. If verification is off, turn it on.
3. Concatenate BACK1 through BACK4 into a new file called FAMLIST. Notice how long the copy takes with verification on.
4. Turn verification off and try the same concatenation again. Can you observe a time difference?

5. Do the concatenation again, this time use the /V switch for verification.
6. Display the contents of FAMLIST, one page at a time. You should see four copies of your family list.
7. Turn verification on and leave it on for the rest of this checkpoint.
8. Concatenate MYADDR.LST, SAVIT, and SAVIT.OUT as BIGFILE. Check the contents of BIGFILE. You should see your name and address followed by a collection of directory entries.
9. Now concatenate FAMLIST into BIGFILE. Check the new BIGFILE.
10. Check the time/date stamp of MYADDR.LST. Change it to the current time and date. Check it again.

---

*1. Enter the command:*

```
VERIFY
```

*DOS responds with a message telling you that VERIFY is on or off.*

*2. If necessary, enter the command:*

```
VERIFY ON
```

*3. Enter the command:*

```
COPY BACK1 + BACK2 + BACK3 + BACK4 FAMLIST
```

*4. Enter these commands:*

```
VERIFY OFF
COPY BACK1 + BACK2 + BACK3 + BACK4 FAMLIST
```

*You probably won't be able to notice a time difference.*

*5. Enter this command:*

```
COPY BACK1 + BACK2 + BACK3 + BACK4 FAMLIST /V
```

*6. Enter the command:*

```
MORE < FAMLIST
```

*8. Enter these commands:*

```
COPY MYADDR.LST + SAVIT + SAVIT.OUT BIGFILE
MORE < BIGFILE
```

*9. Enter these commands:*

```
COPY BIGFILE + FAMLIST
MORE < BIGFILE
```

10.  *Enter these commands:*

```
DIR MYADDR.LST
COPY MYADDR.LST+,,
DIR MYADDR.LST
```

*You should be able to see the date and time change.*

# Extended Copy Functions

Wouldn't it be nice if COPY had some of BACKUP's features? Or if BACKUP produced usable files? The XCOPY (extended copy) command combines some of the best features of BACKUP and COPY. XCOPY makes usable copies like those made with COPY, and it selects modified files as BACKUP does. It also copies from an entire subtree, just as BACKUP does.

XCOPY outperforms COPY on multiple-file copies. Instead of copying one file at a time, XCOPY copies as much data at once as memory can hold. Unlike COPY, however, XCOPY cannot handle devices other than disk drives. Also, XCOPY cannot concatenate files.

XCOPY uses most of the same switches as BACKUP. XCOPY can select files from an entire subtree by their archive attributes or time/date stamps, so you can use XCOPY instead of BACKUP as your main backup function. Many people prefer XCOPY's features. The backup copies are usable "as is"—you don't need a special program, such as RESTORE, to read the files. You also don't need a backup log because you can read the directory of the backup diskette directly. Suppose your fixed disk crashes and is out of use for several days. You can continue to work with your backup files on diskette if they have been made by XCOPY instead of BACKUP.

Furthermore, XCOPY doesn't create several versions of the same file on the backup diskette. If XCOPY backs up a file named POPULATE.DAT on Monday, then backs up a newer version of the same file on Tuesday, Tuesday's version will overwrite Monday's version. Only one version of the file exists on the XCOPY backup diskette—the latest version. In fact, you can start with a full backup, then add modified files to the same backup diskettes each day, overwriting previous versions. At all times, you have one set of backup diskettes containing the latest versions of all your files. (If you want to maintain previous versions, you can do that too. Just back up each day to a fresh set of diskettes.)

You can see that XCOPY has several advantages over BACKUP and RESTORE. Its major disadvantage is in handling full disks. XCOPY, like

COPY, gives up when the target disk is full. It displays a "Disk full" message and terminates itself, even if there are more files to copy. You have to insert another diskette and reenter the command. Furthermore, XCOPY cannot back up a file that is larger than a diskette. Only BACKUP can span a file over two or more diskettes. Therefore, you have to plan for yourself how you will break up your hard disk directory into diskette-sized chunks. You might use one diskette per directory; if a directory is too large to fit onto a diskette, break it up by extensions or filenames. Be sure to leave room to add new files to the diskettes if your plan requires them.

## Command Format

The complete format of the XCOPY command is shown below:

```
XCOPY source [target] [/V] [/A] [/M] [/D:date] [/S] [/E] [/W]
```

In its basic form, without any switches, XCOPY functions just like COPY, except it's faster. For example, to copy all DAT files from the current directory to drive A:, you could enter:

```
XCOPY *.DAT A:
```

## Selecting Modified Files

XCOPY can select modified files in several ways. The /M switch acts just like the BACKUP and RESTORE /M switches. It selects all files in the source directory that have the archive attribute on. The /M switch also turns off the archive attribute when the file is copied. The /A switch selects the same files, but it doesn't turn off the archive attribute. The /D:*date* switch selects files that were created or modified on or after the specified date. This switch does not use or affect the archive attribute. There is no equivalent of BACKUP's /T:*time* switch.

The following command backs up all modified files in the current directory to the diskette in A:. All archive attributes are turned off during the process.

```
XCOPY *.* A: /M
```

The following command backs up all files modified on or after August 1, 1992 to the diskette in B:

```
XCOPY *.* B: /D:8-1-92
```

The following command backs up all modified CAT files but does not change their archive attributes:

```
XCOPY *.CAT A: /A
```

How do you choose between /M, /A, and /D:*date*? That depends on your regular backup system. Suppose your backup routine is built around BACKUP with the /M switch. Every day before you shut down, you use BACKUP with /M to back up modified files. In this case, you don't want XCOPY to turn off archive attributes. Use /A or /D:*date* whenever you want to select modified files with XCOPY.

If you are using XCOPY instead of BACKUP as your main backup function, then use the /M switch so that archive attributes are turned off as files are selected for backup. Whichever method you choose, stick with it. Don't sometimes do one and sometimes do the other, or your backup system won't be consistent.

## Prompted Copies

One especially handy XCOPY feature is the /P (prompt) switch. This switch causes XCOPY to ask you about every file it selects for copying. Figure 9.1 shows a sample interaction. You can see that five files matched the CHAP*.* global filespec and the /A switch. We said "Yes" to four of them but chose not to copy the CHAP01.BAK file. While /P gives you more control, it requires more of your attention. You must respond to each prompt before DOS can continue.

You frequently create or modify files that don't need to be backed up: letters, notes to yourself, temporary scratch pads, WordStar BAK files, WordPerfect BK! files, and so forth. The /P switch lets you reject them when backing up modified files.

```
C:\NOVEL\>XCOPY CHAP*.* A: /A /P
CHAP01 (Y/N)? Y
CHAP02 (Y/N)? Y
CHAP03 (Y/N)? Y
CHAP04 (Y/N)? Y
CHAP01.BAK (Y/N)? N
        4 File(s) copied

C:\NOVEL\>_
```

Figure 9.1. Sample Prompted XCOPY Interaction

You'll also find /P handy when a global filename includes files you don't want to copy. For example, suppose you want to copy CHAP01 through CHAP17, but not CHAP18. Rather than enter 17 separate COPY or XCOPY commands, you could enter this command:

```
XCOPY CHAP* A: /V /P
```

The /P switch slows XCOPY down, and you have to stay at the keyboard for the entire copy operation, but sometimes it's the most convenient way to get a job done.

## Copying Subtrees

XCOPY lets you copy selected files from an entire tree or subtree to a corresponding tree somewhere else. Figure 9.2 shows how this process works. The command for the XCOPY in the figure is:

```
XCOPY \EMAIL A:\ /S /V
```

The source tree starts at C:\EMAIL. The target tree starts at A:\. XCOPY treats the top source directory and the top target directory as parallel directories, even if their names and levels don't match. Thus, in the example, all the files from C:\EMAIL are copied to A:\. Three of the files overwrite existing files; a fourth file is added to the directory.

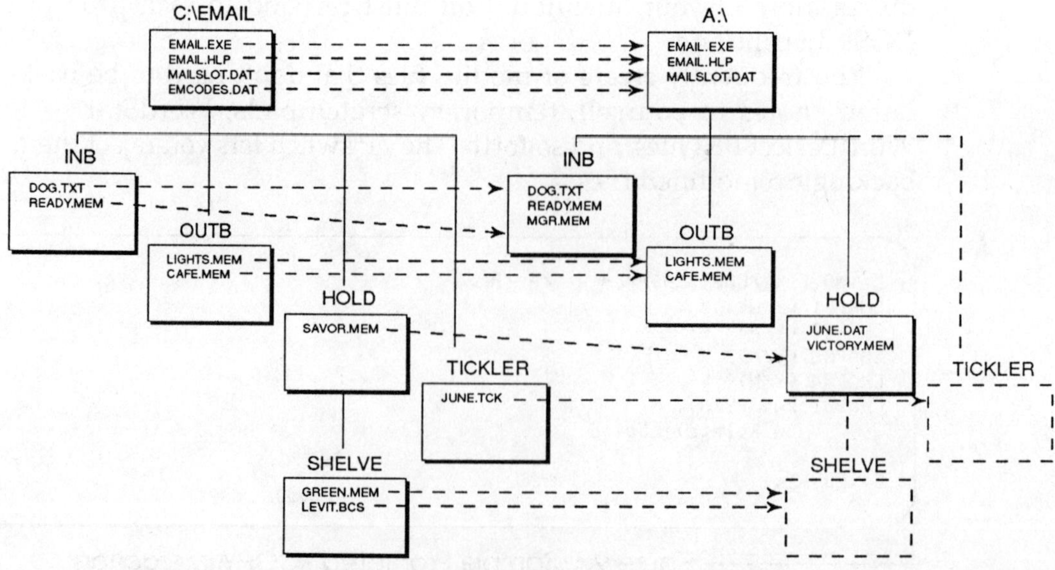


Figure 9.2. Using XCOPY with a Complete Subtree

For each subdirectory in the source subtree, XCOPY looks for a parallel directory in the target tree. The pathnames must match, except for the beginnings, which reflect the top of the trees. In the example, when XCOPY finds C:\EMAIL\INB, it looks for a directory named A:\INB. When it finds C:\EMAIL\HOLD\SHELVE, it looks for A:\HOLD\SHELVE. If XCOPY finds a parallel directory, it copies all the selected files to this directory, overwriting existing files and creating new files as necessary.

If XCOPY doesn't find a target directory parallel to the source directory, it *creates a parallel directory* and copies the source files to this new directory. You can see in the figure that XCOPY created A:\TICKLER and A:\HOLD\SHELVE.

If XCOPY finds a source directory with no files to be copied, it does not look for or create a parallel target directory unless you specify the /E switch. The /E switch causes XCOPY to make the two directory trees parallel. You might use this switch if you are trying to keep your home computer "in sync" with your office computer, for example.

Suppose you want to back up your entire fixed disk using XCOPY instead of BACKUP. You have determined that the entire subtree starting at C:\CLASSES\HIST101 will fit on one diskette with plenty of spare room for later additions. The following command will copy the subtree, including empty subdirectories:

```
XCOPY C:\CLASSES\HIST101 A:\ /S /V /E
```

To add modified files and new subdirectories to the diskette created in the previous command, you could enter:

```
XCOPY C:\CLASSES\HIST101 A:\ /S /V /E /M
```

In both these cases, you might want to include the /P switch to screen out files that don't need to be backed up.

Suppose you need to send a set of files to the home office via diskette. They are contained in the C:\ADMIN\ACCOUNTS subtree, which has several subdirectories. You could create the necessary diskette, while maintaining the tree structure, with this command:

```
XCOPY C:\ADMIN\ACCOUNTS A:\ /S /V
```

Suppose you have received from a vendor a diskette that is structured into a root directory and several subdirectories, some of which are empty. You can copy the entire tree from drive A: to the current directory on drive C: with this command:

```
XCOPY A: /S /V /E
```

## Prompting for Diskettes

The /W (wait) switch causes XCOPY to prompt you for any diskettes. Without /W, XCOPY assumes the diskettes were inserted before the command was entered, and it gets right to work. If you don't have a fixed disk, you must start the XCOPY command with the DOS program diskette in one of your drives. If you want the chance to start the program and then replace the DOS diskette with either the source or the target diskette, use the /W switch. You might also include /W if you put XCOPY in a batch file; this gives you a chance to switch diskettes before the XCOPY operation. You'll learn about batch files in Chapter 13.

## Messages

The following message appears when XCOPY attempts to overwrite a read-only file: "Access denied." Figure 9.3 shows a sample job in which several files were successfully copied, then a read-only file was encountered. The "Access denied" message was displayed and the job terminated. You might also see the "Access denied" message if the source and target files are accidentally the same.

When the same directory is included in both the source and target trees, you'll see "Cannot perform a cyclic copy." For example, refer back to Figure 9.2. If the source directory was EMAIL, the target directory was SHELVE, and the /S switch was used, then SHELVE would be in both trees and XCOPY could not proceed.

If you specify a DOS device name such as PRN as either the source or the target, you'll see "Cannot XCOPY from/to a reserved device."

```
C:\NOVEL\>XCOPY A:*.*

Reading source file(s)...
A:CHAP01
A:CHAP02
A:CHAP03
A:CHAP04

Access denied
        3 File(s) copied

C:\NOVEL\>_
```

Figure 9.3. Access Denied Message with XCOPY

Filenames and directory names look alike. Most of the time, DOS can tell the difference by the context or by looking in the directory to see which type of entry the name has. However, when an XCOPY command specifies a target name that doesn't appear in the target directory, XCOPY doesn't know whether the name is a filename or a directory name. The following message is displayed:

```
Does name specify a file name
or a directory name on the target
  (F = file, D = directory)?_
```

You must enter F or D to tell XCOPY how to treat the name.

If XCOPY is trying to create a directory on the target drive and cannot do so, you'll see "Unable to create directory." Perhaps a file with the same name already exists in the parent directory (you can't have both). Perhaps the disk is full, or the root directory is the parent directory and it's full. Perhaps the specified directory name is a device name. You'll have to figure out what the problem is and correct it before reentering the XCOPY command.

You might want to add XCOPY programs to your **DOS Utilities** screen in the shell if you plan to use XCOPY as your regular backup method. Since XCOPY fails if the target diskette fills up, you'll have to work out a plan for backing up only part of your hard disk to each target diskette. You might want to decide now what source operands you will use, or you might want to build in a dialog box to collect the information when you run the program.

---

Start at the command prompt. Make sure C:\PRACTICE is the current directory.

1. Copy the entire subtree from PRACTICE to a new directory to be created by XCOPY called C:\TARGET1. Notice how much faster XCOPY copies a group of files than COPY does.
2. Get a tree listing (including filenames) of the TARGET1 subtree. You should see the PRACA and PRACY subdirectories created by the XCOPY command.
3. Copy all SYS files from the \PRACTICE subtree to a new directory called \TARGET2.
4. Get a tree listing of the \TARGET2 subtree. The PRACA and PRACY subdirectories were not copied because they contained no SYS files.
5. Try step 4 again, but include the switch to copy all subdirectories, even if they are empty. Get another tree listing to show that the PRACA and PRACY directories were copied, even though they contain no files.

6. Format a blank or reusable diskette. Back up the entire \PRACTICE sub-tree to the diskette using XCOPY instead of BACKUP. Check the tree of A:. You should be able to see which files are backed up there.
7. Use XCOPY to back up only modified files to the diskette in drive A:. Use the switch that retains the archive attributes.
8. Try the same command again, but use the switch that turns off the archive attributes of selected files. Have each selected filename displayed in a yes/no prompt.

---

*1. Enter the command:*

```
XCOPY *.* \TARGET1 /S
```

*3. Enter the command:*

```
XCOPY *.SYS \TARGET2 /S
```

*When DOS asks whether \TARGET1 is a file or directory, enter D.*

*5. Enter these commands:*

```
XCOPY *.SYS \TARGET2 /S /E
TREE \TARGET2 /F
```

*6. Enter these commands:*

```
FORMAT A:
XCOPY *.* A: /S
TREE A: /F
```

*7. Enter the command:*

```
XCOPY *.* A: /S /A
```

*8. Enter the command:*

```
XCOPY *.* A: /S /M /P
```

---

# Upgrading and Replacing Files

One more copy function, REPLACE, gives you some features you might occasionally find useful. The REPLACE command compares the source and target directories and does one of two things: either it copies only matching files, or it copies only nonmatching files.

The format of the command is shown below:

```
REPLACE source [target] [/A] [/S] [/P] [/W] [/R] [/U]
```

You must specify a source filespec. A drivename or path is not enough. If you omit the filespec, you will see the message "No files found." If you omit the target, the current directory is assumed. You can specify a drivename and/or a path for the target. No filespec is permitted. REPLACE treats a filespec as a path and tells you "Path not found."

## Replacing Matching Files

The matching-files function is designed to help you upgrade versions of an application when you receive new copies from a vendor. Figure 9.4 shows how it works. The source diskette contains a new version of SORTER.EXE. Five copies of the previous version reside in various directories on the fixed

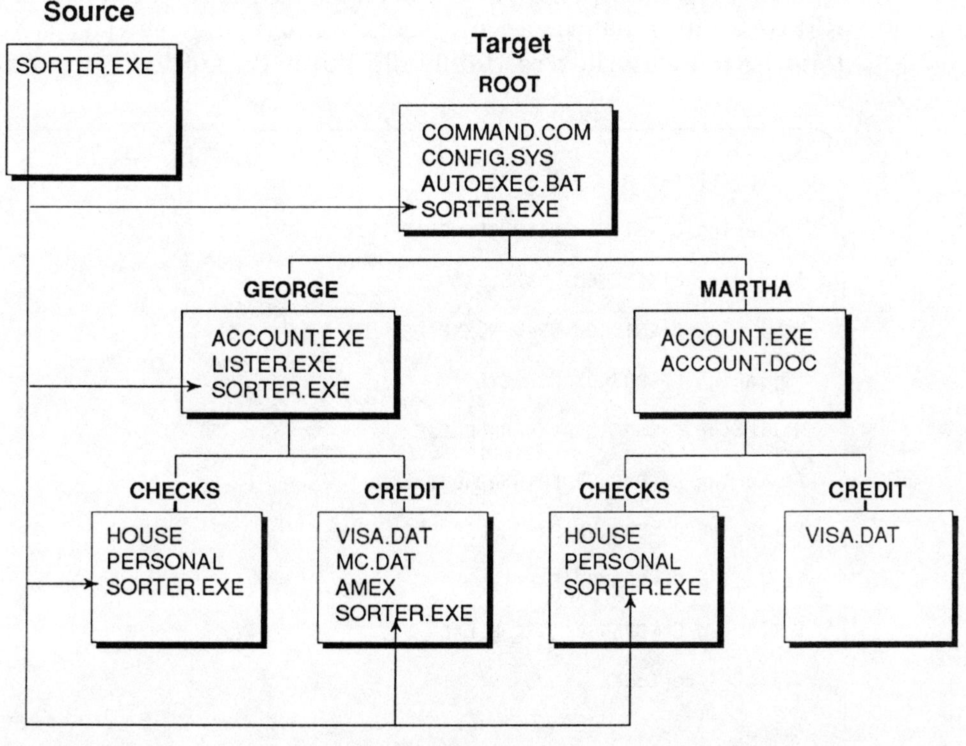


Figure 9.4. Upgrading Several Copies of a File
with REPLACE

disk. REPLACE seeks out and overwrites every existing copy. Thus, RE-PLACE makes it easy to upgrade your software, even if you have several versions of it on the fixed disk.

The command to upgrade the SORTER.EXE application is:

```
REPLACE A:SORTER.EXE C:\ /S
```

The /S switch causes all subdirectories of the target directory to be examined. Since we specified the root directory of C:, the entire fixed disk was examined.

If the source directory contains several files to be upgraded, you can use a global filespec, as in:

```
REPLACE A:*.* C:\ /S
```

Figure 9.5 shows such a REPLACE interaction. In the example, the source disk contained three upgraded files: GRAPH.EXE, GRAPHOUT.EXE, and DRAWGR.EXE. You can see that DOS found several copies of these programs on the fixed disk. All files were replaced automatically.

The /R (read-only) switch is used to replace read-only files. Ordinarily, REPLACE terminates with an "Access denied" message just as XCOPY does if it tries to overwrite a read-only file. But in the software upgrade situation,

```
C:\DOS>REPLACE A:*.* C:\ /S

 Replacing C:\SITCOM\JIMPROPS\GRAPH.EXE

 Replacing C:\SITCOM\GRAPH.EXE

 Replacing C:\SITCOM\DRAWGR.EXE

 Replacing C:\DOS\DRAWGR.EXE

 Replacing C:\DOS\GRAPH\GRAPH.EXE

 Replacing C:\DOS\GRAPH\GRAPHOUT.EXE

 Replacing C:\DOS\GRAPH\DRAWGR.EXE

 Replacing C:\DRAWGR.EXE

 Replacing C:\DOSBOOK\GRAPH.EXE

 9 file(s) replaced

C:\DOS>_
```

Figure 9.5. Upgrading Multiple Files with REPLACE

you frequently need to upgrade program files that have been protected on the fixed disk. This is a case where you want to override the protection. The /R switch lets you do that. Without /R, you would have to go through each directory and turn off the protection with ATTRIB -R before REPLACE could work. That would cause the same work and hassle that REPLACE was designed to prevent. The /R switch lets you avoid the hassle.

The /P (prompt) switch causes each replacement to be prompted with a message like this: "Replace C:\SITCOM\GRAPH.EXE?" This gives you a chance to review and approve (or deny) each replacement. If you use the /R switch to override the read-only attribute, you might want to use the /P switch, just for caution's sake.

## Updating Files

The /U (update) switch helps you update matching files by comparing time/date stamps in both directories. The only files replaced are those that have earlier time/date stamps on the target than on the source. Suppose you have a new copy of INVENTY.DAT on drive A:. You want to update older copies throughout drive C:. You could use this command:

```
C:\>REPLACE A:\INVENTY.DAT C:\ /S /U
```

## Replacing Missing Files

The /A (add) switch reverses the function of REPLACE. It copies only files that don't exist in the target directory. This function helps you replace files that you erased or are missing for some other reason.

Figure 9.6 shows a REPLACE interaction with the /A switch. Only two directories are involved—the source and the target. DOS found three files in the source directory that didn't exist in the target directory and added them.

When you use /P with /A, DOS prompts you for each addition with a message like this: "Add C:\GRAPH.EXE?" You can approve or deny each missing file. Using /R with /A makes no sense, because /A means that no files will be overwritten on the target directory, whether read-only or not. You also can't use /A with /U since they have opposite effects. The /A switch also cannot be used with /S.

## Prompting for Diskettes

The /W switch gives you a chance to change the target diskette before starting the directory search. This switch is useful if you must begin with your

```
C:\PLAY>REPLACE C:*.* A: /A

 Adding A:\PLAY.OUT

 Adding A:\PROPOSAL

 Adding A:\CHAP01.BAK

3 file(s) added

C:\PLAY>_
```

Figure 9.6. REPLACE /A Interaction

DOS diskette in the source or target drive in order to access the REPLACE program. It's also helpful when the REPLACE command is included in a batch file where you don't know what diskettes will be present when the command is executed.

Start at the command prompt. Make sure C:\PRACTICE is the current directory. You will also need a practice diskette in drive A:.
1. Create a new file on A: called WISHLIST. List at least three things you would like to receive as birthday presents.
2. Enter a command to copy missing files from A:\ to C:\PRACTICE. At least WISHLIST should be selected.
3. Copy WISHLIST to PRACA and PRACA\PRACY.
4. Replace all copies of WISHLIST in the C:\PRACTICE subtree with WISHLIST from A:.
5. Make C:\PRACTICE\WISHLIST read-only. Then try the previous REPLACE command again.
6. Try the preceding REPLACE command using the switch to override read-only files.
7. Remove the read-only attribute from WISHLIST.

*1. You can use your ASCII editor, or*

```
COPY CON WISHLIST
```

*or*

```
SORT > WISHLIST
```

*to accomplish this.*
*2. Enter the command:*

```
REPLACE A:\*.* /A
```

*3. Use F3 in the second command.*
*4. Enter the command:*

```
REPLACE A:\WISHLIST C: /S
```

*5. Enter these commands:*

```
ATTRIB WISHLIST +R
REPLACE A:\WISHLIST /S
```

*The program should terminate itself when it encounters the read-only file.*
*6. Enter the command:*

```
REPLACE A:\WISHLIST /S /R
```

*Don't forget to use F3.*

# Summary

In this chapter you have seen several extended copy functions. The COPY command can be used to concatenate files. XCOPY provides several functions that COPY doesn't have, including the ability to copy subtrees and to select files for copying based on their archive attributes and time/date stamps. REPLACE selects files for copying by comparing the source and target directories and selecting either matching files or missing files. You have also seen how to verify files, either by turning verification on with the VERIFY command or by using the /V switch on COPY and XCOPY.

# Exercises

These exercises let you practice using COPY to concatenate, VERIFY, XCOPY, and REPLACE files.

| **What You Should Do** | **How the Computer Responds** |
|---|---|
| 1. If verification is off, turn it on. | 1. Turns verification on, if necessary, but doesn't display a confirmation message unless you ask for it by entering VERIFY without an operand. |
| 2. Format a blank or reusable diskette. (You can use the same diskette that you used to work through the checkpoints for this chapter.) | 2. Formats the diskette as you directed. |
| 3. Copy the entire \PRACTICE subtree to the diskette. | 3. Copies all files from C:\PRACTICE to A:\, creating subdirectories as needed. |
| 4. Delete the C:\PRACTICE\PRACA \PRACY directory. | 4. Deletes the files and subdirectory as you requested. |
| 5. Restore the directory you just deleted from the hard disk. | 5. Copies the subdirectory and its files from the diskette to the hard disk. |
| 6. Copy C:\PRACTICE\BACK1 as C:\PRACTICE\NEWBACK. | 6. Copies the file as directed. |
| 7. Copy all modified files from the \PRACTICE subtree to the diskette. Turn off their archive attributes as they're copied. | 7. Copies at least C:\PRACTICE\NEWBACK as A:\NEWBACK. Might copy other files as well. |
| 8. Update the time/date stamp of A:\MYADDR.LST. (You have to switch to the A: drive to do this.) | 8. Assigns the current date and time to A:\MYADDR.LST. |
| 9. Replace all files in the C:\PRACTICE subtree with more current versions from the A:\ subtree. | 9. Copies A:\MYADDR.LST to C:\PRACTICE\MYADDR.LST. |
| 10. Delete C:\PRACTICE\BACK*.*. | 10. Deletes the files as requested. |
| 11. Replace all of the missing files in the C:\PRACTICE subtree from the back-up diskette. | 11. Replaces the files deleted in Step 10. |

## *What If It Doesn't Work?*

1. If no subdirectories are created on A:, you probably omitted the /S switch from the XCOPY command.

2. If the COPY command to update the time/date stamp results in the message "File cannot be copied onto itself", you didn't enter the two commas at the end of the command.

3. If DOS updates the time/date stamp of C:MYADDR.LST instead of A:MYADDR.LST, you tried to execute the COPY command from C:. You must switch to A:.

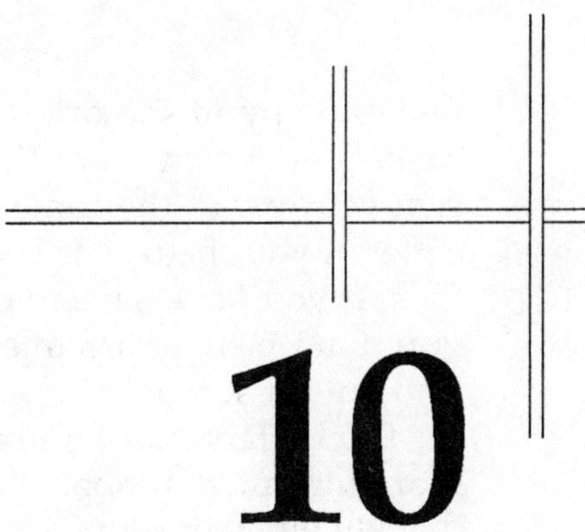

# 10

# Rescuing Files and Disks

You've already seen that files don't always copy correctly. And disks don't last forever. You may have other problems with files as well. For example, you may want to find out how two fairly similar files differ. If you don't verify copies, you may want to compare two files that should be the same but don't seem to be.

You may also want to check the status of memory in your computer or space on your disks. You may want to see if files are stored efficiently or find out whether a disk has developed bad spots (called bad sectors). You may want to recover the good parts of a file or disk that has gone bad.

In this chapter you'll learn to:

- Compare files and display lines that are different
- Compare files and display bytes that are different
- Display how memory is used in the system
- Check a disk for contiguity of storage
- Check for and recapture lost clusters
- Recover files that contain bad sectors
- Recover a disk when the directory has gone bad

## Comparing Files

There are many reasons you might want to compare files. One important reason is that copies may not be perfect. If you've copied a particular program dozens of times, it may suddenly stop working. You can compare the newest copy to the original to see if the two are identical. Then you can make a new copy from the original, using the verify function. If you have two versions of the same data, you could compare them to see how they differ. If your battery is low, you may not have correct date stamps on your files. If you have several different versions of files in different directories, you don't have to assume they are the same; you can compare the files to find out for sure.

DOS offers two commands you can use to compare files. FC gives you more information about how text (ASCII) files differ. COMP can tell you quickly whether two files are identical. You'll learn to use both commands in this section.


## The FC Command

The FC (for File Compare) command compares two files and displays the differences between them on the screen. You can pipe the output to MORE for paging or redirect it to a file or your printer if you prefer. By default, the FC command uses a byte-by-byte binary comparison for all files with extension EXE, COM, OBJ, LIB, or BIN. It uses a line-by-line ASCII comparison for all other files.

For both ASCII and binary comparisons, the FC output displays the differences; you'll see lines for ASCII comparisons and byte contents for binary ones. For ASCII files, FC tries to resynchronize the two files being compared as well. In resynchronizing, FC looks ahead in both files until it finds lines that match. (The matching lines can be at different locations in the files.) The next comparison starts following the matching lines, wherever they were encountered.

To compare two files, just specify the complete filespecs following the FC command. If the two files are identical, you'll see this message: "fc: no differences encountered".

***ASCII Comparison Output*** If files in an ASCII comparison aren't identical, the output shows you what differences exist. An ASCII comparison is done on a line-by-line basis, ignoring spaces at the beginning or end of a line. When FC encounters two lines that aren't the same, it continues searching both files until it finds a match again to resynchronize the operation. For example, if one file contains lines that aren't in the other file, they will be identified, but lines that exist in both files (in the same sequence) are not identified even if they have different line numbers. Figure 10.1 shows the output from the command FC DATA INVENT, which results in an ASCII comparison of two files. Each file contains lines that are not in the other.

```
C:\DOS>FC DATA INVENT
***** DATA
H2345 Hammer, claw                    36        8.50 S-C
H4545 Hammer, sledge            24     14.90 Ben
H4687 Hammer, ball peen               18        8.14 S-C
H9231 Screwdriver, 3 inch             48        1.79 Gen
E1212 Sander, plane                   19       28.50 Mar
E1333 Sandpaper sheets         120        .56 Gen
E1423 Jigsaw, 4 inch blade            10       27.42 Mar
***** INVENT
H2345 Hammer, claw                    36        8.50 S-C
H4545 Hammer, sledge                  24       14.90 Ben
H4687 Hammer, ball peen               18        8.14 S-C
H5897 Screwdriver, 1 inch             28        5.78 Gen
H6980 Screwdriver, 2 inch             38        4.98 Gen
H9231 Screwdriver, 3 inch             48        1.79 Gen
H9987 Screwdriver, cordless           19       19.57 Ben
E1212 Sander, plane                   19       28.50 Mar
E1423 Jigsaw, 4 inch blade            10       27.42 Mar
*****

***** DATA
E4444 Router                           6       20.75 Mar
P1010 Grill, weber                   117       19.40 Web
P2222 Cooler, small                  280        8.40 Coo
***** INVENT
E4444 Router                           6       20.75 Mar
E4477 Router blades                   19        2.60 Gen
P1010 Grill, Weber                   117       19.40 Web
P2222 Cooler, small                  280        8.40 Coo
*****

***** DATA
P2226 Cooler, large                   86       26.00 Coo
Q1111 Picnic Basket                   29       14.30 Gen
***** INVENT
P2226 Cooler, large                   86       26.00 Coo
P2345 Campstove, alcohol              10       29.40 Pil
P1366 Campstove, heet                  9       19.35 Pil
Q1111 Picnic Basket                   29       14.30 Gen
*****

C:\DOS>_
```

Figure 10.1. ASCII Mismatch—FC

The output from an ASCII comparison shows the first filespec (DATA in the figure), followed by the line that precedes the lines that differ (starting with H2345 Hammer in the figure). Following this are the nonmatching lines that appear in the first file, then the first line that matches in both. Then you'll see the name of the second file (INVENT in the figure), the last matching line, followed by the nonmatching lines that appear in the second file and the first line that matches in both. The line containing only ***** marks the end of the first set of mismatched lines. The first and last line for each file are the same in each set of lines. FC assumes the files are resynchronized when it encounters two matching lines in sequence, so you'll see a few isolated matching lines that appear in each group of unmatched lines.

The next set, beginning with ***** and the first filename, shows another difference between the two files, and the third set another.

Notice in the output that spacing (see the line beginning H4545 Hammer) and capitalization (see the line beginning P1010 Grill) cause the lines to be different. You'll learn to make FC ignore these differences shortly.

***Binary Comparison Output*** A binary comparison results in a different style of output since it is byte oriented rather than line oriented. If the files have extension COM, EXE, LIB, OBJ, or BIN, then the FC comparison is done on a byte-by-byte basis. If the fifth byte doesn't match in the two files, that's an error. If the sixth byte doesn't match, that's another mismatch. There is no attempt to resynchronize with a binary comparison. If one file includes a few extra bytes near the beginning, every later set of bytes compared may result in a mismatch. Figure 10.2 shows how the screen looks after a binary comparison of two files that aren't identical.

The output shows the address offset of the byte in hexadecimal, followed by the contents of that byte in the first filespec, followed by the contents of that byte in the second filespec. Many lines are omitted in this listing; you

```
C:\DOS>FC PAYROLL.OBJ PAYTIME.OBJ
000000A3:   39 35
000000C8:   34 32
000000CE:   31 35

  . . . .

0000037F:   1A 20
fc: PAYTIME.OBJ longer than PAYROLL.OBJ
C:\DOS>_
```

Figure 10.2. Binary Mismatch—FC

may get pages of mismatched bytes, but they look pretty much like the ones shown here. The final line shows that one file was longer than the other; this won't appear if the files are exactly the same length. If you aren't a programmer, you shouldn't try modifying binary files. If you wish, however, you can examine them in the shell under the **hex edit** option of **View**.

*Modifying the FC Effect*   As you've seen, if you just want to compare two specific files, you can use the basic format of the FC command along with the filespecs of the two files to be compared. DOS selects the appropriate form of comparison based on the extensions that it finds. The FC command format is shown below:

```
FC [switch(es)] filespec1 filespec2
```

You can modify the effect of the basic comparison by using various switches, as shown in Figure 10.3. You can specify the /L or /B switch to force the comparison to ASCII or binary if the extensions don't select it for you. For a binary comparison, whether by default or with /B, all other switches are invalid. All switches except /B are valid for an ASCII comparison.

*Determining Which Lines Are Different*   Several switches affect the selection of lines that are considered different. The /C switch tells FC to ignore the case of letters in comparing lines. Figure 10.4 shows the output of a command that uses this switch. If you compare it with Figure 10.1, you'll notice

| | |
|---|---|
| /A | abbreviate output of ASCII comparison |
| /B | force byte-by-byte binary comparison; can't be combined with any switches except *nnnn* |
| /C | ignore case in ASCII comparison |
| /L | force ASCII comparison; all other switches are valid |
| /LB *n* | set internal line buffer to *n* lines |
| /N | include line numbers in ASCII comparison |
| /T | don't expand tabs to spaces |
| /W | compress white space (tabs and spaces) during ASCII comparison |
| /*nnnn* | specifies number of lines that must match after FC finds a difference between files to avoid abort |

Figure 10.3. FC Command Switches

```
C:\DOS>FC DATA INVENT
***** DATA
H2345 Hammer, claw                        36        8.50 S-C
H4545 Hammer, sledge                24    14.90 Ben
H4687 Hammer, ball peen                   18        8.14 S-C
H9231 Screwdriver, 3 inch                 48        1.79 Gen
E1212 Sander, plane                       19       28.50 Mar
E1333 Sandpaper sheets             120         .56 Gen
E1423 Jigsaw, 4 inch blade                10       27.42 Mar
***** INVENT
H2345 Hammer, claw                        36        8.50 S-C
H4545 Hammer, sledge                      24       14.90 Ben
H4687 Hammer, ball peen                   18        8.14 S-C
H5897 Screwdriver, 1 inch                 28        5.78 Gen
H6980 Screwdriver, 2 inch                 38        4.98 Gen
H9231 Screwdriver, 3 inch                 48        1.79 Gen
H9987 Screwdriver, cordless               19       19.57 Ben
E1212 Sander, plane                       19       28.50 Mar
E1423 Jigsaw, 4 inch blade                10       27.42 Mar
*****

***** DATA
E4444 Router                               6       20.75 Mar
P1010 Grill, weber                       117       19.40 Web
***** INVENT
E4444 Router                               6       20.75 Mar
E4477 Router blades                       19        2.60 Gen
P1010 Grill, Weber                       117       19.40 Web
*****

***** DATA
P2226 Cooler, large                       86       26.00 Coo
Q1111 Picnic Basket                       29       14.30 Gen
***** INVENT
P2226 Cooler, large                       86       26.00 Coo
P2345 Campstove, alcohol                  10       29.40 Pil
P1366 Campstove, heet                      9       19.35 Pil
Q1111 Picnic Basket                       29       14.30 Gen
*****

C:\DOS>_
```

Figure 10.4. Ignoring Case—FC

that the line beginning P1010 was evaluated as not matching there. In Figure 10.4, those two lines match even though "Weber" appears in one file and "weber" in the other; they both appear as the first line that matches at the end of the second group of unmatched lines.

The /W switch tells FC to compress white space (tabs and spaces) in determining whether lines are the same. FC then considers any string of spaces or tabs as a single white space. FC doesn't ignore the spaces, but it compresses them for the purpose of the comparison. Figure 10.5 shows the effect of FC when /W is used. If you compare this to the listing in Figure 10.1, you'll see that the line beginning H4545 in that figure is no longer considered different in the two files, since the only difference is one of spacing. Notice that the lines containing "Weber" and "weber" are not the same this time, since only one switch was used.

By default, FC expands tabs to eight-column positions for the purpose of ASCII comparison, so a line with spaces is the same as one with tabs if the data appears in the same columns. You can suppress this effect if you wish with the /T switch. Then lines containing tabs won't match lines with spaces.

*Affecting the Output Appearance*   Additional switches let you abbreviate or line-number the output. If you use /A, the output includes only lines that begin and end each set of differences; these are actually the first or last of a set of two consecutive matching lines. The resulting output is greatly abbreviated, including only the lines just before and after each set of differences. Where only one intervening line doesn't match, it is listed. Where more than one line is involved, you'll see three dots in your listing.

If you use /N, the output includes line numbers for each line listed. This can help you identify those lines in your ASCII files. Figure 10.6 shows the output from a comparison of the same two files that used four of the switches. Notice that the line numbers indicate how many nonmatching lines do not appear.

*Affecting FC Operation*   The FC command uses an internal line buffer that holds consecutive nonmatching lines during an ASCII file comparison. By default, the line buffer holds 100 lines. If the files have more than 100 consecutive differing lines, the comparison is aborted with this message:

```
resynch failed. Files are too different.
```

Since a binary comparison isn't resynchronized, it doesn't abort; the line buffer is simply reloaded and the listing continues. You can specify a larger line buffer with the /LB *n* switch. The command FC /LB 300 DATAFILE

```
C:\DOS>FC DATA INVENT
***** DATA
H4687 Hammer, ball peen                  18      8.14 S-C
H9231 Screwdriver, 3 inch                48      1.79 Gen
E1212 Sander, plane                      19     28.50 Mar
E1333 Sandpaper sheets              120         .56 Gen
E1423 Jigsaw, 4 inch blade               10     27.42 Mar
***** INVENT
H4687 Hammer, ball peen                  18      8.14 S-C
H5897 Screwdriver, 1 inch                28      5.78 Gen
H6980 Screwdriver, 2 inch                38      4.98 Gen
H9231 Screwdriver, 3 inch                48      1.79 Gen
H9987 Screwdriver, cordless              19     19.57 Ben
E1212 Sander, plane                      19     28.50 Mar
E1423 Jigsaw, 4 inch blade               10     27.42 Mar
*****

***** DATA
E4444 Router                              6     20.75 Mar
P1010 Grill, weber                      117     19.40 Web
P2222 Cooler, small                     280      8.40 Coo
***** INVENT
E4444 Router                              6     20.75 Mar
E4477 Router blades                      19      2.60 Gen
P1010 Grill, Weber                      117     19.40 Web
P2222 Cooler, small                     280      8.40 Coo
*****

***** DATA
P2226 Cooler, large                      86     26.00 Coo
Q1111 Picnic Basket                      29     14.30 Gen
***** INVENT
P2226 Cooler, large                      86     26.00 Coo
P2345 Campstove, alcohol                 10     29.40 Pil
P1366 Campstove, heet                     9     19.35 Pil
Q1111 Picnic Basket                      29     14.30 Gen
*****

C:\DOS>_
```

Figure 10.5. Ignoring Spacing—FC

```
C:\DOS>FC /A /C /N /W DATA INVENT
***** DATA
      3:   H4687 Hammer, ball peen            18      8.14 S-C
 ...
      7:   E1423 Jigsaw, 4 inch blade         10     27.42 Mar
***** INVENT
      3:   H4687 Hammer, ball peen            18      8.14 S-C
 ...
      9:   E1423 Jigsaw, 4 inch blade         10     27.42 Mar
*****

***** DATA
     10:   E4444 Router                        6     20.75 Mar
     11:   P1010 Grill, weber                117     19.40 Web
***** INVENT
     12:   E4444 Router                        6     20.75 Mar
     13:   E4477 Router blades                19      2.60 Gen
     14:   P1010 Grill, Weber                117     19.40 Web
*****

***** DATA
     14:   P2226 Cooler, large                86     26.00 Coo
     15:   Q1111 Picnic Basket                29     14.30 Gen
***** INVENT
     17:   P2226 Cooler, large                86     26.00 Coo
 ...
     20:   Q1111 Picnic Basket                29     14.30 Gen
*****

C:\DOS>_
```

Figure 10.6. Abbreviated Numbered Listing

INVENTOR.Y allows for a buffer holding up to 300 consecutive differing lines. Each time the command is resynchronized on a matching line, the line buffer is erased; it is refilled again, starting with the next nonmatching line.

FC expects to find at least two matching lines following any set of nonmatching lines. You can modify this with the /*nnnn* switch to specify the number of lines that must match after FC finds a difference between files. If the number of matching lines is less than this number, FC displays the matching lines as differences, as you saw in Figure 10.1. The line beginning "H4687 Hammer" is the same in both groups of unmatched lines. If the last line of an ASCII comparison doesn't contain the ***** indicator, there probably weren't two matching lines at the end of both files.

Start at the command prompt, with \PRACTICE as the current directory.

1. You'll need longer files to compare in this exercise. Using COPY CON or any ASCII editor, create two files called GROCERY and ITEMS containing the lines shown below. Don't worry if you make typos, but try to be consistent in the two files. Notice that some lines are the same, some have spacing differences, and some have capitalization differences.

| GROCERY | ITEMS |
|---|---|
| apples | apples |
| watermelon | watermelon |
| candy bars | candy bars |
| sugar | whole wheat flour |
| whole wheat flour | cantaloupe |
| cantaloupe | casaba melon |
| casaba melon | honey dew melon |
| honeydew melon | strawberries |
| strawberries | raspberries |
| raspberries | peanut butter |
| peanut butter | chicken |
| chicken | lasagna noodles |
| Lasagna noodles | tuna fish |
| tuna fish | sirloin steak |
| eggs | eggs |
| soft drinks | soft drinks |
| pepper | pepper |
| salt | salt |

2. Use FC to compare the two files on screen.

3. Repeat Item 2, except this time use redirection to print a copy so you can compare it with later comparisons.

4. Repeat Item 2, this time ignoring case and compressing white space. Compare the result on the screen with the printed result from Item 3.

5. Repeat Item 2, but specify abbreviated output and line numbers. Compare the result on the screen with the printed result from Item 3.

6. Repeat Item 2, but this time specify that only a single matching line is required for resynchronization. Compare the result on the screen with the printed result from Item 3.

7. Now use FC to do a binary comparison on the two files. Notice the difference in the format of the output.

2. *Enter the command:*

```
FC GROCERY ITEMS
```

3. *Enter the command:*

```
FC GROCERY ITEMS > PRN
```

4. *Enter the command:*

```
FC GROCERY ITEMS /C /W
```

*The new output is shorter than the printed one because fewer lines are considered to be mismatched.*

5. *Enter the command:*

```
FC GROCERY ITEMS /A /N
```

6. *Enter the command:*

```
FC GROCERY ITEMS /1
```

*Fewer mismatched lines are listed because fewer lines are required for resynchronization.*

7. *Enter the command:*

```
FC GROCERY ITEMS /B
```

## *The COMP Command*

Another command you can use to compare files is COMP. You might want to use COMP if you have neglected to verify copies or if you just want to see whether two files are identical. COMP differs from FC in several ways. It provides a message ("Files are different sizes") but no comparison if the two files have different lengths; you'll be offered a chance to enter different file-specs. COMP always does a byte-by-byte binary comparison, but, unlike FC, it aborts after ten mismatched bytes are found in the two files. COMP prompts you for the filespecs if you omit them, and lets you specify a set of files for comparison.

The COMP command output provides the same information as the binary comparison mode of FC, but in a somewhat different format. Figure 10.7 shows typical COMP output when two files are specified. Notice that the offset location is provided on a separate line. At the end of each file comparison with COMP, you'll be offered a chance to enter new filespecs for comparison.

```
C:\DOS>COMP DATA LISTING

C:DATA and C:LISTING

Compare error at OFFSET E
File 1 = 63
File 2 = 6E
Compare error at OFFSET F
File 1 = 6C
File 2 = 65
Compare error at OFFSET 10
File 1 = 61
File 2 = 77
Compare error at OFFSET 11
File 1 = 77
File 2 = 20
Compare more files (Y/N)?N

C:\DOS>_
```

Figure 10.7. COMP Output

To compare two files, just use the filespecs. To compare sets of files, you can use * and ? as needed in the first filespec and use only a drivename in the second. If you omit both filespecs, DOS will prompt you for them. You'll see "Enter primary filename" on the screen. When you have entered the first filespec, you'll see "Enter 2nd filename or drive id". If you're dealing with diskettes, you can insert a new one before responding to the prompt and typing a path. Here's the command format:

```
COMP [drive:][filespec1] [drive:][filespec2]
```

If you omit the second filespec completely, DOS will prompt you for it; you must use at least a drive for the second filespec. If you use just a drive or a path with no filename for either filespec, DOS assumes *.* and compares all files with matching names in the specified location.

If COMP is dealing with a set of files, it displays the name and path of each file, from path1, as it starts. You'll see a message if no matching file in path2 is found or if either path is invalid. If COMP can't identify a match for any file in path1, you are prompted again for both paths.

You'll get a separate message in the output for any location with mismatching information, displaying the offset location and byte contents in hexadecimal code. If the file sizes are different, you'll see an initial message telling you about the size problem and asking if you want to compare more files. If you want to compare two files that aren't the same length, you'll have to use FC.

If the first two files compare OK, COMP then proceeds to the next two files. If you enter a single set of two files, and they match perfectly, you'll see information like this on the screen:

```
C:\DOS>COMP FILE.1 FILE.2
C:\DOS\FILE.1 and C:\DOS\FILE.2
 Files compare OK
 Compare more files (Y/N)?_
```

The COMP command always asks if you want to compare another set before returning to the command prompt. If you respond Y, it prompts you to enter another set of filespecs for the next comparison. If you respond N, you'll see the command prompt next. If fewer than ten mismatches are found, you'll see the same message and have the same options for continuing.

If either file is missing the EOF (end-of-file) mark, you'll see a message to that effect at the end of the comparison. This is not necessarily a problem. If the comparison is fine except for this message, just ignore it.

Start at the command prompt with \PRACTICE current.
1. Use COMP to compare ITEMS and GROCERY.
2. Try COMP again, but don't enter the filespecs until prompted.

*1. Enter the command:*

```
COMP ITEMS GROCERY
```

*2. Enter the command:*

```
COMP
```

*Enter the filespecs in response to the prompts that appear.*

# Checking Memory and Disks

DOS 4 has several commands you can use to check various aspects of memory and disks. As you've seen, the DIR command lets you know how much space remains on a disk. The MEM command lets you check the status of memory in your system and tells you how much, and exactly what, memory is in use. The CHKDSK command gives you information about memory too, but it also provides detailed information about your disk usage. You'll see how to use both commands in this section.

## The MEM Command

The MEM command displays the amount of memory currently in use and the amount of free memory. You can also have it list which areas are allocated and free for programs and other items that use memory. The format of the MEM command is shown below:

```
MEM [switch]
```

You can use either of two switches: /PROGRAM or /DEBUG. If you don't include a switch, you get basic information on the current status of memory. If you include the /PROGRAM switch, you get information on loaded programs as well. If you use the /DEBUG switch instead, you get the most complete information. The listing in Figure 10.8 shows the output from the command MEM /PROGRAM. The memory usage information in the lower third is displayed if no switch is used. The columnar information that makes up the upper two-thirds of the report is added if the /PROGRAM switch is used; it shows where various programs are located in memory and how much space they occupy. You can see that the MEM program is listed here. If you use /DEBUG, more detailed information is added, including information about device drivers.

Since the listing often takes more than one screen, you'll want to use MEM >*filespec* or MEM | MORE when you check your memory with a switch. For basic memory checking, the information fits on the screen just fine.

You'll use MEM when you get a message such as "Not enough memory" or when a program won't run for some reason. The "largest executable program size" value in the lower part of the screen is the crucial value here. This is the largest program you can run.

Special rules govern how extended and expanded memory are displayed. If your memory display doesn't match what you know about your system, you may want to check your documentation for further details on the MEM command.

---

1. Check the basic memory usage with the MEM command.
2. Check the memory to see how it is allocated to manage programs. Page the output.
3. Try the /DEBUG switch if you like.

---

```
Address         Name           Size           Type
DDDDDD          DDDDDDD        DDDDDD         DDDDDD
000000                         000400         Interrupt Vector
000400                         000100         ROM Communication Area
000500                         000200         DOS Communication Area

000700          IO             002510         System Program

002C10          MSDOS          008E20         System Program

00BA30          IO             006A10         System Data
                QEMM           0005A0          DEVICE=
                ANSI           001180          DEVICE=
                               000430          FILES=
                               000100          FCBS=
                               003E70          BUFFERS=
                               000210          LASTDRIVE=
                               000CD0          STACKS=
012450          COMMAND        001A20         Program
013E80          MSDOS          000030         -- Free --
013EC0          COMMAND        000100         Environment
013FD0          MOUSE          000060         Environment
014040          MOUSE          0010C0         Program
015110          GRAB           000060         Environment
015180          GRAB           005990         Program
01AB20          WS             000060         Environment
01AB90          MODE           0001E0         Program
01AD80          WS             03A100         Program
054E90          WS             000010         Data
054EB0          COMMAND        000060         Data
054F20          COMMAND        001640         Program
056570          COMMAND        0000A0         Environment
056620          MEM            000060         Environment
056690          MEM            012F00         Program
0695A0          MSDOS          036A50         -- Free --

  655360 bytes total memory
  655360 bytes available
  301408 largest executable program size

  753664 bytes total EMS memory
  147456 bytes free EMS memory

  393216 bytes total extended memory
       0 bytes available extended memory
```

Figure 10.8. MEM Output

*1. Enter the command:*

```
MEM
```

*2. Enter the command:*

```
MEM /PROGRAM | MORE
```

*3. Enter the command:*

```
MEM /DEBUG | MORE
```

## The CHKDSK Command

The CHKDSK command scans the disk in the specified drive and checks it for errors. It also displays information about memory in your system. When you format a disk, any bad sectors are marked and identified so they won't be used for data. But disks can develop errors after they are formatted and even after they contain data. Whenever you have trouble reading a disk, you should try CHKDSK first to see if there is a problem. Many experts recommend running CHKDSK every week or so on all your active disks to identify errors before they cause problems with your data.

***CHKDSK Output*** Figure 10.9 shows the output from a typical CHKDSK command. Notice that the display gives you detailed information about the disk. At the top, CHKDSK gives you the volume label and creation date, along with the volume serial number. The next and largest group of lines gives information about the disk itself and the directory structure currently in place. The next group of lines gives information about how the disk was formatted. The lower section gives information about RAM, without considering any extended or expanded memory.

The example in the figure gives information about a 1.2MB diskette. You can see exactly how many bytes will fit, as well as how many bytes are taken up by hidden files (IBMDOS.SYS, IBMBIO.SYS, and the volume label), the directory structure, and the user files. If any bad sectors have already been identified, they'll be shown in this section on a separate line. If a file has become unreadable, the disk may have developed a new bad sector or two. In that case, the best thing to do is to copy all files (with COPY or XCOPY, rather than with DISKCOPY) to another disk, then reformat or RECOVER the disk. The last line in the top section provides the amount of space remaining. The number of bytes specified in the first line in this section is equal to the sum of all remaining lines in this group.

The next group of lines refers to allocation units; these are also referred

```
    Volume DOS 4 BOOT   created 08-12-1989 11:02a
    Volume Serial Number is 3725-12C5

     1213952 bytes total disk space
       71168 bytes in 3 hidden files
        1536 bytes in 3 directories
     1061376 bytes in 68 user files
       79872 bytes available on disk

         512 bytes in each allocation unit
        2371 total allocation units on disk
         156 available allocation units on disk

      655360 total bytes memory
      541584 bytes free

C:\DOS>_
```

Figure 10.9. CHKDSK Output

to as clusters. The terms *allocation unit* and *cluster* mean the smallest amount of space that can be allocated for a file. In this example, an allocation unit or cluster is 512 bytes, so every file has a multiple of 512 bytes reserved for it. A hard disk may have allocation units of 2048 bytes (2K), which means a file always has a multiple of 2K bytes reserved for it. As soon as a file requires even one byte over the allocation unit, another allocation unit is reserved for it to hold more of the file.

The final group of lines gives you less memory information than the MEM command, but it is often enough information to solve problems. If a program won't run, you can try CHKDSK to see if there is enough memory. Some programs stay in memory and take up space even when they aren't running, as you saw in the MEM discussion earlier. In general, MEM takes up less space and is quicker than CHKDSK, but gives you much more limited information.

*CHKDSK Options*   With the CHKDSK command, you can check the memory usage and sector status of any disk and get additional information as well. The command format is shown below:

```
CHKDSK [drive:] [filespec] [switch(es)]
```

Each element in the CHKDSK format has a specific effect. If you use only the command name, CHKDSK provides information as you saw in Figure 10.9. It will also report certain types of problems related to lost or shared clusters.

You'll see how to deal with these problems shortly. You can specify a drive to get usage information for the disk in a different drive.

*Contiguity Information*   If you include a filespec or path, you'll get contiguity information on all files in that specification. That means DOS tells you whether the allocation units reserved for each file are in sequence or not. Figure 10.10 shows a CHKDSK report in which several files are not contiguous. If it seems to take longer than before to access files, or if many or most of the files are noncontiguous, you may want to rearrange a file's allocation units to put them in sequence. Just copy all files to another disk using COPY, XCOPY, or BACKUP (not DISKCOPY), then erase them all from the fragmented disk; finally, copy them all back on. If you use DISKCOPY, each disk is copied "as is" and the fragmentation isn't corrected. You can't just copy over the fragmented files because isolated allocation units will be filled in sequence.

*Lost Cluster Errors*   The CHKDSK command can identify errors resulting from lost clusters, which may be single or chained. Lost clusters are allocation units that may at one time have been reserved for files, but now DOS doesn't know if they have been released or not. A power failure or rebooting

```
C:\PRACTICE>CHKDSK A:*.*

   322560 bytes total disk space
     9216 bytes in 2 hidden files
   274432 bytes in 34 user files
    38912 bytes available on disk

     1024 bytes in each allocation unit
      315 total allocation units on disk
       38 available allocation units on disk

   655360 total bytes memory
   545392 bytes free

A:\PURSUIT Contains 3 non-contiguous blocks
A:\RESUME.BAK Contains 3 non-contiguous blocks
A:\SNEAKY.RPG Contains 2 non-contiguous blocks
A:\MAGSYS.GTH Contains 4 non-contiguous blocks
A:\MUSICZ.MNT Contains 2 non-contiguous blocks
A:\BRTHTKNG.BLU Contains 2 non-contiguous blocks

C:\PRACTICE>_
```

Figure 10.10. Noncontiguous File Report

to escape from a program hangup can create these lost clusters, as can various internal disk problems. If you use the /F switch, CHKDSK is prepared to fix any such errors it finds, either by capturing the data in those clusters or by eliminating them so the space can be reused.

If lost clusters are identified, you'll see a message asking if you want CHKDSK to fix them. If you haven't used /F, they won't be fixed no matter what you respond, but CHKDSK lets you know how much space could be freed up if you were to actually fix the problem. If you have used /F and you respond Y, the lost clusters are fixed. If you respond N after using /F, the lost clusters are freed up and any data within them is lost.

When CHKDSK fixes lost clusters, it creates a new file for each chain with a name FILE*nnnn*.CHK, with FILE0001.CHK referring to the first chain, FILE0002.CHK referring to the second chain, and so on. Once the lost clusters are assigned to a file name, DOS no longer considers them lost. You can then examine the contents of new files (use TYPE at the command prompt or **View** with **hex edit** under the shell) and delete them if they don't contain any information you want.

*Listing Filespecs*   If you want a list of the complete filespecs of files stored on the disk being checked, include the /V switch. The result is a listing of all filespecs on that disk. Figure 10.11 shows a partial listing. Notice that the complete filespec is provided.

You might want to generate a listing of files with CHKDSK to have the complete filespecs documented. If you use a filespec to identify noncontiguous blocks along with the /V switch, the /V switch takes precedence. The filespec is ignored and no files are checked for contiguity.

*Redirecting CHKDSK Output*   If you redirect CHKDSK output, you can save it for later reference. If you redirect output with file listing (/V), you can edit the result to remove the space usage information and keep a clean, complete filespec listing. You must be careful not to redirect CHKDSK output to the disk being operated upon. If you do, DOS thinks it finds a lost cluster problem; this problem doesn't really exist. If you get a lost cluster message when you redirect CHKDSK output, try it again without redirection to see if there is a problem. You can redirect the output to another location, then copy the new output to that disk later if it must be there.

**N**ote   CHKDSK doesn't work correctly on disks that have been manipulated with certain commands, such as JOIN or SUBST (covered in Chapter 11). You probably won't use the commands, but if you are having problems with CHKDSK, examine your AUTOEXEC.BAT file to make sure these commands aren't used.

```
     Volume DOS 4 BOOT  created 08-12-1989 11:02a
     Volume Serial Number is 3725-12C5
Directory A:\
        A:\IO.SYS
        A:\MSDOS.SYS

        ...
        A:\PRACTICE.BAT
Directory A:\PRACTICE
        A:\PRACTICE\MYADDR.LST

        ...
        A:\PRACTICE\NEW3
Directory A:\PRACTICE\PRACA
        A:\PRACTICE\PRACA\4201.CPI

        ...
        A:\PRACTICE\PRACA\LCD.CPI
Directory A:\PRACTICE\PRACA\PRACY
        A:\PRACTICE\PRACA\PRACY\ASSIGN.COM

        ...
        A:\PRACTICE\PRACA\PRACY\MYADDR

  1213952 bytes total disk space
    71168 bytes in 3 hidden files
     1536 bytes in 3 directories
  1061376 bytes in 68 user files
    79872 bytes available on disk

      512 bytes in each allocation unit
     2371 total allocation units on disk
      156 available allocation units on disk

   655360 total bytes memory
   541584 bytes free

C:\DOS>_
```

Figure 10.11. CHKDSK with File Listing

Start at the command prompt with \PRACTICE current.

1. Check the space usage on your fixed disk. If CHKDSK reports any problems, don't try to fix them at this time.
2. Check the space usage on an older, often used, diskette.
3. Repeat the above command, but list all files on the diskette as well. Page the output.

4. On the same diskette, check to see if any files have noncontiguous blocks.
5. How can you consolidate files with noncontiguous blocks?

---

1. *Enter the command:*

```
CHKDSK
```

2. *Place the diskette in drive A: and enter:*

```
CHKDSK A:
```

3. *Enter the command:*

```
CHKDSK A: /V | MORE
```

4. *Enter the command:*

```
CHKDSK A:*.*
```

5. *Copy all the files to another disk, reformat the original disk, then copy the files back to it.*

---

# Recovering Disks

You may have a disk that has been having input or output errors. DOS may not let you read data that is on the disk. DOS also may not let you write to the disk. If all data on the disk is backed up, you can reformat the disk with FORMAT, then restore the data from the backup copies. If you don't have a backup, you can rescue what files you can (with XCOPY or COPY), then reformat the disk and hope to be able to recreate the missing files.

DOS provides the RECOVER command to recover parts of a file when some of its sectors are bad. In this section you'll see how to use RECOVER to save most of a file. You won't be able to do much with program files, but you at least should still have the originals or good backups stored on a shelf somewhere.

## The RECOVER Command

RECOVER is the only DOS command that will copy from a file with bad sectors. Ideally, you'll never have to use this command. It's sort of a last resort that attempts to recover the readable part of a file that has developed bad sectors. At best, it will recover most of a file. At worst, it won't recover any. You can use RECOVER in two ways. The easiest way is to recover a single file that has developed one or more bad sectors; you have the best chance of success with this situation. If a directory has gone bad, you'll have to recover all the allocation units on the disk because there is no other way to identify the locations of files. The RECOVER command format is shown below:

```
one file:       RECOVER [drive:]filespec
all files:      RECOVER drive:
```

*Recovering Specific Files*   If you get a "bad sector" or another message indicating that a file can't be read, you can try to recover it. For example, suppose you can't read your \PRACTICE\DATA.2 file and you don't have a current backup of it. Use the command RECOVER \PRACTICE\DATA.2. DOS reads the file, sector by sector, and transfers it to a new file in the same directory; DOS skips over any bad or unreadable sectors. Every bad sector RECOVER encounters is marked, just like the ones identified during FORMAT. No other file will be assigned to the allocation unit containing the bad sector.

You can see that RECOVER is very useful if a sector goes bad on your hard disk, because you don't have to reformat the disk to make it usable. The recovered file, however, will not be complete. After the recovery, you'll see a message telling you how many bytes are missing. You'll be missing at least 512K (or whatever size allocation unit is involved) where the bad sector was located. You'll have to edit the file by figuring out what is missing, then retyping the missing data into the file. But that's better than recreating the entire file from scratch. You won't be able to recover program files at all, since they won't work with a piece missing. You'll have to depend on your backups for these.

If many files on the disk contain bad sectors, recover each file individually. If you can, copy all good files, as well as all recovered ones, to another disk (not with DISKCOPY); then erase the files that have been copied or recovered. If you know the disk contains more files that you can't identify, you'll have to consider recovering the rest of the disk.

*Recovering an Entire Disk*   If you can't read the directories on a disk, this means DOS no longer knows what the files are named. If you don't have a reasonable backup, you have a real problem. You may be able to find a friendly expert or a commercial utility program to help you. Failing that, you can use the RECOVER command, specifying the drivename only. The DOS manuals are very vague about this procedure; be sure to get help from your dealer or a consultant if you try recovering an entire disk.

When used this way, RECOVER ignores directories, which are probably bad anyway, searches the FAT, and creates a file in the root directory for each chain of allocation units. They are given a name in the form FILE*nnnn*.REC, with *nnnn* being 0001 for the first chain, 0002 for the second, and so on.

You'll have to examine each recovered file individually to try to determine what it contains, then rename it. If you determine that it's a program or other unreadable garbage, delete it immediately. Program or binary files are not viewable as such. You may be able to make sense out of some of them by examining them under the **hex edit** option of **View** under the shell. The entire procedure can take hours or even days. If you try this procedure even once, you'll probably never neglect regular backups again!

**N**ote | The RECOVER command won't work on drives manipulated with SUBST or JOIN (see Chapter 11). And it won't work with a network. If you have trouble with RECOVER, make sure none of these are in effect. It may be easier to boot from your A: drive using a diskette with the system but no special configuration files to make sure no strange effects occur. If you want to recover data from a diskette, you can switch to drive C: after booting.

## *Summary*

This chapter has covered several commands you can use to check the status of memory, disks, and files. You've also seen how to solve, or at least approach, problems. The most useful commands in this chapter are CHKDSK and FC. If you use CHKDSK regularly, you might be able to avert major disk problems before they reach a crisis mode. And FC is very useful if you use similar files and want to identify differences between them.

## *Exercises*

These exercises let you practice identifying and correcting disk and memory problems.

| What You Should Do | How the Computer Responds |
|---|---|
| 1. Check how much memory your system has available. | 1. In response to MEM with no operands, displays basic memory statistics. |

2. Check how your system's memory is being used by various programs right now. Page the output to the screen.

3. Compare C:\PRACTICE\GROCERY and C:\PRACTICE\ITEMS as ASCII files.

4. Compare C:\PRACTICE\GROCERY and C:\PRACTICE\ITEMS again. This time, ignore case, compress white space, and require only one line for resync.

5. Compare C:\PRACTICE\GROCERY and C:\PRACTICE\ITEMS as binary files.

6. Compare C:\PRACTICE\GROCERY and C:\PRACTICE\ITEMS using COMP instead of FC.

7. Make a disk copy of any diskette. Put the original diskette away and use the copy as the "exercise diskette" in the following steps.

8. Check the basic space usage on the exercise diskette.

9. If directory and FAT problems were reported in the preceding step, fix them. (Delete lost clusters.)

10. Check the diskette for fragmented files.

11. If any files have noncontiguous blocks, copy all files to a blank, formatted diskette. Check the new diskette for fragmented files.

12. Examine the directory of the exercise diskette. Select a file and recover it.

---

2. In response to MEM /PROGRAM, displays detailed memory layout.

3. In response to the FC command, displays groups of mismatched lines.

4. In response to the /C, /W, and /1 switches, finds fewer mismatched lines.

5. In response to /B switch, compares bytes instead of lines.

6. Produces the same result as in Step 5, but the format is different.

7. Makes the copy as directed.

8. In response to CHKDSK A:, reports basic statistics for the target diskette and memory. Might also report directory and FAT problems, such as lost clusters.

9. In response to CHKDSK A: /F and your answer to the prompt, fixes problems on diskette.

10. In response to CHKDSK *.*, reports any files in the current directory that have noncontiguous blocks.

11. Rejoins fragmented files as it copies them. The new copy should show no noncontiguous blocks.

12. In response to RECOVER *filespec*, shows how much of the file was recovered. Probably recovers all of the file, since no problems should have been experienced.

13. Recover the entire diskette, including the root directory and FAT. Examine its directory again.
14. Switch to the shell and view some of the recovered files. (Try **Hex/ASCII** under **View**.) Can you identify what the files were before you recovered them?

13. In response to RECOVER A: with no filespec, recovers each file and re-names it FILE*nnnn*.REC.
14. Displays files as requested. You will probably be able to recognize ASCII files but not program files.

## What If It Doesn't Work?

1. If CHKDSK doesn't identify any disk problems, skip that portion of the exercises.

2. If CHKDSK doesn't find any fragmented files, skip that portion of the exercises.

3. If CHKDSK still finds noncontiguous blocks after you copied the files to another diskette, the target diskette probably already had files on it. Try again with a blank, formatted diskette.

4. If RECOVER was unable to recover all of a file, the file contained bad sectors. Since this is just an exercise, you can delete the result. In an actual situation, you would have to cope with the problem somehow.

5. There will probably be many files on the recovered diskette that you are unable to identify. In an actual situation, you would have to cope with this problem (and develop a better backup system).

# Controlling the Environment and Search Paths

**11**

This chapter includes a variety of commands that affect the DOS environment and that set up search paths so that DOS can find program and data files.

In this chapter, you will learn to:

- Expand options to terminate a program
- Change the DOS prompt
- Store variables in the DOS environment
- Establish search paths
- Identify commands to reroute directories

## What Is the DOS Environment?

In its general sense, the term *environment* refers to all the background factors that affect the operation of DOS commands and applications. Thus, the system date and time, the country settings, the current directory, and many other factors comprise the environment.

But you can also use the phrase *DOS environment* in a narrower sense. The DOS environment is an area in memory that has been set aside to store certain variables. The current search path, the current prompt, and the file-spec of the command processor are stored there. You can also store other variables there for use by your applications and batch files. The SET command, which you will learn later in this chapter, lets you view the current

241

contents of the DOS environment and lets you store, change, and delete variables there.

When you boot DOS, a default environment is established for you. You can change it any way you like. When you start up the shell, it uses the same environment, including any changes you've made. When you exit the shell and return to the command prompt, the same environment is still in effect.

However, if you select the command prompt from within the shell, something different happens. This command prompt is a child of the original command prompt, and receives a new environment, which is a child of the previous environment. The values of the original environment are taken from the parent environment's current values, so it looks just like the parent. But changes to this environment do not affect the parent. When you type EXIT to return to the shell, the child environment is eliminated and the parent environment is reinstated. The changes you made to the child environment disappear.

For example, suppose you boot DOS, set up a search path of C:\DOS, then start up the shell. The search path will still be C:\DOS. Next you select the command prompt option by pressing Shift+F9. A child environment is spawned, which inherits the parent's search path. Now you change the search path to C:\PRACTICE. After working with that search path for a while, you enter the command EXIT. This takes you back to the parent environment, where the search path is still C:\DOS.

If you return to the shell by using the command DOSSHELL instead of EXIT, you have actually created a new instance of the shell in the child environment. The child environment's variables will continue to be in effect. The only way back to the parent environment at this point is to exit the shell, then enter the EXIT command. You won't exit to the shell, but you will exit back to the parent environment at the command prompt.

For the most part, you need not worry about levels of environments. But if you ever set up an environmental variable that disappears later, you probably set it up at a child level, then exited back to a parent level.

## *Increasing Break Points*

Earlier you learned to terminate a program by using Ctrl+Break (or the equivalent Ctrl+C). However, Ctrl+Break terminates a program only when the program reads information from the keyboard or writes information to the screen or to some external device, such as the printer. Some programs work for long periods of time without reading from the keyboard or writing to the screen or printer. For example, COPYing a file from disk to disk involves only disk I/O and so cannot be interrupted.

If you wish to have DOS check for Ctrl+Break more often, you can use the BREAK command. This slows your programs down slightly because checking for Ctrl+Break takes time. But you probably won't notice the difference. The BREAK command is similar to VERIFY in format:

```
BREAK [ON or OFF]
```

Like VERIFY, you can use BREAK three ways: BREAK with no parameter results in a message that tells you whether BREAK is on or off; BREAK ON turns it on; and BREAK OFF turns it off.

After you boot, BREAK is off, and DOS checks for Ctrl+Break only when doing external I/O. If you turn break on, DOS checks for Ctrl+Break whenever it does any kind of I/O, including disk I/O. Some programs are designed to ignore the BREAK status; these cannot be broken into at all, whether BREAK is on or off.

Start at the command prompt. Make C:\DOS the current directory.
1. Check whether BREAK is on or off.
2. If BREAK is on, turn it off.
3. Find the largest file in the current directory. Copy it to C:\PRACTICE and try to interrupt the copy with Ctrl+Break.
4. Turn BREAK on.
5. Redo the copy and try to interrupt it again.
6. Redo the copy twice more, once with BREAK on and once with it off. Can you notice any time difference? Leave BREAK on or off, as you wish.

1. *Enter the command:*

```
BREAK
```

*DOS will respond with a "BREAK is on" or "BREAK is off" message.*
2. *Enter the command:*

```
BREAK OFF
```

3. *If the largest file is SHELLC.EXE, enter this command:*

```
COPY SHELLC.EXE \PRACTICE
```

*You should not be able to interrupt the copy until the "1 File(s) copied" message is displayed on the monitor.*
4. *Enter the command:*

```
BREAK ON
```

5. *Enter the same COPY command as in Item 3. This time, Ctrl+Break should work immediately. (The interrupted copy is removed from the directory.)*

# Changing the DOS Prompt

You might want to show a different system prompt on your screen. For example, you can display the current time in the system prompt. Or you can include a standard message, such as "Enter command here." The PROMPT command lets you change the prompt. Its format is shown below:

```
PROMPT [prompt text]
```

Your prompt can include any letters or numbers as well as special characters. To use regular letters or numbers, just type them in the prompt text. The following command sets up a prompt of "Enter data here":

```
C:\DOS>PROMPT Enter data here
Enter data here_
```

On the second line, you can see the new command prompt, which reflects the change made by the PROMPT command. The new prompt remains in effect until you change it again or reboot. The following command changes the prompt to "GOOD MORNING!":

```
Enter data herePROMPT GOOD MORNING!
GOOD MORNING!_
```

You can reset the default prompt by entering PROMPT with no operands, but if you have a hard disk, the result might surprise you:

```
GOOD MORNING!PROMPT
C>_
```

The default prompt is the default drivename followed by an angle bracket; the current directory is not included. You are used to the prompt set up by a PROMPT command entered in your AUTOEXEC.BAT file by SELECT when you installed DOS. If you want to get back to that prompt, you have to use some of the special prompt codes, shown in Figure 11.1. Suppose you want to include the time in your prompt. You could enter the following command:

```
C>PROMPT $T$G
12:14:23.06>_     (or whatever the current time is)
```

| | |
|---|---|
| $B | Vertical bar (\|) |
| $D | The current date |
| $E | Escape character |
| $G | Greater than character (>) |
| $H | Backspace (erases previous character; could be used with time, for example, to erase hundredths) |
| $L | Less than character (<) |
| $N | Current disk drive |
| $P | Current drive and directory |
| $Q | Equal sign (=) |
| $T | The current time |
| $V | The current DOS version |
| $$ | Dollar sign ($) |
| $_ | New line (carriage return and line feed) |

Figure 11.1. Prompt Codes

Suppose you want DOS to show the default current directory name, including drive, then start a new line for your entry. You could enter the following command:

```
PROMPT $P$_
```

You can use the special characters and standard characters, including spaces, in any combination. Figure 11.2 shows an example that creates a prompt containing the time and date on the first line, and the phrase "Enter command here" on the second line.

```
C>PROMPT $T  $D$_Enter command here

19:13:58.91  Sun  6-04-1989
Enter command here_
```

Figure 11.2. Sample PROMPT Interaction

Perhaps the most useful prompt is the one containing the current directory followed by >, as set up for you by SELECT. The command to set up that prompt is shown below:

```
PROMPT $P$G
```

Whichever prompt you work with, you'll probably want to put the necessary PROMPT command in your AUTOEXEC.BAT file so the prompt you like comes up every time you start DOS.

1. Change the command prompt to read "Your wish is my command..."
2. Reestablish the default command prompt.
3. Set up the command prompt you're used to—the current directory followed by an angle bracket.

*1. Enter the command:*

```
PROMPT Your wish is my command...
```

*2. Enter the command:*

```
PROMPT
```

*3. Enter the command:*

```
PROMPT $P$G
```

# *Other Environmental Variables*

The PROMPT command adds a parameter to the environment. So does the SET command, which adds any parameter you specify, even if DOS doesn't recognize the parameter or know how it will be used. You've already seen how to use SET to create a value for a dummy parameter used in a batch file. You can also use SET to establish values for parameters used by applications. Any application program can look in the DOS environment for values for PROMPT or any other parameter. For example, WordPerfect looks for a variable called WP containing any of its startup options. Suppose you always want to use these WordPerfect startup options: /R/NC/M-SETDIR. You would include this command in your AUTOEXEC.BAT file:

```
SET WP=/R/NC/M-SETDIR
```

DOS has no earthly idea what this parameter does, but dutifully stores the parameter in the environment. When you start up WordPerfect, it will find the parameter there.

Do not put spaces around the equal sign in a SET command or DOS will treat the spaces as part of the text. DOS sees these commands as setting up two different parameters:

```
SET WP=/R/NC/M-SETDIR
SET WP = /R/NC/M-SETDIR
```

WordPerfect would find the first parameter, but not the second one, since the program doesn't look for a parameter called WP followed by a space. To change a parameter, simply enter another value for the same name. For example, to change the WP parameter, you could enter:

```
SET WP=/NC/X
```

To remove a parameter from the environment, enter it with a null value. All you have to do is press Enter immediately after typing the equal sign. For example, to remove the WP parameter you would enter this command:

```
SET WP=
```

Figure 11.3 shows the output when you use SET with no operands. A list of the environment variables is shown, including the standard environment variables, such as PATH and PROMPT, as well as any you may have set yourself.

COMSPEC is a standard DOS variable that tells DOS where to find the command processor. The SET command example in Figure 11.3 shows that COMMAND.COM is in C:\DOS. COMSPEC is a required variable; DOS cannot survive long without it. You can change the standard value with the SET command if you want DOS to use another command processor or a different directory.

```
C:\DOSBOOK> SET
COMSPEC=c:\dos\command.com
PROMPT=$p$g
PATH=C:\;C:\DOS;D:\HSG;D:\WS5;D:\WINDOWS

C:\DOSBOOK>_
```

Figure 11.3. Sample SET Display

1. View the current parameters in the DOS environment.
2. Store a parameter called MYPARM in the environment. Give it your name as a value. Check to make sure the parameter has been recorded in the environment.
3. Change the stored value of MYPARM to George Washington. Check it.
4. Remove MYPARM from the environment. Check to make sure it's gone.

1. *Enter the command:*

```
SET
```

*DOS should list at least COMSPEC, PROMPT, and PATH parameters. It might list other values as well.*
2. *Enter the command:*

```
SET MYPARM=yourname
```

*followed by*

```
SET
```

*You should see MYPARM in the listing.*
3. *Enter the command:*

```
SET MYPARM=George Washington
```

*followed by*

```
SET
```

*You should see the changed parameter in the listing.*
4. *Enter the command:*

```
SET MYPARM=
```

*followed by*

```
SET
```

*MYPARM should no longer appear in the listing.*

# Setting Up Search Paths

When you enter an external command—such as FORMAT, LABEL, or DISKCOPY—DOS looks for an executable file (extension COM, BAT, or EXE) in the current directory only. You can reach the desired program file by using the CHDIR command to switch to the directory it's in. Alternatively, you can prefix the command name with a path, as in this example:

```
C:\DOS\FORMAT A:
```

In response to the pathname, DOS will look for the FORMAT.COM file in the C:\DOS directory.

## Program Search Paths

It's time consuming and error prone to constantly change directories and/or prefix command names with directory paths. You can set up a standard search path in the DOS environment with the PATH command, which has this format:

```
PATH [;] or [path[;path...]]
```

The path you specify is automatically searched for any external commands (that is, programs or batch files) that are not in the current directory. This path is not used for locating operands, which are set up in the APPEND command (covered next). Suppose you have FIXIT.BAT and PARTS.EXE in different directories, and you've specified a path that includes both directories. The command shown below causes the path to be searched for FIXIT, but only the current directory is searched for PARTS.EXE:

```
FIXIT PARTS.EXE
```

If PARTS.EXE is in another directory, you'll have to include the path in the filespec, set up an APPEND path, or change to that directory before entering the command.

The PATH command sets up a chain of directories to be searched for all future command references. DOS searches for a program file starting with the current directory, then proceeds from directory to directory in the order specified in the search path, until the file is found. For example, the following command tells DOS to search first the current directory, then directory C:\GEORGE\CHECKS, then C:\GEORGE\CREDIT, and finally B:\ (the root directory on drive B:):

```
PATH C:\GEORGE\CHECKS;C:\GEORGE\CREDIT;B:\
```

Semicolons separate pathnames in the list. Don't include spaces in the operand, or DOS will tell you that it has too many operands. You need to use absolute pathnames for each directory, including the drivename. Otherwise, when DOS tries to use the path from drive A: or drive B:, it won't work properly. DOS does not check pathnames for validity; as long as the format is correct, DOS accepts the path and stores it in the environment. When using the path, DOS ignores invalid directories (except there must be diskettes in drive A: and B: if these drives are included in the path).

When entering your path, put the most likely directory first, the least likely last. DOS searches the directories in the order you list them in the PATH command, so the search will be briefer if the program is found in the first or second directory.

To change the search path, simply enter another one. To search only the current directory, use the command name followed by a semicolon, as in this command:

```
PATH;
```

To see the current path, enter PATH with no operands, like this:

```
C:\>PATH
PATH=C:\GEORGE\CHECKS;C:\GEORGE\CREDIT;B:\

C:>_
```

The reason you've been able to access all your DOS external programs from any directory is that SELECT automatically included a PATH command in your AUTOEXEC.BAT file, like this:

```
PATH C:\DOS
```

Every time you boot, this command is executed, giving you access to all the DOS external command files, which are all stored in C:\DOS. Whatever path you eventually decide to use should always include C:\DOS as one component so that your DOS programs are always available to you. (Your internal commands are available because the COMSPEC variable is provided in the environment.)

## Data Search Paths

To set up a path for nonprogram files, use APPEND in the same way you use PATH. Its format is shown below:

```
APPEND [;] or [path[;path...]
```

The following command sets up a search path comprising three directories:

```
APPEND C:\GEORGE;C:\GEORGE\CHECKS;C:\GEORGE\CREDIT
```

Suppose FIXIT.BAT is in C:\DOS and PARTS.EXE is in C:\GEORGE. If the above append path is in effect, and the program search path includes C:\DOS, then the following command will work from any directory in the system:

```
FIXIT PARTS.EXE
```

DOS will find FIXIT.BAT by using the program search path and PARTS.EXE by using the append search path.

The following command deletes the nonprogram search path:

```
APPEND;
```

The APPEND search path affects reading operations but not writing operations. That is, DOS looks in the APPEND search path to find an input file if it isn't in the current directory. But output operations, such as COPY, always place the output in the current directory unless another directory is specified in the command. Be cautious about using APPEND when you work with applications that update files, such as word processors. The application might read the file from somewhere else in the search path, but when it goes to save the updated version, it will save the file in the current directory. Thus, the original version of the file is unchanged in its original directory, and the updated version is in the current directory. If this happens to you, you'll probably spend a lot of time wondering what went wrong. If you don't use APPEND, you'll have to specify the exact path for a file, but the software then knows exactly where to put updated files.

APPEND is a TSR program. The first time you use it after booting, the program is read into memory like any other external program. Then it stays in memory and acts like an internal program until you boot again.

1. Check the program search path.
2. Check the data search path.
3. Delete the program search path.
4. Make C:\ the current directory. Then try using some of the DOS external commands, such as XCOPY and ATTRIB. You should get "Bad command or file name" messages since DOS can no longer find the program files.
5. Reset the search path to C:\DOS. Try the same external commands again. They should work now.
6. Try typing the file named BIGFILE without supplying a path. You should get a "File not found" message since BIGFILE is in C:\PRACTICE.
7. Set the data search path to C:\PRACTICE. Then try typing BIGFILE again. This time, DOS should be able to find the file even though C:\ is the current directory.
8. Eliminate the data search path.
9. Reboot to reestablish your default paths.

1. *Enter the command:*

```
PATH
```

   *DOS should display the current PATH.*
2. *Enter the command:*

```
APPEND
```

   *DOS should display the current APPEND path, if one has been established.*
3. *Enter the command:*

```
PATH;
```

4. *Enter:*

```
CD \
```

   *Then try commands such as:*

```
ATTRIB *.*
```

   *and*

```
XCOPY COMMAND.COM \PRACTICE
```

5. *Enter the command:*

```
PATH C:\DOS
```

   *Then enter the same commands you entered in Item 4.*
7. *Enter the command:*

```
APPEND C:\PRACTICE
```

   *followed by*

```
TYPE BIGFILE
```

8. *Enter the command*

```
APPEND;
```

# *Manipulating Directories*

Several commands let you manipulate the layout of directories. Ordinarily, PATH and APPEND should serve all your needs. But some applications have special needs. For the most part, these are programs that were released many years ago—before fixed disks, tree-structured directories, and paths were in widespread use. DOS has created several commands that let you use drivenames and paths with these programs. You probably won't have to use any of these commands, but we'll overview them just in case. If you use one or more of these commands, some of your other DOS commands won't work properly, as explained below.

The SUBST command substitutes an imaginary drivename for a path. This facility helps with programs that can handle drivenames, but not paths. Here is its format:

```
SUBST [d:path] [d: /D]
```

To establish a substitution, specify an imaginary drivename and pathname, as in:

```
C:\>SUBST E: C:\GEORGE\CHECKS
```

Now you can use E: in filespecs and DOS will substitute C:\GEORGE\CHECKS. To display all the substitutions currently in effect, enter SUBST with no operands. To delete a substitution, enter the imaginary drivename with the /D switch, as in:

```
C:\>SUBST E: /D
```

The highest drivename you can use in DOS is E: unless you enter a LAST-DRIVE statement in your CONFIG.SYS file to specify a higher last drive name. LASTDRIVE is discussed in Chapter 13.

The JOIN command adds one drive's directory tree to another. This command accommodates applications that recognize paths but not drivenames. The format of JOIN is shown below:

```
JOIN [d: d:subdirectory] [d: /D]
```

To join the entire tree structure on drive C: to the root directory on drive A:, you would enter:

```
C:\>JOIN C: A:\TEMP
```

Now you can reference any directory on C: from the A:\TEMP path. To list all the joined directories currently in effect, enter JOIN with no operands. To cancel a particular join operation, enter the original drivename with the /D switch, as in:

```
A:>JOIN C: /D
```

The ASSIGN command substitutes one drivename for another. It is meant for very old applications that assume the only available drives are A: and B:. The format of ASSIGN is shown below:

```
ASSIGN [d=d...]
```

To rename drive C as drive B, you would enter:

```
A:\>ASSIGN C=B
```

To break an assignment, enter ASSIGN with no operands. This clears all the current assignments.

When directories have been manipulated, you might be confused about the real path for a file. The TRUENAME command causes the full, real filespec for a file to be displayed. For example, if you want to find out the real name of X:CAUTION, you might enter this:

```
C:\>TRUENAME X:CAUTION
C:\PRACTICE\PRACA\CAUTION

C:\>_
```

The SUBST, JOIN, and ASSIGN commands are powerful and dangerous. They can cause major problems if used together or in conjunction with APPEND. If you try to use such DOS programs as FORMAT, DISKCOPY, and DISKCOMP on manipulated directories, you could do actual harm to your directories and suffer severe data loss. Programs that search directories for files to handle—such as BACKUP, XCOPY, REPLACE, RECOVER, and CHKDSK—could access files you didn't mean to include. Some of these commands will identify and refuse to work with manipulated directories, but others won't. In general, don't use SUBST, JOIN, or ASSIGN unless you have to.

If you suspect you must use one of these programs to make an application work, read your DOS documentation thoroughly beforehand to learn all the techniques and pitfalls. We haven't spelled them out here. Then enter the command immediately before starting the application and cancel the command or reboot immediately after terminating the application so it doesn't affect any other operations.

# Summary

In this chapter, you have seen how to manipulate the DOS environment and search paths. The PATH, PROMPT, and SET commands all add variables to the DOS environment. The PATH command sets up a program search path, while the APPEND command sets up a data search path. The JOIN, SUBST, and ASSIGN commands manipulate directories in various (somewhat dangerous) ways to accommodate applications that don't work with the full directory structure of DOS.

# *Exercises*

These exercises let you practice and reinforce the various environmental commands you have learned in this chapter.

| **What You Should Do** | **How the Computer Responds** |
|---|---|
| 1. Turn the BREAK feature on. | 1. In response to BREAK ON, turns BREAK on as directed. You will not see any confirmation, but Ctrl+Break will work better with many programs. |
| 2. Set the prompt to "Summary Exercise Prompt>". | 2. In response to PROMPT Summary Exercise Prompt$G, displays the new prompt. |
| 3. Store the following variables in the DOS environment:<br><br>*Variable*    *Value*<br>CHAPTER    11<br>EXERCISE    FINAL<br><br>Check the environmental variables to make sure the new ones are set correctly. | 3. In response to SET CHAPTER=11 and SET EXERCISE=FINAL, stores the variables in the DOS environment. In response to SET with no operands, displays all the environmental variables. |
| 4. Set the program search path to include C:\DOS, the root directory on C:, and any other directory on C: that contains programs you use. | 4. In response to PATH C:\DOS;C:\, stores the new search path in the environment. You won't see any confirmation, but the path will affect other commands you enter. |
| 5. Set the data search path to C:\PRACTICE, C:\PRACTICE\PRACA, and C:\PRACTICE\PRACA\PRACY, in that order. | 5. In response to the command<br><br>`APPEND C:\PRACTICE;C:\PRACTICE\`<br>`   PRACA;C:\PRACTICE\PRACA\PRACY`<br><br>stores the new search path in the environment. You won't see any confirmation, but the path will affect other commands you enter. |
| 6. Restore the prompt you want to use. | 6. In response to PROMPT $P$G, displays the current directory and an angle bracket as a prompt. |

7. Remove the two variables you stored in the DOS environment (CHAPTER and EXERCISE).

7. In response to SET CHAPTER= and SET EXERCISE=, removes the two variables from the environment. You won't see any confirmation unless you enter SET with no operands to display all the environmental variables.

8. Remove the data search path from the environment.

8. In response to APPEND;, removes the data search path from the environment. You won't see any confirmation unless you enter SET with no operands to display all the environmental variables.

## What If It Doesn't Work?

You shouldn't encounter any problems in this exercise.

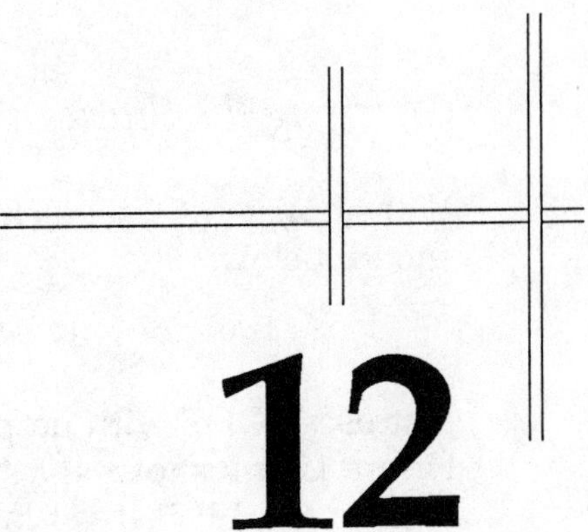

# Controlling Hardware

**D**OS 4 provides several commands you can use to control various hardware facilities. For example, the MODE command lets you control aspects of the display, the keyboard, parallel printers, and communications devices. Other commands let you control how DOS uses memory, disks, and such internal features as graphics.

In this chapter, you'll learn to:

- Check the status of attached hardware devices
- Control the console display and keyboard action
- Control the density of print on parallel printers
- Control the signal sent to a communications port
- Redirect data from a parallel to a serial port
- Print graphics screens with the Shift+PrtSc key combination
- Speed up directory access

## Controlling Hardware Devices

One of the most useful commands DOS provides for controlling hardware devices is MODE. With MODE, you can control the display, the keyboard, your printer through the parallel ports, and your serial or communication ports. The command has different options for each device, so we'll discuss it in several sections.

## Checking the Status

You can use MODE to check the status of any or all devices. The format is shown below:

```
MODE [device] [/STA or /STATUS]
```

Just use MODE with no parameters to get a display like the one shown in Figure 12.1. It shows the status of up to three parallel ports and the console. In this case, LPT1 (the first parallel port) has been rerouted, LPT2 and LPT3 have not been rerouted, and CON (the console) is set for a display of 80 columns and 25 lines. As you continue, you'll see how to change the values that appear here.

You can check the status of any device (refer back to the list in Figure 4.2) by specifying it in the MODE command. If you check the status of a redirected parallel printer individually, you must include the /STATUS switch as well; otherwise the redirection is undone. You'll see how to set up printer redirection later in this chapter. The status report may not give you enough information, but it's a start.

```
Status for device LPT1:
-------------------------
LPT1: rerouted to COM1:
RETRY=NONE
Code page operation not supported on this device

Status for device LPT2:
-------------------------
LPT2: not rerouted

Status for device LPT3:
-------------------------
LPT3: not rerouted

Status for device CON:
-------------------------
COLUMNS=80
LINES=25
Code page operation not supported on this device
```

Figure 12.1. MODE Status Display

## Controlling the Console

You can use MODE to control several aspects of the monitor. You can control the color and number of characters per line by specifying the appropriate value following the command. Figure 12.2 shows the values you can use to tell DOS how to set the display. If your system has only a monochrome board, only MODE MONO is valid. If you have any color/graphics board, you can use any value except MONO; your system may freeze up if you try MODE MONO when it isn't valid. If your system has both types of monitor, you can use all the values and switch between monitors with MODE MONO and MODE CO80, or whatever is appropriate.

The DOS command prompt screen is always in monochrome, so you won't see any effect there no matter what option you choose. The shell screen has its own control built in; if you've changed the display mode and then you enter the shell, the shell appears as it always does. And when you return to command mode, the default console mode is reestablished. However, you may see the effect of a modified console display in software applications entered from command mode.

If you want large character display on a color monitor, use one of the values containing 40. Since this results in fewer characters per line, it may not be appropriate for all applications. You'll have to experiment a bit. You can switch back to an 80-character line display with any of the options that contain 80.

You can add a parameter to set the number of lines on EGA or VGA screens to 25, 43, or 50. If you want to use a display option, such as BW80, as well as set the number of lines per screen to 43, use MODE BW80,43.

Another form of the MODE command lets you control the number of

| | |
|---|---|
| 40 | Use 40 characters per line (large text) |
| 80 | Use 80 characters per line (normal text) |
| BW40 | Use 40 characters per line and disable color |
| BW80 | Use 80 characters per line and disable color |
| CO40 | Use 40 characters per line and enable color |
| CO80 | Use 80 characters per line and enable color |
| MONO | Use the monochrome monitor as the console monitor |

Figure 12.2. Valid Console Values for MODE

lines and columns on EGA or VGA monitors with specific parameters; in this case, you must use the following format:

```
MODE CON [LINES=l] [COLS=c]
```

In order for DOS to execute this command, a device driver named ANSI.SYS must be loaded. If ANSI.SYS isn't loaded automatically in your CONFIG.SYS file, you'll have to add it; you'll learn to load ANSI.SYS in the next chapter. You can use MODE CON LINES=25 to set the number of lines to 25 (the default); other valid values are 43 and 50. MODE CON COLS=80 is the default, but you could use MODE CON COLS=40 to use a shorter line. If your console seems off and you want to restore it to normal appearance, try MODE CON LINES=25 COLS=80 and review the effect. The nondefault line counts and character counts don't have an effect on all consoles, but you might want to experiment.

You can also use MODE to adjust the display on a color/graphics screen if it isn't centered the way you like it. Use MODE ,R to shift the display to the right; use MODE ,L to shift it to the left. Add ,T to the end of the command if you want to see a test line to help you adjust the display. The command MODE ,L,T results in a screen like the one shown in Figure 12.3. If you respond N, the screen is shifted one position to the left. This repeats until you press Y, at which point DOS assumes you are satisfied with the display and terminates the MODE command.

You can add shifting options to the end of a MODE command, as in MODE CO80,L; you would do this if you know that the screen must be shifted one position to the left. Some screens can't be shifted. Others can be shifted only within limits. The message "Unable to shift screen left/right" means the screen can't be shifted in that direction.

```
0123456789012345678901234567890123456789012345678901234567890123456789012345678901234567890123456789

Do you see the rightmost 9? (y/n)
```

Figure 12.3. Shifting the Display with MODE

## Controlling the Keyboard

You can use MODE in some systems to adjust the speed at which keys repeat on your keyboard by changing the typematic rate. You might want to speed up key repetition if you frequently repeat many keys and want to save some time. You might want to slow it down if you frequently get repeated keys when you didn't expect them. Here's the format:

```
MODE CON RATE=r DELAY=d
```

You must specify both the rate and the delay. The $r$ value, which specifies the interval, must be between 1 and 32; the default is about 20. The higher the number, the faster the repeat. At RATE=20, a key repeats about 10 times per second. The $d$ value specifies how long the keyboard waits until the repeat starts; this value must be 1, 2, 3, or 4. Each represents approximately 1/4 second, so DELAY=3 means the typematic effect won't start for about .75 seconds.

Start at the command prompt with your DOS directory current. The features you will use in this checkpoint are somewhat dependent on your system and what it supports. If a particular command hangs up, just reboot and modify that command to use an option your system supports.
1. Check the status of all your devices.
2. Check the status of your console.
3. Your console probably displays 25 lines and 80 columns. Change the display to 40 columns, then get a directory listing.
4. Change the console so that it displays 43 lines and 80 characters. Then get another directory listing.
5. Try shifting the display on your console. If shifting left doesn't work, try shifting right.
6. Try adjusting the speed of your typematic keys. First hold down a key to gauge its delay and rate. Then change it to a very high speed and short delay time. Then hold the same key and compare the result.
7. Reboot to reset the environment and the features you have changed.

*1. Enter the command:*

```
MODE
```

*2. Enter the command:*

```
MODE CON
```

3. *Enter the command:*

```
MODE 40
```

*followed by:*

```
DIR
```

4. *Enter the command:*

```
MODE CON LINES=43 COLS=80
```

*or*

```
MODE CON 80,43
```

*followed by:*

```
DIR
```

5. *Enter the command:*

```
MODE ,L,T
```

*or*

```
MODE ,R,T
```

*You should see a test screen or a message that you can't shift in that direction. (You might not be able to shift in either direction.)*

6. *Enter the command:*

```
MODE CON RATE=30 DELAY=1
```

## Controlling the Printer (Parallel Ports)

You can use MODE to control the output of a parallel printer by changing the number of characters per line or the number of lines per inch. You can also tell DOS to continually try to send data to the port if it is busy. You can use named parameters or place the values in the correct sequence. The two formats are shown below:

```
MODE LPTn [c][,l][,x]

MODE LPTn COLUMNS=c LINES=l RETRY=x
```

If you use the first format, the values must be entered in the sequence shown. If you use the second format, you can put the parameters following LPTn, in any sequence.

The value *c* indicates the number of columns; it can be 80 or 132. Most printers default to 80 characters per inch. If you set the number of columns to 132, most dot matrix printers will compress the type so that 132 characters fit in the space allowed for 80.

The value *l* indicates the number of lines per inch; it can be 6 or 8. Most printers default to six lines per inch. If you set the number of lines per inch to 8, the lines will be compressed. Figure 12-4 shows a partial page of standard print (LINES=6 COLUMNS=80) and compressed print (LINES=8 COLUMNS=132) so you can see the difference. To see the effect on your printer, you'll have to experiment.

The value *x* gives a RETRY parameter. Earlier versions of DOS used the value P here to request a retry if the port is busy. DOS 4 provides several values. The most common is B, which is equivalent to the former value P and causes continuous retry. If you use B and the printer is busy, your entire system may just wait until it is free. Use N to request no retry or to restore the default. In this case, you'll have to reenter the command if the printer is busy the first time. Check your DOS reference manual if you need some other effect here.

Suppose you want to set your printer for eight lines per inch and continuous retry. You could use either of these commands:

```
MODE LPT1 LINES=8 RETRY=B

MODE LPT1 ,8,B
```

**Default print format**
**(6 lines per inch, 80 characters per line)**

```
Volume in drive B is BACKUP    002
Directory of B:\

PROCESS           5376   11-30-88      9:53a
PROCESS5          6912   12-01-88     10:53a
NEWLIST             82   2-26-89      11:05a
PRESBACK           180   5-25-89      12:38p
PRESIDEN           180   5-26-89      12:38p
PRESSORT            65   2-26-89      11:34a
PRESCOPY           180   5-25-89      12:38p
        7 Files(s)   327680 bytes free
```

**Condensed print format**
**(8 lines per inch, 132 characters per line)**

```
Volume in drive B is BACKUP    002
Directory of B:\

PROCESS       5376   11-30-88    9:53a
PROCESS5      6912   12-01-88   10:53a
NEWLIST         82   2-26-89    11:05a
PRESBACK       180   5-25-89    12:38p
PRESIDEN       180   5-26-89    12:38p
PRESSORT        65   2-26-89    11:34a
PRESCOPY       180   5-25-89    12:38p
    7 Files(s)   327680 bytes free
```

Figure 12-4. Standard and Compressed Print

## Controlling Communications (Serial) Ports

One major use of MODE is to configure communications or serial ports; your system may have up to four of these. You can check them individually with MODE to see how many you have. When you try MODE COM1, you might see RETRY=NONE; even if you don't know what this means, the message tells you that COM1 exists. When you try MODE COM2, you might see "Illegal device name", which tells you that your system doesn't have a COM2 port.

Communications ports can be used for a variety of devices. You might use COM1 for a serial printer, COM2 for a mouse, and COM3 for a modem. Each one probably needs different configuration information. You can use either named parameters or the shorter, sequenced list of values in the command. Here's the format:

```
MODE COMn[:]b[,p[,d[,s[,r]]]]

MODE COMn BAUD=b [PARITY=p]  [DATA=d]  [STOP=s]  [RETRY=r]
```

You'll find it easier to use the named parameters in MODE commands to control communications ports. If you use the sequenced parameters, they must be in the sequence shown here. If you omit any sequenced parameters before the last one you use, you need commas to mark the position. Notice that the colon is optional if you don't use named parameters; you can't use it with the named parameters.

You'll need a separate MODE command for each serial port; always specify COMn in the command so DOS knows which one you are defining.

You must specify the baud rate for each communications port; this is the transmission rate for data passing through the port. The MODE command tells DOS at what speed to send data; this must match the speed the device is actually capable of handling. Valid values are 110, 150, 300, 600, 1200, 2400, 4800, 9600, and 19200. DOS can deal with just the first two characters of the value, but you might as well use the entire value, so you will remember it later. A modem may need 300, 1200, or 2400. A serial printer may need 9600. You can find the value to specify in the documentation for the device you will connect to that port.

Parity is an error-checking technique the device or software uses to help ensure that only valid data is sent through the port. Valid values here are N (none), E (even), O (odd), M (mark), and S (space). Even parity is the default. Like the baud rate, you'll find the appropriate value to include in the MODE command in the device documentation. The MODE command for a modem to use COM2 might read MODE COM2 BAUD=2400 PARITY=N or MODE COM2 24,N.

DATA refers to the number of bits that make up one character, or *byte*, of data; this value can be 5, 6, 7, or 8. Most devices use 7 or 8; the default is 7. If you use any parity (except N), you can't use 8 data bits. If you use 8 data bits, you must specify no parity. You might use this command:

```
MODE COM1 BAUD=9600 PARITY=N DATA=8
```

or

```
MODE COM1:9600,N,8
```

The STOP parameter refers to stop bits, which are extra bits sent to mark the end of a data character or block. You can specify 1, 1.5, or 2 stop bits. If the baud rate is 110, the default number of stop bits is 2; for all other baud rates, the default is 1.

The TRY parameter specifies what type of action you want DOS to take if the port is busy. Use B for continuous retry (this is equivalent to the value P in earlier versions), E if the device is a shared printer, or N for no retry.

Suppose you use COM1 for a serial printer that requires 9600 baud input, no parity, eight data bits, and one stop bit. You want continuous retry so that you won't have to enter a command twice. Here are several ways you could code the command:

```
MODE COM1 BAUD=9600 PARITY=N DATA=8 STOP=1 RETRY=B
MODE COM1 BAUD=9600 PARITY=N DATA=8 RETRY=B
MODE COM1:9600,N,8,1,B
MODE COM196,N,8,,B
```

In the first and third examples, we've included every parameter, even if we used the default. In the second and fourth examples, default values are omitted.

## Redirecting Printing

DOS uses LPT1 (also called PRN) as its default printer for screen prints and echo printing. Other applications may also send their print output to LPT1. If you want to use a serial printer instead, you'll have to tell DOS to redirect LPT1 output to a serial port You can use MODE to redirect printing from any parallel port to any serial port. Here's the format:

```
MODE LPTn[=COMn]
```

If you omit the second part of the command, redirection is canceled. To reestablish it, just specify the appropriate parallel and serial ports; they must both be available on your system. You have to use MODE to configure the serial port first, then use this one to redirect the parallel printer output. If you have reconfigured the parallel port, redirecting to that port cancels the configuration. The only configuration that comes through is whatever you specified for the serial port.

Suppose you want to use your serial printer as your primary printer. You could use this set of commands:

```
MODE COM1 BAUD=9600 PARITY=N DATA=8 STOP=1 RETRY=B
MODE LPT1=COM1
```

All output directed to LPT1 will be sent to COM1, configured as above. If you want to send data to a parallel printer, you could use MODE LPT1 to cancel the redirection.

Do the part of the checkpoint that corresponds to the equipment and ports you have available.

**Parallel Printer:**
1. Print the file named BACK1. Keep the printout as a reference.
2. Change the printer characteristics to eight lines per inch and 132 characters per line. Print BACK1 again.

**Serial Printer:**
3. If you have a serial printer that has been working fine, you undoubtedly have a MODE command in the AUTOEXEC.BAT file that sets up the characteristics for the port. Display AUTOEXEC.BAT on your screen and examine the MODE command. Don't change it!
4. If you have been getting DOS print output from your serial printer, it is probably redirected in your AUTOEXEC.BAT file. Look for the MODE command that redirects LPT1 to a serial port.

2. *Enter these commands:*

```
MODE LPT1 COLUMNS=132 LINES=8
PRINT BACK1
```

3. *The command might look like this:*

```
MODE COM1 9600,N,8,1
```

*or*

```
MODE COM1 BAUD=9600 PARITY=N DATA=8 STOP=1
```

*4. The command might look like this:*

```
MODE LPT1=COM1
```

# Controlling Graphics Output

Normally, when you print screens from your console (by pressing Shift+PrtSc), DOS prints a text screen. It converts any graphics characters to the closest it can come to a text character. If you want the screen printed in graphics mode, you must first use a DOS command. Some printers provide their own software for handling graphics screens. Standard DOS command-mode screens are in text mode, while most shell screens are in graphics mode. If you want to print shell screens on your IBM compatible printer, you'll have to first use the GRAPHICS command. Printers that work well with this command are generally dot-matrix printers of some type.

The GRAPHICS command has no effect if your system has no graphics adapter; it supports CGA, EGA, VGA, and 8514/A display adapters. If your system has one of these features, and your printer is IBM compatible, type GRAPHICS at the command prompt to establish graphics print mode. Then whenever you request a screen print, DOS will use graphics mode if the screen demands it. The GRAPHICS program knows how to interpret screen displays and convert them so they print correctly on your printer. A text-mode screen prints in about 30 seconds or less. Graphics mode takes at least three minutes on most printers.

A graphics screen prints in up to four patterns or shades of gray. The orientation on the page depends on the graphics mode in effect. In 320 x 200 mode, the screen is printed across the top of the page. In 640 x 200 mode, the screen is printed sideways on the page; the upper-right corner of the screen appears on the upper-left corner of the page.

## GRAPHICS Command

The GRAPHICS command allows several options you can use to vary the default effect. The format is shown below:

```
GRAPHICS type [profile] [/R] [/B] [LCD] [/PRINTBOX:id]
```

The first value in the GRAPHICS command indicates the type of printer involved. As you can see in Figure 12.5, the GRAPHICS type includes the largest number of printers; this is the default and need not be specified. If you have another listed type of printer, you'll have to specify it in the command. If your printer wasn't manufactured by IBM, it may still be compatible with an IBM printer. Try the one that seems closest. If you don't get the effect you want, try another option.

A printer profile is a special file that contains formatted information about your printer and how DOS can use it for graphics printing. If your printer is compatible with any of the IBM printers listed in the figure, GRAPHICS uses a file named GRAPHICS.PRO, which is part of DOS. This file should be stored in the same directory as the GRAPHICS.COM program. If it is stored elsewhere, you'll have to include the path and name it in the program. For example, you might use GRAPHICS \UTILITY\GRAPHICS.PRO if GRAPHICS reports that it can't locate the profile. You won't have to name GRAPHICS.PRO if DOS doesn't report a problem in finding it. If you have a nonstandard printer, check its documentation for details on installing its graphics features. In most cases, you'll have to store its profile in your DOS files directory and name it in the GRAPHICS command.

## GRAPHICS Switches

The GRAPHICS command provides several switches you can use to control its output:

**/R** The /R switch tells GRAPHICS to reverse the normal printing of black and white. The screen normally displays white characters on a black background; graphics screens such as those in the shell may display dark characters on a light background. When you use GRAPHICS to print a shell screen, the background will be dark. If you use /R, the situation is reversed and

| | |
|---|---|
| COLOR1 | IBM Color printer with one-color ribbon |
| COLOR4 | IBM Color printer with RGB ribbon |
| COLOR8 | IBM Color printer with YMC ribbon |
| GRAPHICS | IBM Graphics, IBM PagePrinter, IBM Proprinter, or IBM Quietwriter, all with 8.5 inch wide paper |
| GRAPHICSWIDE | IBM Proprinter or IBM Quietwriter with 13.5 inch wide paper |
| THERMAL | IBM PC Convertible Thermal printer |

Figure 12.5. Valid Printer Types for the Graphics Command

DOS leaves the background white, using shades of gray for the design. Before trying /R, you'll want to use GRAPHICS without this switch, to see the effect. Then rerun GRAPHICS with /R to get the reverse if you need it.

**/B** The /B switch tells GRAPHICS to print the background colors on your color printer. Normally, the background is left white during printing.

**/LCD4** This is the same as /PB:LCD, described below; it was used like this in earlier versions and is still valid.

**/PB:** or **/PRINTBOX:** This value lets you tell GRAPHICS if the screen to be printed is from a CRT (cathode ray tube) or LCD (liquid crystal display) monitor. The default is /PB:CRT. If you are printing screens from a LCD monitor, try the default first. If you don't like the effect, try using /PB:LCD or /PRINTBOX:LCD. In most cases, you'll get a better print with the default (CRT).

## Printing Foreign Text Characters

Some earlier computers with CGA boards can't handle foreign text characters in text mode. If yours has trouble, try entering the GRAFTABL command, then print the file or screen again.

GRAFTABL makes the upper 128 ASCII characters available to the system. They will then appear on the display and be printed as usual.

If your monitor and printer don't both have graphics capability, skip this checkpoint.

1. At the command prompt, list any directory. Print the current screen as a reference.
2. Enter the **File System** and print the screen display.
3. Return to the command prompt. Determine which of the options in Figure 12.5 is closest to your printer. Enter the GRAPHICS command, specifying the printer type if you decided on one.
4. Enter the **File System** again and print the screen display. Does it print this time?
5. Return to the command prompt. If you printed the **File System** screen display in the preceding item, enter a command to reverse the colors. Then print the **File System** screen display again.

1. *Enter the command:*

```
DIR
```

   *Then press Shift+PrtSc.*
2. *The **File System** screen display will probably not print because it is a graphics screen.*
3. *Enter the command:*

```
GRAPHICS type
```

   *If GRAPHICS.PRO is not in C:\DOS, determine where it is and add the correct path to the command.*
4. *If the **File System** screen display still doesn't print, you probably need a different profile file. Check your printer documentation, or ask your dealer or your printer manufacturer for help.*
5. *Enter the command:*

```
GRAPHICS type [path] /R
```

   *All black and white images should be reversed in the resulting printout.*

# Speeding Up Directory Access

Accessing a disk is very slow compared to working in memory. Therefore, any time a program must access a file on disk, it is slowed down. The microprocessor sits idle until the disk access is done. If you run software applications that do a great amount of file access—such as accounting programs, online retrieval, or desktop publishing—a great deal of time is spent just waiting for file access.

You can speed up the process with a FASTOPEN command. FASTOPEN lets DOS save disk address information in memory as it looks up directories, files, and even data within files. Then, when DOS needs to access a file again, it checks first in the FASTOPEN area. If it locates the directory path, it can start there. If it locates the filename, it can go directly to the file. If it locates the appropriate part of the file, it can go directly to the cluster needed. This can save DOS from searching through several levels of directories, which may require six or seven separate disk accesses. Instead, DOS can find information in the FASTOPEN area and access the disk only once—to read or write the data. With applications that do a great deal of disk access, such as databases or desktop publishers, FASTOPEN can make a noticeable difference in speed.

## The FASTOPEN Command

FASTOPEN can be used only with fixed disks. If you try to use it on a diskette that was changed, the contents of the current diskette could be seriously damaged. Here is the FASTOPEN format:

```
FASTOPEN drive:[=(files,clusters)] ... [/X]
```

In its simplest form, you use FASTOPEN to set up a number of file entries for a fixed disk; the command FASTOPEN C: tells DOS to keep track of 34 files and 34 separate clusters that make up files. You can specify up to four fixed disks. The command FASTOPEN C: D: E: sets up the default number of files and clusters for three different fixed disks.

You can specify from a minimum of 10 files per drive to a maximum of 999 files for all specified drives. Similarly, you can specify from a minimum of 10 file clusters to a maximum of 999 clusters for all specified drives. A good ratio is about four or five times as many clusters as files; this will be plenty unless your files are highly fragmented. (You can use CHKDSK to determine if many files have noncontiguous blocks.) The command below requests 50 files and 200 file clusters to be remembered for each of two fixed disk drives and the default number on a third.

```
FASTOPEN C:=(50,200) D:=(50,200) E:
```

You don't have to specify both a number of files and a number of clusters for each drive. If you use just a file value, as in (50), the default number of clusters are saved as well. If you use the comma, as in (50,), no clusters are saved. If you want to save information on clusters only, without any filename information, you can omit the file value, as in (,200).

If your system has extended memory, you can use the /X switch to cause the FASTOPEN area to be placed in extended memory. If you use /X when you don't have extended memory, you'll see a message letting you know that the program isn't installed.

## Installing FASTOPEN

You can enter the FASTOPEN command at the command prompt or in your AUTOEXEC.BAT file, which is executed automatically when you boot or reboot your computer. You can only use it once, however. The first time you use FASTOPEN, you'll see a message that "FASTOPEN is installed." If you want to change any of its features, you'll have to reboot. If you enter the FASTOPEN command a second time, you'll see an error message.

FASTOPEN takes up a certain amount of space in memory, depending on how many files and clusters you ask DOS to keep track of. If you use one drive with the default number of files and clusters, FASTOPEN needs about 10K of space. If you want to track three drives with a total of 200 files and 950 clusters, FASTOPEN needs about 30K of space. You can use the MEM command with the /PROGRAM switch to see how much space (in hex) is set aside for FASTOPEN. You'll have to experiment with different settings to find a value that both saves time and doesn't impinge on the memory requirements of the software.

Start at the command prompt.
1. Enter the default FASTOPEN command.
2. Run the MEM command with the /PROGRAM switch and notice the FASTOPEN entry.
3. Try installing FASTOPEN again to change it to save 80 files and 400 clusters. You'll get a message that FASTOPEN is already installed; it won't be changed.
4. Reboot and try the preceding FASTOPEN command again. Check the amount of memory allocated in MEM.
5. If you have extended memory, reboot the system and install FASTOPEN as above, but in extended memory. Check memory allocation with MEM.

1. *Enter the command:*

```
FASTOPEN C:
```

*You'll see a message that FASTOPEN either is installed or is already installed.*
2. *Enter the command:*

```
MEM /PROGRAM | MORE
```

*You'll see that FASTOPEN occupies about $2880_{16}$ bytes ( about 10K in decimal).*
3. *Enter the command:*

```
FASTOPEN C:=(80,400)
```

4. *Now FASTOPEN takes about $4480_{16}$—nearly twice as much space.*
5. *Enter the command:*

```
FASTOPEN C:=(80,400) /X
```

*The FASTOPEN space is now removed from extended memory instead of regular memory.*

# Summary

In this chapter, you've learned several ways to control various hardware devices attached to your computer system. Of these, the MODE command is the most often used, since it has useful effects on several different devices. All the commands covered in this chapter are most often contained in AUTOEXEC.BAT files, which are executed automatically when you boot or reboot. You'll learn to create these files in Chapter 14.

# Exercises

These exercises let you practice some of the hardware management techniques you have learned in this chapter.

| **What You Should Do** | **How the Computer Responds** |
| --- | --- |
| 1. Display a status report for all the devices in your system. | 1. In response to the command MODE with no operands, displays a status report of all the hardware devices. |
| 2. If possible, set your monitor to display 43 lines. Display GROCERY. | 2. In response to the command MODE CON LINES=43, displays 43 lines per screen. |
| 3. If possible, shift the display on your monitor left or right four columns. | 3. In response to MODE CON ,L,T or MODE CON ,R,T, displays a test screen and shifts the screen left or right one column each time you enter N. Returns to the command prompt when you enter Y. |
| 4. Adjust the speed of your typematic keys to be very slow. | 4. In response to MODE CON RATE=5 DELAY=4, slows the typematic rate. |
| 5. Reboot to reset your monitor and keyboard. | 5. Restores all the default values for your console. |
| 6. If you have a parallel printer, set it to print 132 characters per line, eight lines per inch. Print GROCERY. | 6. In response to the command MODE LPT1 LINES=8 COLUMNS=132, prints the file in a condensed mode. |
| 7. If you can use the GRAPHICS program to print graphic screens, print the **DOS Utilities** screen. | 7. In response to the GRAPHICS command, which must be tailored to your system, starts up the GRAPHICS program in memory. Prints the graphics screen as requested. |

8. Reboot to reset your system.
9. If your system doesn't automatically set up FASTOPEN when you boot, enter a command to allocate FASTOPEN buffers for 20 files and 100 clusters.

8. Restores all values to their defaults.
9. In response to FASTOPEN C:=(20,100), sets up the appropriate number of FASTOPEN buffers in memory. Uses those buffers as you access other files.

## What If It Doesn't Work?

1. If any of these commands result in a "Bad command or file name" message, you probably need to check your PATH variable. It should include C:\DOS in the search path.

2. If your monitor won't display 43 lines per screen, make sure you entered the correct command. If the command is correct, your screen is probably not capable of displaying this number of lines.

3. If MODE won't shift your screen to the left, try shifting it to the right. If MODE won't shift the screen in either direction, your screen is probably not capable of being shifted.

4. If you can't adjust the typematic rate, your keyboard is probably not capable of being controlled by this particular MODE command.

5. Your printer might not be capable of printing 132 columns per line or eight lines per inch. If not, skip that part of the exercise.

6. If your printer is not capable of printing a graphics screen, or if the DOS GRAPHICS program will not drive your printer, skip that part of the exercise.

7. If the FASTOPEN command responds with a message that FOSTOPEN is already installed, it has already been installed in your system. It is probably installed by the AUTOEXEC.BAT file. Skip that part of the exercise.

# 13

# CONFIG.SYS

During booting, DOS always looks for a file named CONFIG.SYS, which contains statements that tailor the hardware configuration. You can put statements in this file to control the amount of memory to be set aside as buffers, to select a set of country codes different than the ones built into your hardware, to create a RAM drive, and so on.

In this chapter, you will learn to:

- Create a CONFIG.SYS file
- Initialize the break feature
- Install device drivers
- Create and use RAM drives
- Set aside various types of buffers
- Increase the number of available drivenames
- Identify commands to establish a non-U.S. environment for your system
- Install DOS commands during CONFIG.SYS processing
- Document your CONFIG.SYS file with comments

## Creating CONFIG.SYS

You create a CONFIG.SYS file just like you create any ASCII text file. You can use any editor or word processor capable of producing an ASCII file, or you can use COPY CON:. The file must be located in the root directory of the boot drive.

If you installed DOS on your hard disk using SELECT, then a CONFIG.SYS file was probably generated for you. Be sure to add to that file instead of overwriting it. If you must use COPY CON:, put your new statements in another file and concatenate it into CONFIG.SYS. For example, if you put the new statements in a file called CONFIG.ADD, you would then enter this command:

```
COPY CONFIG.SYS+CONFIG.ADD
```

The DOS programs don't need a CONFIG.SYS file to operate correctly. Many applications, however, require nondefault settings for configuration values. The information you need in order to set up the configuration correctly should be included in the application's documentation. Also, many of the configuration options make your entire system run faster.

## Initializing the Break Feature

One value you can set in CONFIG.SYS is BREAK, which controls how often DOS checks for the Ctrl+Break (or Ctrl+C) key combination. The default BREAK status is off. If you want it initialized to on instead, you can put a BREAK statement in your CONFIG.SYS file. The BREAK configuration statement has a different format from the BREAK command you've already learned. You must include an equal sign in the statement. The following interaction adds a line that initializes the break feature to the CONFIG.SYS file in the root directory.

```
C:\>COPY CON: CONFIG.ADD
BREAK=ON
^Z

C:\>COPY CONFIG.SYS+CONFIG.ADD
CONFIG.SYS
CONFIG.ADD
  1 File(s) copied

C:\>DEL CONFIG.ADD

C:\>_
```

The CONFIG.SYS file now includes a BREAK=ON statement. Whenever you boot from the fixed disk, the break feature is turned on. If you don't want it on, you can turn it off by entering BREAK OFF at the command prompt.

# *Device Drivers*

DOS needs device drivers to support any peripheral device, including the screen, the keyboard, the disk drives, and the printer. A device driver is a program that controls a peripheral device. All the standard device drivers are loaded automatically when you boot the system—you don't have to worry about them. You use the DEVICE statement in the CONFIG.SYS file to load other device drivers, as specified in your device manuals. DOS includes several device drivers you might need under certain circumstances. Specialized hardware, such as a mouse or a digitizer, might have its own device driver.

Most device drivers are designed to be loaded via CONFIG.SYS and cannot be installed any other way. If a driver's filespec ends with SYS or BIN, then you cannot install the driver from the command prompt. Instead, you must use a DEVICE statement in the CONFIG.SYS file. And you must reboot to make the statement take effect.

Suppose you want to install the driver that came with your mouse. The driver's on C:\MOUSE and is called PMOUSE.SYS. You would use this statement in CONFIG.SYS to install it:

```
DEVICE=C:\MOUSE\PMOUSE.SYS
```

The following sections explain some of the device drivers included in DOS.

## *ANSI.SYS*

The ANSI.SYS driver lets DOS use "Extended Screen and Keyboard Control." These are features that give an application better control over screen facilities—such as background and foreground color, flashing, highlighting, cursor location, and number of lines per screen—and over keyboard input. Some DOS features require ANSI.SYS. You might also have applications that require the ANSI.SYS driver to be installed; their documentation should tell you to install it. You can also use the ANSI.SYS features yourself in your PROMPT command. You could create a flashing red prompt, for example, or assign the DIR command to the F10 key. If you're interested in learning more about customizing your prompt and keyboard with the ANSI.SYS features, look up these capabilities in your DOS reference manual. To install the ANSI.SYS driver, include this statement in your CONFIG.SYS file:

```
DEVICE=ANSI.SYS
```

If the ANSI.SYS file is not located in the root directory of the boot drive, be sure to include the correct path in the filespec.

Start at the command prompt. Make C:\ the current directory.

1. Check the directory to see if you have a CONFIG.SYS file.
2. If you have a CONFIG.SYS file, copy it to a backup diskette. This will save your original configuration so that you can restore it after experimenting with the options in this chapter. As a safeguard, write-protect the backup diskette. Print CONFIG.SYS.
3. Locate the file named ANSI.SYS. It's probably on C:\DOS. Remember where it is, but return to the C:\ directory.
4. If you do have a C:\CONFIG.SYS file, examine the printout you made in Item 2. Does CONFIG.SYS load the ANSI.SYS driver? If not, add a line to the file to load that driver. Don't forget to include a path to tell DOS where to find ANSI.SYS.
5. If you don't have a CONFIG.SYS file, create one that loads the ANSI.SYS device driver. Don't forget to include a path to tell DOS where it is.
6. Reboot and get back to the C:\ command prompt. Now that you have changed CONFIG.SYS, watch carefully for any error messages during booting.
7. Display your detailed memory usage. You should be able to see the ANSI driver listed in the **System Data** section.
8. The following command will create a flashing red prompt. Enter it at the command prompt, exactly as shown, and be sure to use lowercase letters in the prompt text:

```
PROMPT $e[5;31m$p$g$e[0m
```

   Your prompt should now be flashing red (unless you have a monochrome monitor).
9. Restore the conventional prompt.

1. *Enter the command:*

```
DIR CONFIG.SYS
```

   *If a CONFIG.SYS file is listed, it exists; "File not found" means no CONFIG.SYS file exists in this directory.*
2. *Enter these commands:*

```
COPY CONFIG.SYS A: /V
PRINT CONFIG.SYS
```

3. *Enter the command:*

```
DIR C:\DOS\ANSI.SYS
```

*If you get a "File not found" message, enter the shell, start the **File System**, set the **Display Options** filespec to ANSI.SYS, and select **System file list**. If ANSI.SYS exists anywhere on the fixed disk, it will show up in the file list. Then, you can highlight ANSI.SYS to determine the directory it's in. Return to the command prompt for C:\ when you know the correct directory.*

4. *Use your ASCII editor to add this line to CONFIG.SYS:*

```
DEVICE=path\ANSI.SYS
```

*If you don't have an ASCII editor or don't know how to use one, you can create a file named CONFIG.ADD containing the DEVICE statement and then concatenate CONFIG.ADD with your CONFIG.SYS file.*

5. *Use your ASCII editor or COPY CON to create a file named C:\CONFIG.SYS containing the statement DEVICE=path\ANSI.SYS.*

6. *Be sure to remove the diskette from drive A: so the system boots from C:. If you see a message about an error in the CONFIG.SYS file, you might have typed the DEVICE statement incorrectly, or you might have put the wrong path in the ANSI.SYS filespec. Correct the error and try again. (If you must use COPY CON, copy the backed up CONFIG.SYS from the diskette to C:\, then add the new line to CONFIG.SYS, as you did before.)*

   *If you see an "Insufficient memory" message, you don't have enough memory to load the ANSI.SYS driver. Restore your original CONFIG.SYS by copying it from the backup diskette. Skip the remainder of this checkpoint.*

   *If ANSI.SYS loads properly, you won't see any confirmation message, but there will be no error messages during booting.*

7. *Enter the command:*

```
MEM /PROGRAM | MORE
```

8. *If the prompt doesn't flash red, you didn't enter the correct PROMPT text. It's especially important to use lowercase m's in the PROMPT text. Try once more, but don't spend too much time on this.*

9. *Enter the command:*

```
PROMPT $P$G
```

## Expanded and Extended Memory

For many years, DOS was limited to managing 640K of memory, even if more was installed in the computer. But now two methods let DOS and applications running under DOS access more memory: expanded memory and extended memory. If you have more than 1MB of memory in your machine, you have either one or both of these. You should configure your system so that DOS can use the extra memory. As you'll see in this chapter, your system can be made to run much faster, dramatically faster, by using the higher memory areas as disk buffer space and RAM drives.

If you have more than 1MB of memory in your machine, it's important to know which type you have. If your machine is a PC or XT compatible, then you have expanded memory. Other machines might have either or both types. Some extra memory boards are capable of switching from one type to the other. Also, drivers exist that make one type act like the other. You can tell which type you have by using the MEM command. (Expanded memory shows up as EMS on the display.)

For DOS to use either type of extra memory, a memory device driver must be installed. Check your memory board documentation to find out how to install your driver. Most likely, it will require a CONFIG.SYS statement in the following format:

```
DEVICE=[path]name.SYS
```

The DOS diskettes include some memory drivers, called XMAEM.SYS and XMAE2EMS.SYS. You might need to use one of these drivers, or you might use one that came with your memory board. Check your memory board documentation to find out.

Whichever driver you choose, its DEVICE statement should be the first statement in the CONFIG.SYS file so that other configuration features, such as RAM drivers and extra buffers, can use the higher memory areas.


## RAM Drives

RAMDRIVE.SYS is a device driver that lets you turn part of your memory into virtual drives. A virtual drive is an area of memory set aside to be used like a disk drive. Of course, it isn't really a disk drive; you lose all the data stored in the virtual drive when the machine loses power. But you can store files there during a session.

DOS can access memory hundreds of times faster than a disk, so programs that do a lot of disk access run much faster when you use a RAM drive. You can copy a program, such as a word processor, to a RAM drive area and make this the default drive. You'll actually see the difference in performance. Of course, your system must have plenty of memory, since space being used as a RAM drive is not free for other uses. However, you can put the RAM drive into extended or expanded memory, which is ordinarily not used by DOS.

Again, keep in mind that a virtual drive isn't actually a disk drive; when the machine is rebooted or loses power, any data in memory, including the RAM drive, is lost. If you use a RAM drive, be sure to copy any files to be saved to actual disks before turning off the computer or rebooting. Since you could lose all your work in a power outage, many experts recommend that you don't put data files in a RAM drive, just programs. Your program files are already recorded on disk, so you don't need to worry about losing the RAM drive copy. You won't save as much work time when your data files are on actual disks, but you also don't take the chance of losing a day's work. If you do put your data files in a RAM drive, copy them to a real disk at least once per hour.

DOS lets you create as many RAM drives as you need; they are lettered in sequence after your real drives. If you go beyond drive E:, you will need to place a LASTDRIVE statement in your CONFIG.SYS file as well. LASTDRIVE is explained later in this chapter.

Suppose you have created a CONFIG.SYS file containing the statement DEVICE=RAMDRIVE.SYS. When you reboot the fixed-disk system, you'll see the message shown in Figure 13.1. Notice the RAM drive has been assigned the name D:. The disk size tells you the size of the RAM drive; 64K is the default. The sector size tells you the size of each sector in the RAM drive; 512 bytes is the default. The allocation unit size shows the fewest number of sectors that will be allocated to one file; 1 is the default. The default number of entries in the root directory is 64. You can specify different values with the DEVICE=RAMDRIVE.SYS statement for all these factors except allocation units. Its format is shown below:

```
DEVICE=RAMDRIVE.SYS [buffer-size] [sector-size] [directory-size] [/E or /A]
```

```
Microsoft RAMdrive version 2.12 virtual disk D:
    Disk size: 64k
    Sector size: 512 bytes
    Allocation unit: 1 sectors
    Directory entries: 64
```

Figure 13.1. RAMDRIVE Messages

The buffer size is given in kilobytes. You can enter any size between 16K and the available memory size in your system. To create a RAM drive of 240K, you would place this statement in your CONFIG.SYS file:

```
DEVICE=RAMDRIVE.SYS 240
```

In the DEVICE statement that sets up the RAM drive, you can also specify the sector size as 128, 256, 512, or 1024 bytes. DOS uses 512 as the default on RAM drives. You might as well use the default size unless you have reason not to. A large sector size works well with large files; a smaller size works better with small files.

You can also specify the number of directory entries for a RAM drive, from 4 to 1024. The default is 64. The directory takes up storage space just as files do. The more entries you specify (each entry takes up 32 bytes), the more drive space you use. There's a relationship between directory entries and sector size, because DOS won't use just part of a sector for directory entries. Say your sector size is 128 bytes and you request 75 directory entries, 2400 bytes altogether. That's 18 complete sectors plus part of a nineteenth. DOS will make the entire nineteenth sector into directory entries, so you actually get 76 entries, not 75, for a total directory size of 2432 bytes. The message you see reflects the amount allocated, not what you requested.

If you request more directory entries than can fit in your RAM drive, the directory request is scaled down until it fits. Just allow enough space for the programs you want to run and the files you want to store.

The /E options tells RAMDRIVE to use extended memory, while the /A option uses expanded memory. If you have either of these memory options, you'll want to use /E or /A to put your RAM drives in the higher memory, so the RAM drives won't decrease available memory by much—a nice advantage. (A few bytes of conventional memory, below the 640K mark, are taken up by control information for the RAM drives.)

Figure 13.2. shows portions of a session using a RAM drive. You can see the message resulting from the DEVICE=RAMDRIVE.SYS statement in the CONFIG.SYS file at boot time. Then we copied all the necessary word processing files into the RAM drive. Next we copied the file we want to edit (PRACTICE) into the drive. Then we started up the word processor and edited the file. At the end of the session, before shutting down, we copied the edited file back to the real drive.

In planning your RAM drive size, keep your other memory needs in mind. DOS needs about 115K for its own use if you gave it the minimum space during installation. It needs more if you gave it more space. DosShell takes up room. Every TSR you load takes up memory room. Features that reserve extra buffers in memory, such as FASTOPEN and the BUFFERS

```
Microsoft RAMdrive Version 2.12 virtual disk D:
                                                 This message results from
                                                 the Device statement in
                                                 CONFIG.SYS
      Disk size: 64k
      Sector size: 512 bytes
      Allocation unit: 1 sectors
      Directory entries: 64
    .
    .
    .

C:\DOS>COPY C:\CX5\CX*.* D:                      This command copies the
C:CX.EXE                                          word processing program
C:CX.MSG                                          to the RAM drive
C:CX.DCT
        3 File(s) copied


C:\DOS>COPY C:\TEXTS\PRACTICE D:                  This command copies the
        1 File(s) copied                         text file to be edited
                                                 to the RAM drive


C:\DOS>D:                                         This command makes the
D:\>                                              RAM drive the default
                                                 drive


    .                                            Use the word processor to
    .                                            edit PRACTICE
    .


D:\>COPY PRACTICE C:\TEXTS                        Save PRACTICE on a real
                                                 disk
```

Figure 13.2. Using a RAM Drive

statement that you will learn later in this chapter, take up memory space. If you see the message "RAMDrive: Insufficient memory" during booting, your RAM drive is too big for the rest of your DOS configuration—even before trying to load any TSRs. If the RAM drive is created successfully, but you later see another message stating that there isn't enough memory space—to load a program or install buffers, perhaps—then you need to reduce or eliminate your RAM drive (or put it in higher memory if possible). This involves adapting CONFIG.SYS and rebooting.

One error can result in an awkward situation. If DOS installs the RAM drive but then cannot install the rest of the configuration, it will stall with the message "Configuration too large for memory." Until you change your CONFIG.SYS, you can't successfully boot. You have just discovered a Catch 22: You can't boot until you change CONFIG.SYS, and you can't change CONFIG.SYS until you boot. You have to boot from a diskette with a different CONFIG.SYS so that you can fix your regular CONFIG.SYS. If you don't have a usable diskette (even one that has an earlier version of DOS or some other operating system), borrow one from a friend or get help from your dealer. You can also try booting from your original DOS diskettes; avoid booting with the INSTALL diskette so that you don't have to reinstall the system.

## Other DOS Drivers

The DRIVER.SYS driver lets you assign alternate names to your diskette drives. If you have two different types of diskette drives, it's difficult to do single-drive copies. DRIVER.SYS lets you assign alternate names to each drive. For example, you could assign the name E: to the A: drive. Then, to copy a file from one diskette to another of the same size, you could enter: COPY A:MYFILE E:. DOS will tell you when to insert the diskette in drive E:. Check your DOS reference manual for the details to follow in using DRIVER.SYS.

The IBMCACHE.SYS driver is available only if you have a PS/2 model 50, 60, or 80. It is a hidden file, so you won't see it in the directory brought up by DIR at the command prompt, although you can see it on the **File System** screen. It creates a buffer in memory to cache (store) fixed disk data to reduce the number of disk accesses required and to greatly speed up fixed disk operations. If you have one of the above PS/2 models, you will probably want to use the IBMCACHE.SYS driver. You must run a program called IBMCACHE to install the driver. IBMCACHE gives you menus from which to choose your options. Check your DOS manual for details.

1. Use MEM to find out the largest-sized program you can run. Decide how large a RAM drive you could create and leave at least 300K of memory available for the shell and other DOS features. (If the answer is less than 16K, skip this checkpoint.)
2. Add a line to CONFIG.SYS to create a RAM drive of the size you determined. Use the default sector and directory sizes. Don't worry about using expanded or extended memory now.
3. Reboot. Watch the booting messages and note the name DOS assigns to

the RAM drive. Watch carefully; the RAMDRIVE message might disappear from the screen if other drivers are installed by CONFIG.SYS or if AUTOEXEC.BAT executes some programs.

4. Make C:\DOS your current drive. Look through this directory to find the largest file that will fit in your RAM drive. Copy it to C:\PRACTICE and notice how long the copy takes when you don't use the RAM drive.

5. Now copy the same file to your RAM drive and notice how long it takes. The copy should take noticeably less time with the RAM drive.

6. Try using DIR and CHKDSK on your RAM drive. Notice how much less available memory you have.

If you need to use your computer for other tasks before the next checkpoint in this chapter, you might want to restore your original CONFIG.SYS from the backup you made at the beginning of the chapter.

---

1. *Enter the command:*

```
MEM
```

2. *If you decided to add an 80K drive, you would add this statement to CONFIG.SYS:*

```
DEVICE=path\RAMDRIVE.SYS 80
```

3. *You should see the RAMDRIVE message, confirming the creation of the RAM drive. If you see any error messages that indicate insufficient memory, restore your original CONFIG.SYS from the backup copy and try this checkpoint again with a smaller RAM drive. (If you get stuck with the "Configuration too large for memory" message, you'll have to find another disk to boot from in order to fix the problem.)*

   *If you see error messages indicating that DOS can't find RAMDRIVE.SYS or that there is a mistake in the CONFIG.SYS file, then figure out what the problem is, correct the DEVICE statement, and try again. (If you're using COPY CON, you can correct the DEVICE statement by restoring the original CONFIG.SYS from diskette and concatenating it again.)*

5. *If you are copying SHELLC.EXE, and the RAM drive is named D:, enter the command:*

```
COPY SHELLC.EXE D:
```

6. *If the RAM drive is named D:, enter these commands:*

```
CHKDSK D:
DIR D:
```

# Disk Buffers

You can dramatically speed up your system by increasing the number of buffers set aside for disk access. Every time you read something from a disk, DOS saves the data in these buffers. The next time you read from the same disk, DOS first looks in the buffers to see if the desired data is already there. If it is, DOS doesn't have to access the disk itself. Not only does this save an enormous amount of time (because reading from memory is so much faster than reading from a disk), it also saves wear on the disk drive.

The more buffers you specify, up to a practical limit, the faster your disk access will be because DOS can save more data in memory. DOS allocates a default number of buffers, from 2 to 15, based on the configuration of your disk drives and the amount of memory you have.

How many buffers should you specify? Because your system configuration and file allocation needs are unique, it's impossible to give a "right" answer. Experimentation is the best guide. If you allocate too many buffers, DOS spends more time searching the buffers than it would accessing the disk. Also, each buffer takes .5K, so if you don't have expanded memory, specifying too many buffers will seriously cut into the available memory space. Try allocating 30 buffers for a start (if you have the memory space). Then periodically add 5 or 10 buffers until you reach the point where your applications start running slower instead of faster.

The format of the BUFFERS statement is shown below:

```
BUFFERS=number[,lookahead] [/X]
```

You can specify from 1 to 99 buffers in the basic statement. If you use the /X switch, which places the buffers in expanded memory, then you can specify as many buffers as expanded memory has room for, up to 10,000 buffers. Suppose you want to use 500 buffers in expanded memory. You would place the following statement in your CONFIG.SYS file:

```
BUFFERS=500 /X
```

To enhance system performance even more, you can define up to 8 *lookahead* buffers. DOS tries to predict what sectors you are going to read next and places them in the lookahead buffers. For example, if you have defined three lookahead buffers and your application reads sectors 25 and 26, DOS will store sectors 27, 28, and 29 in the lookahead buffers. If those are the next sectors read, the disk access time is circumvented. To define 30 regular buffers and 8 lookahead buffers, you would place the following statement in your CONFIG.SYS file:

```
BUFFERS=30,8
```

or

```
BUFFERS=30,8 /X      (if you have expanded memory)
```

Start at the command prompt. Make C:\ the default directory.
1. Add a line to CONFIG.SYS that creates 99 buffers and 8 lookahead buffers. Put them in expanded memory if you have it.
2. Reboot and watch for any error messages.
3. You can't really experience the effects of the extra buffers without using your applications. For now, examine your detailed memory usage. You should be able to see the buffers in the listing. If they are in expanded memory, you can see them by subtracting available expanded memory from total expanded memory. The difference should be about 50K.

   This is the last checkpoint for this chapter. The remaining topics cannot be easily practiced. Restore your original CONFIG.SYS from the backup diskette unless you want to continue to use the features you have added to it in this chapter.

1. *Add this line to CONFIG.SYS:*

   ```
   BUFFERS=99,8
   ```

   *Or, if you have expanded memory, add this line to CONFIG.SYS instead:*

   ```
   BUFFERS=99,8 /X
   ```

2. *If no error messages result, everything should be okay. If any error messages imply that you don't have enough memory, restore your original CONFIG.SYS from the backup diskette, reboot, and skip the remainder of this checkpoint. If any error messages imply that there is a mistake in the BUFFERS statement, fix the statement and try again.*
3. *Enter the command:*

   ```
   MEM /PROGRAM | MORE
   ```

## File Handles and FCBs

Many programs require that several files be available at once. Programs such as WordStar 2000 or WordPerfect need to work with up to 20 files at a time. An accounting package may need as many as 40. Every open file needs a small memory area (39 bytes) for the file's *handle* (control information about the file). By default, DOS creates eight file areas. You can raise that limit, up to 99, with the FILES statement. If the CONFIG.SYS file contains a statement like FILES=20, the file limit is set to the indicated number. If an application needs more than the default amount, its documentation should tell you how many to allocate. Leaving space for more file handles than you need doesn't do much harm, since each one takes up only 39 bytes.

Some older programs require File Control Blocks (FCBs) rather than file handles. FCBs are created with the FCBS statement, as in FCBS=30. Your application documentation will tell you if you need to use the FCBS statement in a CONFIG.SYS file, and it should show you the statement you need.

## Making More Drives Available

The LASTDRIVE statement tells DOS the highest lettered drivename it can accept in commands. The default value is E. You can use LASTDRIVE to pretend you have more drives than you really do. This allows you to create imaginary drives with DRIVER.SYS and RAMDRIVE, beyond drive E:. Some of your applications might also require LASTDRIVE, as described in their documentation. Suppose you have a 1.2MB drive (A:) a 1.44MB drive (B:) and two hard drives (C: and D:). You want to assign alternate drivenames to your diskettes so you can do single-drive copies (E: and F:), and you want to use two RAM drives (G: and H:). You would need to insert this statement in CONFIG.SYS:

```
LASTDRIVE=H
```

To allocate the maximum number of drives, you would include this statement in your CONFIG.SYS file:

```
LASTDRIVE=Z
```

## Country and Language Formats

DOS was developed in the United States and, naturally, its default formats are appropriate for this country. For example, the date is reported as 1-15-90, the time is reported as 9:15:25.19 or 9:15a, and monetary values are displayed as $5,238.26. If you use your system in a different country, you can do several things to adapt DOS to use your country's formats and alphabet.

The COUNTRY statement in CONFIG.SYS affects the date and time formats. It also provides information to applications about numeric formats (the decimal point and thousands separator), sort sequence (how to alpha-betize such characters as â, à, and å), and currency symbols. Its format is shown below:

```
COUNTRY=xxx[,,filespec]
```

Figure 13.3 lists the country codes. For example, if you want to use the Swedish formats, you would include the following statement in your CONFIG.SYS file:

```
COUNTRY=046
```

After rebooting, your date and time formats would look like this:

```
C:>DATE
Current date is Wed  1992-01-15
Enter new date (yy-mm-dd):_

C:>TIME
Current time is 18.12.26,32
Enter new time:_
```

DOS needs the COUNTRY.SYS file to obtain the country information. If the information isn't in the root directory of the boot disk, then you need to tell

| | | | |
|---|---|---|---|
| Arabic | 785 | Korea | 082 |
| Australia (international English) | 061 | Latin America | 003 |
| Belguim | 032 | Netherlands | 031 |
| Canada-English | 001 | Norway | 047 |
| Canada-French | 002 | Peoples Republic of China | 086 |
| Denmark | 045 | Portugal | 351 |
| Finland | 358 | Spain | 034 |
| France | 033 | Sweden | 046 |
| Germany | 049 | Switzerland | 041 |
| Israel | 972 | Taiwan | 088 |
| Italy | 039 | United Kingdom | 044 |
| Japan | 081 | United States | 001 |

Figure 13.3. Country Codes

DOS where to find it. The filespec must be preceded by two commas, as in this example:

```
COUNTRY=044,,C:\DOS\COUNTRY.SYS
```

## Codepages

Your monitor display and printer have *codepages* built into them. A codepage is a table that tells the device what character to issue for each of the 256 possible values of a byte. For example, in the U.S. codepage, code 157 is displayed or printed as ¥. In the multilingual and Nordic codepages, the same code yields Ø. In the Portuguese and Canadian-French codepage, the same code produces Ú.

When DOS displays or prints data, it sends numeric codes to the monitor or printer. How these codes are interpreted depends on the codepage that is installed in the device. Usually the codepage depends on the country where you buy the hardware. If you buy a printer in the U.S., it will probably have the U.S. codepage built in. If you buy a monitor in Portugal, it might have the Portuguese codepage built in.

Many printers and monitors are able to use codepages different than the ones that are built-in. You can download software codepages. Thus, even though you bought your system in the U.S., you can display and print files prepared in Nordic languages. DOS has five software codepages available, as shown in Figure 13.4. You can download a single codepage or set up your system to switch among several codepages.

The monitors that can handle software codepages are EGA, VGA, and LCD. The older monochrome and CGA monitors are not capable of doing this. The printers that can handle software codepages are the IBM ProPrinter Model 4201 or 4208 and their compatibles, and the IBM Quietwriter III

| Canada-French | 863 |
|---|---|
| Multilingual | 850 |
| Norway and Denmark | 865 |
| Portugal | 860 |
| United States | 437 |

Figure 13.4. DOS Software Codepages

Model 5202 and its compatibles. If you don't have one of those models, the best thing to do is to try switching codepages on your printer and see if it works.

Downloading a software codepage is not a simple task. It requires careful coordination of several CONFIG.SYS statements and DOS commands. We will overview the necessary facilities here. If you actually need to do this downloading operation, check with your DOS reference manual or your dealer for more details.

In your CONFIG.SYS file, you need:

- The COUNTRY statement (as discussed earlier) to establish the desired country formats and to tell DOS where COUNTRY.SYS is.

- A DEVICE=DISPLAY.SYS statement with operands to tell DOS which codepage is the monitor hardware codepage and to allocate buffers for every software codepage you want to be able to use with the monitor. (The DISPLAY.SYS file, provided by DOS, must be available at boot time for this statement to have its proper effect.)

- A DEVICE=PRINTER.SYS statement with operands to tell DOS which codepage is the printer hardware codepage and to allocate buffers for every software codepage you want to be able to use with the printer. (The PRINTER.SYS file, provided by DOS, must be available at boot time for this statement to have its proper effect.)

After booting, you need these commands:

- MODE CON: CODEPAGE PREPARE must be used to prepare the various codepages you want to use on the monitor. You can only prepare as many codepages as you allocated buffers for in the DEVICE=DISPLAY.SYS statement. The EGA.CPI or LCD.CPI file, provided by DOS, must be available when this command is executed.

- MODE LPT*n* CODEPAGE PREPARE does the same thing as MODE CON: CODEPAGE PREPARE, but for printer codepages. The 4201.CPI or 5202.CPI file, provided by DOS, must be available when this command is executed.

- MODE CON: CODEPAGE SELECT downloads a codepage to the monitor. The codepage must have been prepared first.

- MODE LPT*n* CODEPAGE SELECT downloads a codepage to the printer. The codepage must have been prepared first.

- NLSFUNC (National Language Support FUNCtions) loads the CHCP program into memory as a resident program. You must execute NLSFUNC before you can execute CHCP.

- CHCP (CHange CodePage) can be used instead of MODE...SELECT to download a codepage to all eligible devices at once. The codepages must have been prepared first and NLSFUNC must have been executed first.

- MODE *device* CODEPAGE REFRESH refreshes the software codepage after a hardware error (such as turning off the printer).

### Keyboard Codepages

Your keyboard also has a built-in codepage that determines what code is sent to DOS for each key you press. If you want to use a non-U.S. layout on a U.S. keyboard, you might need the KEYB command to tell DOS what keyboard layout you want to use and what monitor codepage it should be associated with.

# Executing Commands in CONFIG.SYS

You can use the INSTALL statement to execute any of the following commands during the processing of CONFIG.SYS: FASTOPEN, KEYB, NLSFUNC, and SHARE. You might want to do this to keep these commands out of your AUTOEXEC.BAT file. Then you can run AUTOEXEC.BAT to reinitialize your system without rebooting. Also, SELECT might have generated some INSTALL statements for your CONFIG.SYS file, depending on your answers to various options during the installation process. The format of the statement is:

```
INSTALL=filespec [parameters]
```

Include whatever parameters are appropriate for the command you are executing. For example, to install FASTOPEN from CONFIG.SYS, you might include this statement:

```
INSTALL=C:\DOS\FASTOPEN.EXE C:=(50,200)
```

# Documenting Your CONFIG.SYS File

You can include comments in your CONFIG.SYS file with the REM statement. These don't appear on the screen when the file is processed, but they do show up when the file is displayed. A typical CONFIG.SYS file might look like this:

```
REM The following statement installs the expanded memory
REM device driver.
DEVICE=C:\DOS\EMDRIVER.SYS
REM
REM
REM The following statement sets up 500 buffers in expanded
REM memory.
BUFFERS=500 /X
REM
REM
REM The following statement installs the mouse driver.
DEVICE=C:\MOUSE\MOUSE.SYS /COM2
REM
REM
REM The following statement sets up RAM drive D: in expanded
REM memory.
DEVICE=C:\DOS\RAMDRIVE.SYS 32000 /A
REM
REM
REM The following statement installs FASTOPEN in expanded
REM memory.
INSTALL=FASTOPEN C:=(100,500) /X
```

It pays to document your CONFIG.SYS file, not only for other users of your system, but also for yourself. You might have difficulty remembering, say a year from now, what that INSTALL statement is doing there.

# Summary

In this chapter, you have learned to create a CONFIG.SYS file to control how your hardware is configured during booting. You have seen how to install device drivers, initialize the break feature, install a limited number of programs, create and use a RAM drive, allocate disk and file buffers, and use more drivenames. You have also been introduced to the commands and statements necessary for changing the country settings in your computer.

# *Exercises*

These exercises let you practice using CONFIG.SYS features.

| **What You Should Do** | **How the Computer Responds** |
|---|---|
| 1. Save your current CONFIG.SYS file on a backup diskette so you can restore it at the end of this exercise. | 1. Copies the file as directed. |
| 2. Add each of the following features to your CONFIG.SYS file (unless the feature is already there):<br><br>ANSI.SYS<br>50 buffers and 5 lookahead buffers<br>20K RAM drive<br><br>(If you don't have a CONFIG.SYS file, create one for this exercise.) | 2. Revises the file as directed, but doesn't recognize the new features. |
| 3. Reboot with your new CONFIG.SYS file. If you see any messages that indicate a syntax or logic error in the CONFIG.SYS file, correct the file. | 3. Reboots using the new CONFIG.SYS. Installs ANSI.SYS, sets aside the requested number of buffers, and establishes the RAM drive. Displays a message about the RAM drive, but not about the other features. If the configuration is too large for memory, or if it takes up so much room that other CONFIG.SYS features or programs started in AUTOEXEC.BAT cannot function, displays error messages to that effect. |
| 4. If you have extended or expanded memory, revise your CONFIG.SYS file to put the following features in higher memory:<br><br>200 buffers and 8 lookahead buffers<br>100K RAM drive<br><br>Reboot to establish the new configuration. | 4. Reboots using the new CONFIG.SYS. Allocates the requested number of buffers and the RAM drive in higher memory. Displays a message about the RAM drive, but not about the other features. |

5. Check out your detailed memory. You should be able to see the ANSI.SYS driver, the RAM drive, and the buffers in the report.
6. Restore your original CONFIG.SYS file.
7. Review the contents of your current CONFIG.SYS file and the various configuration features available to you. Could you benefit from extra buffers, RAM drives, device drivers (such as ANSI.SYS and DRIVER.SYS), extra drivenames, and alternate country formats and codepages? If so, decide what statements to put in your CONFIG.SYS file, revise the file, reboot and try it out.

5. In response to MEM /PROGRAM | MORE, displays a detailed report of memory usage.

6. Copies the file as directed.
7. Obeys your commands.

## *What If It Doesn't Work?*

1. If new CONFIG.SYS doesn't take effect, you probably didn't put it in the root directory of the boot drive.

2. If you get a message that there's not enough memory, try again using fewer buffers and a smaller RAM drive (16K is the minimum size). If the configuration still won't fit, restore your original CONFIG.SYS file and go on to the next step in the exercise.

3. If you get a "Configuration too large for memory" message, you'll have to boot from a diskette so that you can fix the CONFIG.SYS file before rebooting from the hard disk.

# 14

# *Basic Batch Files*

Batch files provide a great shortcut and convenience in working with computers. While these files can become quite complex, even the simple ones can help make your life easier. In this chapter, you'll learn to:

- Use standard DOS commands in a batch file
- Create a batch file to be processed automatically
- Use REM commands to document a batch file
- Use ECHO commands to display messages in a batch file
- Use the PAUSE command to let the user decide when to continue
- Use CLS to clear the screen
- Include replaceable parameters to use command-line values
- Include and process named parameters

## *What Is a Batch File?*

In earlier chapters, you've seen some applications of files with extension BAT that contain a few DOS commands and can be executed by typing the filename. These are called batch files, and their application possibilities are much greater than you've seen so far. Figure 14.1 shows several batch files made up of commands you already know.

```
LISTA.BAT
     DIR A: | SORT | MORE

CHECKA.BAT
     CHKDSK A:
     DIR A:\*.COM

VERVOL.BAT
     VER
     VOL
     CHECKA

EDIT.BAT
     C:
     CD \WS5
     WS

SPREAD.BAT
     C:
     \MOUSE
     CD \SPREADSH
     GENICS /N
```

Figure 14.1. Sample Batch Files

If you frequently use a complicated FIND command, you might include it in a batch file called FINDIT.BAT. Then you can execute the complex command by just typing FINDIT. Or you might go through a series of five or six commands to accomplish your weekly backup routine. These too can be placed in a batch file and executed with a single command at the command prompt, much as commands that make up a program added to the shell can be executed by selecting the program title in the shell.

Batch files can be set up to send messages to the screen, to make decisions, and even to use specific parameters. Normally, the commands in a batch file are executed in sequence. However, they can be programmed to include loops, decisions, and branching much like a computer program. The next chapter covers programming applications of batch files.

## Batch File Contents

A batch file can contain any DOS commands as well as some special commands. For example, the PAUSE command causes information to stay on the screen and puts the program on hold until you press a key.

## General Rules for Batch Files

A batch file must be in ASCII format. COPY CON produces ASCII files. Nearly all editors and word processors have some facility for creating ASCII (or text) files. You can use any of these for creating new batch files or modifying existing ones.

Within a batch file, each command must begin on a separate line; this is comparable to the command separator ( || ) produced in the **Add Program** dialog box when you press F4. DOS must know where one command ends and the next begins. You can use redirection and piping within a batch file just as you can at the keyboard. Wherever you have to press Enter when entering a command at the keyboard, you have to start a new line in a batch file.

## Executing a Batch File

When you execute a batch file, you enter just its name, without the extension. Whenever DOS sees a filename at the prompt, it tries to run the program. It looks first for a file with extension COM; if no file of the specified name with that extension exists, DOS looks for a file with extension EXE. Only if no file of that name exists does DOS look for a file with extension BAT. If it still hasn't found a file to use, DOS moves on to the next directory in the search path.

Make sure you don't give a batch file a name that DOS uses for its programs. For example, FORMAT.BAT or CHKDSK.BAT would never be executed in the same directory as FORMAT.COM or CHKDSK.EXE. You could put batch files with those names in different directories and execute them with complete paths, but it is easier and safer to use unique names. Use FORMAT1.BAT, for example, or CHKDSKA.BAT to distinguish your batch files from programs that use the same filenames.

## Batch Files in the Shell

While batch files are generally designed to be executed at the command prompt, they can be executed through the shell as well. In the shell, you can include a batch file command in a program added to a group. If you use just the filename, as in FORMAT1, DOS will exit the shell permanently and proceed to execute the batch file, as shown in the example in Figure 14.2. You'll have to use DOSSHELL to restart the shell. If you want shell reentry to be automatic after batch file execution, use CALL FORMAT1 instead.

```
 09-14-89                     Start Programs                  2:17 pm
  Program  Group  Exit                                       F1=Help
                           DOS Utilities...
               To select an item, use the up and down arrows.
            To start a program or display a new group, press Enter.

 Set Date and Time
 Disk Copy
 Disk Compare            ┌──────────── Add Program ────────────┐
 Backup Fixed Dis        │ Required                            │
 Restore Fixed D         │                                     │
 Format                  │   Title . . . .  │Arrange system disks│→│
                         │                                     │
                         │   Commands  . .  │←│IR ║ PAUSE ║ FORMAT1│→│
                         │ Optional                            │
                         │                                     │
                         │   Help text . .  │                 │→│
                         │                                     │
                         │   Password  . .  │        │         │
                         │                                     │
                         │  ( Esc=Cancel )  ( F1=Help )  ( F2=Save )│
                         └─────────────────────────────────────┘
 F10=Actions   Esc=Cancel   Shift+F9=Command Prompt
```

Figure 14.2. Batch File Command in Shell

## The AUTOEXEC.BAT File

Whenever you boot or reboot your computer, several steps are executed in sequence. First some internal procedures (and chip checking for the initial boot) are done. Then DOS processes a file called CONFIG.SYS, if one exists (you've seen how to use this file in Chapter 13). Finally, DOS looks for a file in the root directory called AUTOEXEC.BAT. If DOS finds one, this batch file is executed automatically before you get the command prompt.

The commands in the AUTOEXEC.BAT file depend on the needs of your system and the kind of work you do. You might set the path, set a prompt, initialize your mouse, initialize the printer, or send a message to the user. You might include DOSSHELL, as the last command, to start the shell.

If DOS doesn't find an AUTOEXEC.BAT file, it asks you for the date and time. If your date and time must be reset every time you start up your computer, you should include both the DATE and TIME commands in your AUTOEXEC.BAT file.

When you installed DOS 4, an AUTOEXEC.BAT file was created automatically, using your responses as given to the SELECT program. The AUTOEXEC.BAT file may contain commands similar to these:

```
@ECHO OFF
SET COMSPEC=A:\COMMAND.COM
VERIFY OFF
VER
```

You can use your editor to add standard DOS commands and special batch commands to this file.

Start at the command prompt. Make \PRACTICE the current directory.
1. Create a file called DISK.BAT that contains these commands:

```
CHKDSK
VER
```

2. Execute the batch file you just created. You should see the CHKDSK and VER (version) output on the screen for the current disk.
3. Examine your C:\AUTOEXEC.BAT file by displaying it on the monitor. You'll probably recognize some of the commands. If you see unfamiliar commands, don't change them! Your system probably needs them.
4. Add a DIR command to the end of your DISK.BAT file.
5. Try out the modified batch file.
6. Add the command:

```
TREE C:\
```

to the beginning of your DISK.BAT file.
7. To the **DOS Utilities** group in the shell, add a program that executes DISK.BAT. After executing DISK, DOS should stay at the command prompt.
8. Try out your new shell program.
9. Change your new shell program so that it returns automatically to the **DOS Utilities** screen upon termination. Try out your newly revised shell program.

*1. Use your ASCII editor or COPY CON.*
*2. Enter the command:*

```
DISK
```

*Correct the batch file until it produces the desired result.*
*3. Enter the command:*

```
TYPE \AUTOEXEC.BAT
```

*4. Use your ASCII editor. If you must use COPY CON, create a new file containing the added command and concatenate it with DISK.BAT. Alternatively, you could use one of these interactions:*

```
C:\>ECHO DIR >> DISK.BAT
C:\>_
```

*or*

```
C:\>SORT >> DISK.BAT
DIR
^Z
C:\>_
```

5. *If the batch file doesn't work properly, correct it until you get the desired results.*

6. *Use your ASCII editor. If you must use COPY CON, make a new file that contains the command to be added. Then concatenate DISK.BAT into the new file (so that the new command is at the beginning of the concatenated file). Finally, delete the previous DISK.BAT and rename the new file as DISK.BAT.*

7. *Go to the **DOS Utilities** screen, pull down the **Program** menu, and select **Add**. In the **Add Program** dialog box, enter a title such as "Try a batch file." In the **Commands** box, enter "\PRACTICE\DISK". Then select **Save**.*

8. *Double-click on the new title or highlight it and press Enter. If you don't get the desired results, correct the **Commands** box until you do.*

9. *Highlight the title, pull down the **Program** menu, and select **Change**. Change the **Commands** box to read "CALL C:\PRACTICE\DISK", then select **Save**.*

# Messages in Batch Files

DOS offers two commands you can use to include messages in a batch file. While these commands can be used at the keyboard as well, they are most useful in batch files. The REM commmand is used primarily for remarks that document the batch file internally. The ECHO command is used primarily to control messages and displays to the user when the batch command is executed. As with other DOS commands, batch commands can be in uppercase or lowercase characters. We will continue to show them in uppercase.

## The REM Command

The REM command format is shown below:

```
REM [message]
```

You can include any message up to 127 characters (including the word REM), or none if you want a blank line.

Figure 14.3 shows a batch file in which REM commands explain what the file does. The REM command without any message is used for spacing.

```
REM This file copies all files from the virtual D drive
REM to the newly created TEMP directory on drive C.
REM
REM It then sorts and displays the directory before ending.
C:
CD \
MD TEMP
XCOPY /S D:*.* C:\TEMP
DIR C:\TEMP | SORT
```

Figure 14.3. Batch File with REM Command

When you run this program, the REM lines are sent to the screen. You'll see all commands and their standard output on the screen as well. The screen looks something like the one in Figure 14.4 after you run the batch file.

## The ECHO Command

The ECHO command can also be used to send a message to the screen. In addition, the echo status can be turned on and off with ECHO. The echo status determines visual effects of other batch commands. For example, when echo is off, REM commands do not display on the screen. Neither do any DOS commands that would otherwise appear at the command prompt. Program output continues to be sent to the screen even when echo status is off. For example, SORT or FIND output comes to the screen (unless you redirect it elsewhere) no matter what the status of echo.

The ECHO batch command can include a comment or it can be used to change the echo status. The formats are shown below:

```
ECHO [comment]
ECHO [ON or OFF]
```

If you use ECHO without any following value, the current echo status is displayed.

The ECHO message format looks much like the REM command and has the same limitations. The command can contain up to 127 characters. If necessary, excess characters will wrap to the next line when the message is displayed. When echo status is on, the ECHO command is displayed, followed by the ECHO message. The advantage of ECHO over REM is that ECHO messages also display when the echo status is off. And the word ECHO doesn't appear on the screen when echo status is off. ECHO is useful

```
C:\DOS>FIXD
C:\DOS>REM This file copies all files from the virtual D drive
C:\DOS>REM to the newly created TEMP directory on drive C.
C:\DOS>REM
C:\DOS>REM It then sorts and displays the directory before ending.
C:\DOS>C:
C:\DOS>CD \
C:\>MD TEMP
C:\>XCOPY /S D:*.* C:\TEMP
Reading source file(s)...
D:\SUPPLIES.JAN
D:\SUPPLIES.FEB
D:\SUPPLIES.MAR
D:\MARKETS
        4 File(s) copied

C:\>DIR C:\TEMP | SORT

        6 File(s)  9576448 bytes free
        Directory of C:\TEMP
    Volume in drive C is DUOTECH INC
.               <DIR>        09-13-90
..              <DIR>        09-13-90
MARKETS            40986     08-17-90
SUPPLIES.FEB       60239     09-13-90
SUPPLIES.JAN       78900     09-11-90
SUPPLIES.MAR       67870     09-11-90
C:\>
C:\>_
```



for displaying messages on the screen to whomever is using the batch file. Such messages might alert the user to insert a diskette, warn of possible loss of data, or provide a format for user input. You can insert blank lines on the screen by following ECHO with one or more spaces. If you just use ECHO by itself, you'll see a status message ("ECHO is on" or "ECHO is off") in its place.

The batch file from Figure 14.3 can be enhanced with ECHO commands to look like the one in Figure 14.5. When the file is run this time, the screen looks like the one shown in Figure 14.6. You can see that the screen display is much easier to understand.

```
ECHO OFF
REM This file copies all files from the virtual D drive
REM to the newly created TEMP directory on drive C.
REM
REM It then sorts and displays the directory before ending.
C:
CD \
MD TEMP
XCOPY /S D:*.* C:\TEMP
DIR C:\TEMP | SORT
ECHO
ECHO The root directory of Drive C is now active.
```

Figure 14.5. Batch File with ECHO Commands

```
C:\DOS>FIXD
C:\DOS>ECHO OFF
Reading source file(s)...
D:\SUPPLIES.JAN
D:\SUPPLIES.FEB
D:\SUPPLIES.MAR
D:\MARKETS
        4 File(s) copied

        6 File(s)  9576448 bytes free
      Directory of C:\TEMP
    Volume in drive C is DUOTECH INC
.               <DIR>        09-13-90
..              <DIR>        09-13-90
MARKETS              40986   08-17-90
SUPPLIES.FEB         60239   09-13-90
SUPPLIES.JAN         78900   09-11-90
SUPPLIES.MAR         67870   09-11-90
ECHO is off
The root directory of drive C is now active.
C:\>_
```

Figure 14.6. Batch File Execution with ECHO OFF

## Suppressing a Single Command

To suppress display of an ECHO command when echo status is on, use @ as the first character of the command. For instance, the command ECHO OFF would display if echo is on, but the command @ECHO OFF would be suppressed. You can use @ before any command to suppress it when echo status is on.

## Suppressing Normal Message Output

You can suppress certain normal output messages, such as "1 File(s) copied", by redirecting them to NUL, which gets rid of messages for good. If you use COPY *.COM C:\TEMP > NUL, the messages specifying the selected filespecs and the number of copies will not appear. This is especially useful in batch files to avoid cluttering up the screen, but it works from the keyboard as well. Error messages such as "File not found" may still be displayed as usual.

## Getting Keyboard Input

When you create a batch file, you generally want it to run without any further action from you. Some commands, however, require keyboard input. If you include DEL *.* in a batch file, for example, DOS asks "Are you sure (Y/N)?" and waits for a keyboard response. You can have a response ready in another ASCII file and redirect it to the program when you run the batch file. Suppose you have a batch file called SAVED.BAT that erases all the files from drive A: then copies the root directory from virtual drive D: to drive A:. The file ANS.Y contains one character, Y. SAVED.BAT contains these commands:

```
@ECHO OFF
ECHO Insert a disk in A: that contains nothing useful.
PAUSE
DEL A:*.* < ANS.Y
XCOPY D:\*.* A:
```

When you run the program with SAVED, the commands are executed in sequence. You insert an appropriate disk and press a key to continue. When a response is needed to the question following the DEL command, DOS uses the file ANS.Y as input.

If you know all the responses a command requires, you can place them all in a single file, in the correct sequence, then redirect that file as input to the command. The redirection must be applied to the individual command. If several commands in a batch file require standard input, you'll need a separate redirection file for each.

## The PAUSE Command

The PAUSE command causes the batch program to pause and wait until you press a key. You've already seen how it works in shell programs. The command format is shown below:

```
PAUSE [comment]
```

You can include a comment in the PAUSE command, as shown in the format. The comment appears before the standard pause message only when echo status is on (the default state).

When the echo status is off, the PAUSE command still has an effect and you'll see the message "Press any key to continue...", but you won't see the PAUSE command or any comment included in it. You can use a preceding ECHO command to display the message, much like this:

```
@ECHO OFF
VER
ECHO When you have examined the screen,
PAUSE
VOL
```

When the PAUSE command is executed, the screen will look something like this:

```
IBM-DOS Version 4.00
When you have examined the screen,
Press any key to continue . . .
```

Another way to handle the problem is to use this series of commands in the batch file:

```
@ECHO ON
@VER
PAUSE When you have examined the screen,
@VOL
```

In either case, when the file is executed, the screen shows the VER command output without the command itself, the message while the execution is suspended, then the VOL command output. Finally, the command prompt reappears.

## The CLS Command

When batch files are executing, the screen can fill with messages and extraneous output. You can remove the output from the screen with the CLS command, which has no arguments or options. CLS clears the screen and places the command prompt and the cursor on the top line of the screen. You can use CLS to clear the screen at any time, even when you aren't in a batch file. CLS is most useful in a batch file or shell program, especially to remove distracting commands and output for novice users. Many people routinely use CLS as the second command in a batch file, immediately following @ECHO OFF.

## Interrupting Batch Files

You can interrupt a batch file by pressing Ctrl+C or Ctrl+Break. You'll see the message "Terminate batch job (Y/N)?" If you press Y, the batch file is ended. If you press any other key, the current command is canceled and the batch file continues with the next command. The batch job must be available at the time. If you've changed diskettes, you'll be prompted to replace the diskette that contains the batch file. Changing directories doesn't hurt; DOS keeps the path and program name in a special location for later use.

Start at the command prompt, with C:\PRACTICE as the current directory.
1. Modify your DISK.BAT file to first clear the screen. Include several REM commands to document the file.
2. Try out your revised batch file.
3. Modify DISK.BAT to turn off command echoing. Try it out again.
4. Modify the file again to add @ before ECHO OFF. Try it out again.
5. If you use an editor, add messages to the file to tell the user what is coming up next. These messages should be displayed even though ECHO is off. (Don't try to do this with COPY CON.) Try out the file again.
6. If you use an editor, add a PAUSE command before the VER command. Display a message telling the user what the next command does and providing a message to press Ctrl+Break to terminate, if desired. Execute

the batch file at least twice, once terminating it with Ctrl+Break and once with any other key.

---

1. *Edit the file to look something like this:*

```
CLS
REM This file checks things out.
REM First it lists the tree.
REM Then it checks the current disk for problems.
REM Then it displays the DOS version number.
REM Then it lists the current directory.
TREE C:\
CHKDSK
VER
DIR
```

2. *Enter the command:*

```
DISK
```

*The screen should clear. Next, each REM command should be displayed at a command prompt. Then the commands should execute as before. If they don't, correct the file until it produces the desired results.*

3. *Add ECHO OFF as the first command in the file. When you try it out, you will no longer see any of the commands displayed, except ECHO OFF. This means the remarks won't appear. You will see only the results of the commands.*

4. *Now the ECHO OFF command is also suppressed.*

5. *You might want to create a file that looks something like this:*

```
@ECHO OFF
CLS
REM This file checks things out.
REM First it lists the current directory.
REM Then it checks the current disk for problems.
REM Then it displays the DOS version number.
ECHO First you will see a directory of the current drive...
DIR
ECHO Next you will see a report of the current disk's
ECHO statistics...
CHKDSK
ECHO Finally you will see DOS version information...
VER
ECHO That's all folks!
```

6. *You would need to insert these commands before VER:*

```
ECHO If you want to suppress the version information,
ECHO press Ctrl+C now. Any other key causes the version
ECHO information to be displayed.
PAUSE
```

# Parameters in Batch Files

So far, you have been creating and using batch files that need no information to run except the filename. Sometimes you may want to enter additional information. For example, suppose you have a batch file named D.BAT that contains only the command DIR | SORT | MORE. When you type D and press Enter, the current directory is sorted automatically and paged to the screen. This file would be more useful if you could include a directory name or a global filename, just as you can with DIR. Then you could type D *.EXE or D A:\ to get a nondefault directory. In this section, you'll learn to use replaceable parameters in defining a batch file so that you can supply information when you execute the file.

## Numbered Parameters

When you define a batch file, you can include replaceable parameters in commands within the file. Then, when you run the batch file, these parameters are replaced by corresponding values from the command line. DOS uses the names %1 through %9 to refer to up to nine values included on the command line following the batch file name. You can use these names in the batch file to indicate where the command line values should be inserted.

The D.BAT file can use a replaceable parameter for the directory name. For example, the command can be modified as DIR %1 | SORT | MORE. When you run the program with D *.EXE, the parameter is inserted into the command, which then becomes DIR *.EXE | SORT | MORE. The result is a paged and sorted directory as requested. If you run the program without a value, DOS uses a null value; the missing parameter doesn't interfere with the program, so you'll still get the paged, sorted current directory.

Replaceable parameters can be used in many batch files. For example, suppose you want a file named MOVE.BAT that copies a named file to a named target and removes the original. The batch file would contain this:

```
COPY %1 %2
DEL %1
```

To execute the program, you would use this format:

```
MOVE source-filespec target-filespec
```

DOS replaces %1 with the source-filespec and %2 with the target-filespec. Notice that the replaceable parameters can be reused in the batch file.

## Parameters in Messages

You can include parameter values in messages as well as in commands. For example, you might want to include these commands in the MOVE.BAT file to tell the user what has happened:

```
@ECHO OFF
CLS
COPY %1 %2
DEL %1
ECHO File %1 has been moved to %2.
```

The screen output when you use MOVE is shown in Figure 14.7. If you use MOVE *value* > NUL to run the batch file, the message giving the number of files copied does not appear. Notice that each variable is used "as is" in the messages. If you have to use a percent symbol for some other purpose in a message, you'll have to double it, as in %%. If this symbol occurs in a file-name in your batch file, you'll also have to double it. A file named 88%.DOC would be referred to in a batch file as 88%%.DOC.

## The %0 Parameter

DOS uses %0 to refer to the command name itself, and assigns the complete filespec of the command to the parameter. If you include a command like "ECHO Currently running the %0 program" in a batch file, the %0 will be replaced with the program name. You can use %0 value either to display the program name or to restart the same batch file.

```
C:\DOS>MOVE TEMP.4 \SAVETEMP\TEMP4.JAN

        1 File(s) copied
File TEMP.4 has been moved to \SAVETEMP\TEMP4.JAN.

C:\DOS>_
```

Figure 14.7. MOVE.BAT Output

## More Replaceable Parameters

A simple batch file can use variables numbered up to %9. If you need more than that, you can use a special command, SHIFT (covered in Chapter 15), to adjust variables.

## Example

You can create batch files to accomplish many different functions. Suppose you have a file that contains mailing information. You might want to be able to create a printout of just the records from a certain city, state, or ZIP code. You would first use the FIND command to extract the lines containing the desired string, then sort the resulting lines and send them to the printer. You could use this command: FIND "CA" CUSTOMER | SORT > PRN.

Suppose you want to carry out a slightly more complex process: You want to be able to enter the string and the file to be searched, you want the number of identified lines displayed on the console, and you want to be able to enter either PRN or a filespec to hold the sorted output. You might use a batch file like this:

```
@ECHO OFF
CLS
FIND /C "%1" %2
FIND "%1" %2 | SORT > %3
```

When you run the program, the resulting interaction looks like the one in Figure 14.8. The output from FIND /C is sent to the screen, and the output from the second FIND command goes to the file or device identified by %3.

## Named Parameters

Numbered parameters work fine for values that are entered with the command line. However, sometimes you might want to use other parameters within the batch file. You can do this with named parameters. Named parameters are given a value in the SET command, which stores the value in the environment. As you learned earlier, you can use SET *parameter=value* to establish a value for any parameter. When you use SET without arguments, all currently established parameter names and their values are displayed on the screen.

```
C:\DOS>FIX CA CUSTOMER PRN

---------- CUSTOMER:  45

C:\DOS>_
```

======= Figure 14.8. Typical Screen Output

***Named Parameters in a Batch File***   You might want to create a named parameter for a value that is to be used several times in a session or by several different people. If everybody uses a named parameter, they don't have to be concerned with the value of the parameter.

Suppose you use a temporary directory to save a copy of any file before deleting it. This provides a copy of deleted files in case you need them later. As part of the daily backup routine, you save the temporary directory. As part of your startup routine, you run a batch file named SETDELS.BAT, which requires a command line parameter specifying the directory. The file contains these commands:

```
MD C:\%1
SET DELSAVE=%1
```

If you run the file with SETDELS \DELTODAY, the commands create a directory of the name you specify (\DELTODAY) and also establish a named parameter (DELSAVE) with the value \DELTODAY. You use the named parameter in a batch file by enclosing it with percent symbols; %DELSAVE% now refers to \DELTODAY. Then instead of using DEL or ERASE when you want to remove a file, you use a batch file that specifies the named parameter. The KILL.BAT file contains these lines:

```
@ECHO OFF
ECHO The file will be saved in the %DELSAVE% directory.
COPY %1 %DELSAVE%
DEL %1
ECHO %1 has been deleted from its former location.
```

When you execute the program, the screen might look like the one in Figure 14.9. You can use KILL ADDISON.LET > NUL to eliminate the copy file message.

```
C:\DOS>KILL ADDISON.LET
The file will be saved in the \DELTODAY directory.
        1 File(s) copied
ADDISON.LET has been deleted from its former location.
C:\DOS>_
```

Figure 14.9. Batch File Interaction

Figure 14.9. Batch File Interaction

1. Create a DVOL.BAT file that displays volume information for the disk specified in the command to invoke the batch file.
2. Try out DVOL.BAT several times, getting the volume information for several different disks. Be sure to try invoking the command with no drive parameter.
3. Create a batch file that will sort a directory by size, then store the sorted output in a file. The directory to be sorted and the name of the output file will both be supplied in the invoking command line.
4. Try out the new batch file and correct it until it works.
5. Create an environmental variable named DFILE that contains the name of a new file. Then modify the sorted directory batch file so the output is appended to the named file.
6. Try out the changed batch file and correct it until you get the desired results.

*1. DVOL.BAT should containing the following line:*

```
VOL %1
```

*2. Enter commands such as the following:*

```
DVOL
DVOL A:
DVOL B:
```

*3. The file should look something like this:*

```
DIR %1 | SORT /+14 > %2
```

*4. If the batch file is named DSORT, you might enter the following command to run it:*

```
DSORT *.* ALL.DIR
```

*Then use the following command to see the result:*

```
MORE < ALL.DIR
```

5. *To use the filename CHEKFILE, enter this command:*

```
SET DFILE=CHEKFILE
```

*Then revise the DSORT file to read:*

```
DIR %1 | SORT /+14 >> %DFILE%
```

6. *You might enter the following commands:*

```
DSORT *.*
MORE < CHEKFILE
```

## Summary

This chapter has introduced you to the use of basic batch files. You can now manage comments, messages, screen appearance, and the use of replaceable and named parameters in a batch file. The next chapter covers various methods of programming a batch file; it expands on many of the concepts and commands covered in this chapter.

## Exercises

These exercises let you practice creating and using basic batch files. Try out all the jobs you create in these exercises and revise them until they work.

| What You Should Do | How the Computer Responds |
|---|---|
| 1. Create a file called MOVE.BAT that moves a file from one directory to another. The source and target filespecs should be entered in the command that invokes the batch job. Document the file and display informative messages to the user. | 1. Creates the file as directed. When you test the file, should copy the specified file to the target directory, then delete it from the source directory. |

2. Create a file called DELBUT.BAT that deletes all files on drive A: *except* those matching a filespec entered in the invoking command. (Hint: Use the filespec to set the read-only attribute; then use the DEL *.* command.) Document the file and display informative messages to the user. Set up a practice diskette in drive A: to test this batch job; copy files to the diskette from the hard disk as needed.

2. Creates the file as directed. When you test the file, should delete all files in the current directory except those that are write-protected. The write-protected files should include the ones matching the input filespec.

3. Create a file called ADDPATH.BAT that adds a directory to the existing path. (The present path can be accessed by the name %PATH%.)

3. Creates the file as directed. When you test the file, should add the input directory name to the end of the PATH variable.

4. Set up a **DOS Utilities** option for ADDPATH. Collect the input directory name in a dialog box.

4. Adds the program to the **DOS Utilities** screen as directed. When you test it, it should display a dialog box to collect the directory name, then execute ADDPATH as above.

## What If It Doesn't Work?

1. If you have problems with MOVE.BAT, compare your file to the version below. Your logic should be similar, although your messages and comments are probably different:

```
@ECHO OFF
CLS
REM Moves a file by copying it to the target directory, then
REM deleting it from the source directory.
COPY %1 %2
DEL %1
ECHO %1 moved to %2
ECHO End of %0.BAT
```

2. If you're having trouble with DELBUT.BAT, compare it with the following version. Your logic should be similar, although your messages and comments are probably different:

```
@ECHO OFF
CLS
REM This batch job deletes all but the specified files.
ATTRIB A:%1 +R
DEL A:*.*
ECHO The following files remain in the directory...
DIR A:
ATTRIB A:%1 -R
ECHO End of %0.BAT
```

3. If you're having trouble with ADDPATH, compare your batch file with the version below. Your logic should be similar, although your messages and comments are probably different:

```
@ECHO OFF
CLS
REM This batch job adds a new directory to the end of the
REM current search path.
PATH %PATH%;%1
ECHO The new path is shown below...
PATH
ECHO End of %0.BAT
```

4. If you're having trouble invoking ADDPATH from the shell, compare your **Commands** box to the following version. Yours should be very similar:

```
C:\PRACTICE\ADDPATH [/T"ADDPATH"/I"Enter the directory name
to be added to the PATH variable"/P"Directory: "]
```

# 15

# *Batch File Programming*

In the previous chapter, you learned to create and use basic batch files—with commands that are executed in sequence. In this chapter, you'll see how to program batch files.

In this chapter, you'll learn to:

- Manipulate batch parameters
- Cause branching in a batch file
- Perform decision making in a batch file
- Create loops in a batch file

## *Handling Parameters*

You have already seen how to define and use parameters from the command line as well as named parameters. In a batch file, you may occasionally want to use more than nine command-line parameters. Or you may want to pass a parameter from one batch file to a nested one. In this section you'll see how to achieve these effects.

### *Shifting Numbered Parameters*

The SHIFT command adjusts command line parameters down by one. After SHIFT, the former parameter %0 no longer exists, the former %1 is now %0, and so on until %9 now refers to the tenth value included in the command line. You can use SHIFT even if you have fewer than nine command line parameters. In most cases, however, you won't need it unless your batch file requires more than nine parameters.

## Passing Parameters

When you start a batch file, it takes its numbered replaceable parameters from the command line. If you start another batch file from within a batch file, you can use a numbered parameter or a named parameter in the new command. If you don't want to use the numbered parameter as such, you can assign it to a named parameter, then insert it in the command that calls the new batch file. The sample batch file below is called MOVE.BAT:

```
COPY %1 %2
SET SAVE=%1
CALL FIXLOG %SAVE%
DEL %1
```

After the file is copied, the named parameter SAVE is set to the value of the first named file. Then the batch file FIXLOG.BAT is called using the named parameter; since %SAVE% is the first command line parameter, it will be %1 in FIXLOG. When control returns to MOVE.BAT, the first file is deleted. While you can use numbered parameters in nested batch file calls, it often makes the file easier to read and understand if you use named parameters instead.

# Branching

One way to control any program is with branching. By default, commands are executed in sequence. With branching, you can cause control to jump to another part of the program. Batch files, like many programming languages, use the GOTO command for this function. In order to use GOTO, however, you must include a label in the batch file; a label occupies a line by itself and starts with a colon. Then the GOTO command branches to that label. Suppose that, every week or so, you copy a bunch of diskettes from drive A: to drive B:, copying the entire diskette with all subdirectories. You could create a batch file to do one iteration, like this:

```
XCOPY /S A:*.* B: > NUL
```

Here's a batch file that you could use to copy an indefinite number of diskettes:

```
@ECHO OFF
:DOAGAIN
   ECHO Place the diskette to be copied in drive A:
   ECHO and the target diskette in drive B:
   ECHO To stop the program, press Ctrl+C now.
   PAUSE
   XCOPY /S A:*.* B: > NUL
   GOTO DOAGAIN
```

Spaces at the beginning of lines are ignored, so you can use indentation to show the commands that follow a label. When a GOTO command specifies a label, DOS branches to the command following the named label. Labels are not case sensitive; in the example, "GOTO doagain" would have the same effect as GOTO DOAGAIN. There is no space in the word GOTO. You can include the colon before the label name in the GOTO command if you wish. If you put a label at the beginning of the file, then branch back to the label repeatedly, the batch file is repeated until you press Ctrl+Break. As in the example, it's a good idea to include on-screen instructions for terminating the job.

A label is defined by its appearance in the batch file on a line by itself, starting with a colon. The label can include up to eight characters (in addition to :), and it must start with a letter and be terminated with a space. Don't use special characters such as <, >, |, % or a space in a label. Since DOS ignores lines that start with a colon while processing a batch file, you can include comment lines this way if you wish. Make sure you don't use a comment line beginning with : that is followed by the same word you use as a label elsewhere in the file; DOS might branch to the wrong line.

Start at the command prompt, with \PRACTICE as the current directory.
1. Create a batch file that will produce a sorted, paged listing of the diskette in drive A:. You want to be able to replace the diskette and press any key to check another diskette, and you want to be able to press Ctrl+Break to terminate the loop.
2. Try out your program several times. Correct it until you get the desired results.

*1. The batch file should look something like this:*

```
@ECHO OFF
CLS
:START
  ECHO Please insert next diskette to be checked in drive A:
  ECHO or press Ctrl+Break to cancel this job.
  PAUSE
  DIR A: | SORT | MORE
  GOTO START
```

*2. If the batch file is named DIRBAT.BAT, you would enter the DIRBAT command to run it. When you get tired of checking diskettes, press Ctrl+Break.*

# Making Decisions

Suppose you want a batch file to make a decision based on some current condition. For example, if no parameters are entered on the command line, the batch file should display a special message and ask the user to try again. If a file that is requested doesn't exist, you may want to cancel the batch file. At some point in a batch file, if a condition is true, you want to do one thing. If the condition is false, you want to do something else. The general format of the IF batch command is:

```
IF [NOT] condition command
```

The IF command always includes a condition. Figure 15.1 shows the three forms the condition can take, along with an example of each.

The IF command always includes a second command to be executed if the condition is true. When the IF includes NOT before the condition, the

```
            ERRORLEVEL number

            string1==string2

            EXIST filespec


IF ERRORLEVEL 1 COPY %1 %2
IF %1.==%DELSAVE%. ECHO Please try another directory.
IF NOT EXIST DATA.JAN GOTO MESSAGE
```

Figure 15.1. Conditions in the IF Batch Command

second command is executed if the condition is false. The command can be any DOS or batch command. If the command isn't GOTO (to branch to another location) or CALL (to start another batch file), the command following IF is processed next.


## Conditions

IF commands can handle three types of conditions, as shown in Figure 15.1. You can use any of the three, but only one in each IF command.

***Does a File Exist?***   The EXIST condition always includes a filespec or a parameter that represents one. For example, any of these commands are valid:

```
IF EXIST MACHINES.XX ECHO The file MACHINES.XX was located
IF NOT EXIST \INVENT\MACHINES.XX GOTO END
IF EXIST %2 FIND "%1" %2
IF NOT EXIST %2 ECHO File %2 not located.
```

The first two examples each use a specific filespec; in the first, the ECHO command displays an appropriate message, while in the second, the GOTO command transfers control. The third IF command checks for the existence of the filespec provided as the second parameter in the command line; if the filespec does exist, the FIND command is executed using the first parameter as the string to be located. The last example displays a message if the same file cannot be found.

You can use EXIST conditions to check for the existence of any files. If you create batch files for other people to use, it's a good idea to make sure a filespec included in the command line represents an existing file if the batch uses it as a source or input. It's also a good idea to make sure a file specified in the command line as a target or output doesn't exist before overwriting it. In either case, you can then give the user a very specific message about the problem rather than relying on the rather terse error messages that DOS provides.

***Do Two Strings Match?***   The second condition type compares two strings. This comparison is case sensitive, so both strings must use the same arrangement of uppercase and lowercase characters. This is an ASCII comparison, so "0" is not equal to "0.0", and "2." is not equal to "2" (without a decimal point). Either string or both can be a parameter or an actual value; there isn't much point in comparing two actual strings, however. You can compare a command line parameter to a named parameter or constant. For example, suppose you have a named parameter containing a secret code that is changed regularly. A protected batch file may require that users enter that code as the first parameter. If the codes don't match, a different batch program (BADCODE.BAT) is processed. The basic IF command might look like this:

```
IF NOT %CODE%==%1 CALL BADCODE
```

Another way to do this is to branch to a certain part of the batch file only if the entered value is correct, as in:

```
IF %CODE%==%1 GOTO GOODCODE
```

Notice that this condition form requires a double equal sign with no embedded spaces. If you include a space before or after the double equal sign, DOS uses the space as part of the string to be compared.

If there is any chance that a value might not exist on either side of the == symbol, you must include a dummy character to avoid an error message. Most people use a period or question mark. For example, the command IF NOT .%CODE%==.%1 CALL BADCODE is valid even if either of the parameters is null. If the named parameter wasn't set and the first command line parameter has the value USER, the condition will be .==.USER; while they don't match, the comparison is valid. Without the period, the command would be IF NOT ==USER, which is not valid syntax. If both parameters are null, the command is IF NOT .==. CALL BADCODE; in this case, the strings match since they are both null.

You can also code within your batch file specific values to be matched. Suppose the people who use a particular batch file are all assigned user codes with directories based on those codes. When they start working for the day, they each use a batch file called STARTIT.BAT followed by the user ID. The batch file looks like the one in Figure 15.2. This batch file makes extensive use of IF and GOTO. Notice that the command following the last IF transfers control to BADID; DOS won't execute this command if the parameter matched any of the valid values. Notice also that each user-specific segment (such as RUTHGO) ends with a GOTO command to bypass other user-specific segments and to go directly to the end of the batch file. You could use a technique like this to establish some security and to control who uses batch files that execute sensitive programs.

Figure 15.3 shows three batch files that work together to verify that a diskette inserted in drive A: is the one you want by comparing the volume label. The user runs just the first batch file, GETV.BAT, with a drivename if appropriate. The VOL command redirects its output to another batch file VOLNAME.BAT (shown as the second batch file), then saves the drivename in a named parameter DRIVE. The next command executes the VOLNAME

```
@ECHO OFF
IF %1==RUTH GOTO :RUTHGO
IF %1==JUDI GOTO :JUDIGO
IF %1==PAULA GOTO :PAULAGO
IF %1==DAVID GOTO :DAVIDGO
IF %1==AUSTIN GOTO :AUSTINGO
IF %1==STEVE GOTO :STEVEGO
GOTO BADID
:RUTHGO
        CD \RUTH
        DIR
        GOTO END
:JUDIGO
        CD \JUDI
        DIR
        GOTO END
        ...
:BADID
        ECHO You didn't enter a valid user ID.
        ECHO See your manager.
:END
        ECHO End of program.
```

Figure 15.2. Batch File with Decisions and Branching

batch. When a batch file is executed without using CALL, the effect is to chain batch files; control will never return to the GETV.BAT file. Whenever a batch file command is the last one in the file, you won't need to use CALL.

VOLNAME.BAT contains the output from the VOL command. The first word, VOLUME, is treated as the command name; since CALL isn't included, control won't ever return to this file either. The other values in the first line are treated as parameters. The VOLUME command chains to the third batch file, VOLUME.BAT. The actual volume label is represented by %5; if the label includes spaces, as our example does, it needs additional parameters to represent the entire thing.

VOLUME.BAT sets a named parameter NEWNAME to contain the volume label, represented by a series of replaceable parameters. The result won't include any spaces, but will otherwise be a copy of the volume label. If you want to maintain spaces, you could simply insert them between the numbered parameters. The IF command compares the named parameter to the desired volume label, then executes the appropriate commands.

```
GETV.BAT
    @ECHO OFF
    VOL %1 > VOLNAME.BAT
    SET DRIVE=%1
    VOLNAME

VOLNAME.BAT
    Volume in drive A is DUOTECH INC

VOLUME.BAT
    @ECHO OFF
    ECHO Volume name is %5%6%7
    SET NEWNAME=%5%6%7
    IF .%NEWNAME%==.DOS4BOOT GOTO RIGHT
    ECHO  Wrong disk inserted.  Find the right one.
    GOTO END
    :RIGHT
        ECHO That's the correct diskette all right.
    :END
        ECHO End of routine to check the volume label
```

Figure 15.3. Checking Volume Labels

***Checking Exit Codes*** Many DOS commands return an exit code when they are finished; you can't see what this code is directly, but you can test for it with the ERRORLEVEL condition. If the command returns exit codes, 0 always indicates a normal completion of the command. Whatever you asked DOS to do was done correctly. Higher numbers indicate some sort of problem, ranging from user termination with Ctrl+C to a fatal disk error. Your DOS documentation includes the applicable exit codes in the description of each command that returns them. The most common commands that return exit codes are FORMAT and XCOPY; Appendix C shows a list of the documented exit codes returned by specific DOS commands. Application software can also return exit codes; you can find information about them in the documentation.

When you use the ERRORLEVEL condition, you specify a number. The condition will be true if the last exit code returned had a value greater than or equal to that number. The condition ERRORLEVEL 0 is always true, because an exit code is always 0 or greater. If you want to test whether a command was completed successfully, use ERRORLEVEL 1 insteadof ERRORLEVEL 0. The command IF ERRORLEVEL 1 ... is true when the command was not completed successfully; use IF NOT ERRORLEVEL 1 ... if you want successful completion to be the true result.

Suppose you have a batch file to copy files by using XCOPY. If the copy is successful, you want a batch file called PROCESS.BAT to be executed. The resulting batch file might look like the one shown in Figure 15.4. Notice that any exit code greater than 0 is considered unsuccessful.

As soon as the XCOPY command is completed, the IF command checks the exit code. If the code is not 0, indicating an unsuccessful copy, the condition is false, so the ECHO commands are processed. Then the batch branches to the VERYEND label. If the copy was successful, the exit code is 0 and the condition is true. The batch branches immediately to the MESSAGE label, where execution continues.

Suppose you want to know exactly what error occurred if XCOPY doesn't work correctly. Differentiating between successful (exit code 0) and unsuccessful execution in a batch file is fairly straightforward. If you try to identify the exact exit code, however, the programming gets more involved. The batch file in Figure 15.5 shows one way you can identify and display the actual exit code.

First the batch file determines if the operation was successful. If not, it starts with the highest numbered exit code for the command and works down. When a match is found, the condition indicates the exit code setting. A named parameter is set to the appropriate value for each successful condition. When all possibilities have been checked, the named parameter has a value; you can then display the value to find out why the operation failed. In the example, we included a message for display when none of the documented exit codes is identified. Some commands may have undocumented exit codes.

```
@ECHO OFF
CLS
XCOPY %1 %2
IF NOT ERRORLEVEL 1 GOTO MESSAGE
     ECHO Copy not successful
     ECHO Try again with correct values
     GOTO VERYEND
:MESSAGE
     ECHO Files in %1 copied to %2
     CALL PROCESS
:VERYEND
```

Figure 15.4. Checking the Exit Code

```
@ECHO OFF
XCOPY %1 %2
IF NOT ERRORLEVEL 1 GOTO VERYEND
IF ERRORLEVEL 5 GOTO INT24
IF ERRORLEVEL 4 GOTO MISC
IF ERROLEVEL 2 GOTO CTRL-C
IF ERRORLEVEL 1 GOTO NONEFND
ECHO Nonstandard, but unsuccessful, exit code
GOTO VERYEND
:INT24
     SET EXITCD=5
     GOTO SHOWEXIT
:MISC
     SET EXITCD=4
     GOTO SHOWEXIT
:CTRL-C
     SET EXITCD=2
     GOTO SHOWEXIT
:NONEFND
     SET EXITCD=1
     GOTO SHOWEXIT
:SHOWEXIT
     ECHO File %1 not copied.  Exit code is %EXITCD%.
:VERYEND
     ECHO End of batch file
```

Figure 15.5. Identifying the Exit Code

1. Create a batch file called CHECKIT.BAT to copy a file to drive A:. The filespec, which might be global, will be supplied in the invoking command. Make sure the file exists before copying it. If the file doesn't exist, display an appropriate message.
2. Try out CHECKIT and correct it until you get the desired results. Try it with individual filespecs that don't exist, individual filespecs that do, and global filespecs.
3. Create a batch file named START.BAT that expects FORM, GOOD, or VERB as the first parameter. If one of these parameters is entered, the file should branch to a routine that displays a message saying "You entered *word*." If some other value is entered, display a message saying "You did not enter a valid word."
4. Try out START.BAT and correct it until you get the desired results. Be

sure to try it with FORM, GOOD, and VERB, as well as with other words and no word.

1. *CHECKIT.BAT might look like this:*

```
@ECHO OFF
CLS
IF NOT EXIST %1 GOTO NOFILE
COPY %1 A:
ECHO %1 copied to drive A:
GOTO END
:NOFILE
  ECHO No file named %1--copy not made
:END
  ECHO End of program %0
```

3. *START.BAT might look something like this:*

```
@ECHO OFF
CLS
IF %1==FORM GOTO YES
IF %1==GOOD GOTO YES
IF %1==VERB GOTO YES
ECHO You did not enter a valid word.
GOTO END
:YES
  ECHO You entered %1.
:END
  ECHO End of %0 program.
```

# Loops

*Loops* in a program are composed of a set of commands executed repeatedly. Any programming language can use some type of loop. In batch files, you can use simple loops constructed with GOTO and a label, or structured loops created with the FOR command.

## Simple Loops

You have already seen loops created with the GOTO command and labels. Such a loop can be terminated with Ctrl+C.

## The FOR Batch Command

DOS provides a special command that lets you cause a command to be executed for every one of a list of items. The list can be coded directly into the FOR command, it can be derived from command line parameters, or it can be represented with a global filename. Here's the FOR command format:

```
FOR %%variable IN ( list ) DO command
```

The variable is a dummy value used to represent each listed item—as the item is processed by the command. In a batch file, the dummy variable is preceded by two percent signs; a FOR command might look like this:

```
FOR %%Z IN ( A: B: C: D: ) DO DIR %%Z
```

The parentheses are required to enclose items in the list. The command that follows DO is executed once for each value included in the list. During the execution, you use %%variable to represent the item being processed. The example uses Z as the dummy value character; so each time the command is processed, %%Z has a different value. The command above executes these four commands: DIR A:, DIR B:, DIR C:, and DIR D:.

The command FOR %%A IN ( AUTOEXEC.BAT CONFIG.SYS ) DO TYPE %%A results in the screen display of the contents of the two files in the list, in sequence.

You can also use a global filespec to establish the list. The command FOR %%P IN ( *.DOC) DO CALL PROCESS %%P uses P as the dummy value character. The list in this example is a global filename, so the command following DO is processed once for each file that matches *.DOC. DOS executes PROCESS once for each file that matches *.DOC, using the current filespec as the first command-line parameter.

## Using FOR in Batches

Suppose you frequently have to copy a file to three other locations: drive A:, drive B:, and C:\TEMP. You can save time by creating a batch file that will accept the name of the source file as input, then perform the copies. Here's how you could create such a file, without using a loop:

```
@ECHO OFF
IF NOT EXIST %1 GOTO NOTRIGHT
ECHO Insert target disks into drives A: and B:
PAUSE
COPY %1 A:
ECHO File %1 copied to A:
```

```
COPY %1 B:
ECHO File %1 copied to B:
COPY %1 C:\TEMP
ECHO File %1 copied to C:\TEMP
GOTO END
:NOTRIGHT
  ECHO File %1 not located. Check it out and try again.
:END
  ECHO End of batch %0.
```

You could accomplish the same effect by using a loop with FOR. Here's how it might look:

```
@ECHO OFF
IF NOT EXIST %1 GOTO NOTRIGHT
ECHO Insert target disks into drives A: and B:
PAUSE
FOR %%S IN ( A: B: C:\TEMP ) COPY %1 %%S
ECHO File %1 copied to A: B: and C:\TEMP
GOTO END
:NOTRIGHT
  ECHO File %1 not located. Check it out and try again.
:END
  ECHO End of batch %0.
```

When DOS encounters the FOR command, it executes COPY for each item in the list.

Suppose that, each day, you want to save a complete list of the files in each disk drive into a file you'll name when you run the batch. You can use the FOR command to accomplish this. Here's how:

```
IF EXIST %1 GOTO SKIPOVER
  FOR %%D IN ( A:\ B:\ C:\ D:\ ) DO TREE /F %%D >> %1
  GOTO END
:SKIPOVER
  ECHO File %1 already exists. Please name a new file.
:END
```

## Using FOR at the Command Prompt

As mentioned earlier, you can use any of the batch commands at the command prompt. The FOR command is the only one that is a bit different. When you use FOR at the keyboard, use only a single percent symbol before the dummy parameter. If you want to copy four files to another directory, you might use this command:

```
C:\DOS>FOR %F IN ( WILLS TRUSTS MONEY STORMS ) DO COPY %F
A:\TEMP
```

Each file in turn is copied to the \TEMP directory on drive A:. You can use FOR to do many operations at the keyboard; it is especially useful to handle a group of files that can't be referenced with a global filename.

You can also use FOR to process the FIND command repeatedly. For example, suppose you want to find all lines in the INVENTORY data file that contain Silver, Gold, or Bronze. You could use a command like this at the command prompt:

```
C:\DOS>FOR %M IN ( "Silver" "Gold" "Bronze" ) DO FIND %M
INVENTORY >> SAVEMET
```

The FIND command is executed once for each value supplied in the set. If you were to use the same command in a batch file, you would have to use %%M instead of %M. If the batch file takes the search strings as command-line parameters, you might code the command like this:

```
FOR %%M IN ( "%1" "%2" "%3" ) DO FIND %%M INVENTORY >>
PRODS.FND
```

The command line that invokes this batch file would not require quotation marks around the search strings, since they are provided in the list.

---

Start at the command prompt, with \PRACTICE as the current directory.
1. Copy files BACK1, BACK2, BIGFILE, and FAMLIST to directory \PRACTICE\PRACA\PRACY. Do it all with one command. If the command doesn't work, keep trying until you get the desired results.
2. Ordinarily, the FIND command does not accept global filespecs. Create a batch file named FINDALL.BAT that searches all files in the current directory for a specific string, displaying the output on the screen. The string will be entered in the invoking command.
3. Try out FINDALL and correct it until you get the desired results.
4. Ordinarily, the PRINT command does not accept global filespecs. Create a batch file that lets you submit a global filespec for printing.

---

*1. Enter this command:*

```
FOR %F IN (BACK1 BACK2 BIGFILE FAMLIST) DO COPY %F
\PRACTICE\PRACA\PRACY
```

*2. Your FINDALL.BAT file might look like this:*

```
@ECHO OFF
CLS
FOR %%F IN (*.*) DO FIND "%1" %%F
```

*3. You can pause the output with the Pause key (Ctrl+NumLock).*
*4. Your batch file might look like this:*

```
@ECHO OFF
CLS
FOR %%F IN (%1) DO PRINT %%F
```

# Summary

You can now use all the batch file commands that DOS provides. By now, you can use loops, branching, and decisions in any batch file; you can even combine them with called batches to create fairly extensive programs. In practice, however, keep batch files as simple as you can. Debugging is awkward at best.

# Exercises

These exercises let you practice creating and using programmed batch files. Be sure to try out each of the batch files you create in these exercises and correct it until you get the desired results.

| What You Should Do | How the Computer Responds |
| --- | --- |
| 1. Modify MOVE.BAT, which you created in Chapter 14, so that it doesn't erase the file from the source directory unless the file is successfully copied to the target directory. | 1. Modifies the batch file as directed. When you test the file, should copy the file to the target directory, then erase it from the source directory. If anything goes wrong with the copy—for example, if the target file is write-protected or the target directory doesn't exist—then the source file should not be deleted. |

2. Modify DELBUT.BAT, which you created in Chapter 14, so that up to nine filespecs can be entered with the command.

2. Modifies the batch file as directed. When you test the file, should delete all files in a directory except the ones specified in the invoking command. You should be able to specify anywhere from zero to nine filespecs in the invoking command, and all matching files should be protected from deletion.

3. Create a batch file with the name PRINTDIR.BAT that prints the directories of any number of diskettes in drive A:.

3. Creates the batch file as directed. When you test the file, should tell you to place a diskette in drive A:, print the directory of that diskette, then ask for another diskette. Program should stop when you press Ctrl+Break.

4. Create a batch file named BIGDEL.BAT that will delete any number of files. Filespecs, which can be individual or global, are entered with the invoking command. (Hint: Create a loop that deletes %1. Use SHIFT to set up %1 for the next loop. Stop the loop when %1 is null.)

4. Creates the batch file as directed. When you test the file, should delete all files listed in the invoking command.

## What If It Doesn't Work?

1. If you're having trouble with MOVE.BAT, compare it with this version. Your logic should be similar, although your messages and comments are probably different:

```
@ECHO OFF
CLS
REM Moves a file by copying it to the target directory, then
REM deleting it from the source directory.
REM XCOPY is used because it sets an exit code.
XCOPY %1 %2
IF NOT ERRORLEVEL 1 GOTO BADEND
   DEL %1
   ECHO %1 successfully moved to %2
   GOTO END
:BADEND
   ECHO XCOPY unsuccessful. %1 not moved.
```

```
:END
   ECHO End of %0.BAT
```

2. If you're having trouble with DELBUT.BAT, compare it with this version. Your logic should be similar, although your messages and comments are probably different:

```
@ECHO OFF
CLS
REM This batch job deletes all but the specified files.
REM Up to nine filespecs can be excepted.
FOR %%F IN (%1 %2 %3 %4 %5 %6 %7 %8 %9) DO ATTRIB A:%%F +R
DEL A:*.*
ECHO The following files remain in the directory...
DIR A:
FOR %%F IN (%1 %2 %3 %4 %5 %6 %7 %8 %9) DO ATTRIB A:%%F -R
ECHO End of %0.BAT
```

3. If you're having trouble with PRINTDIR.BAT, compare it with this version. Your logic should be similar, although your messages and comments are probably different:

```
@ECHO OFF
CLS
:PRINTLOOP
   ECHO Insert the next diskette to be printed
   ECHO or press Ctrl+Break to quit.
   PAUSE
   DIR A: > PRN
   GOTO PRINTLOOP
```

4. If you're having trouble with BIGDEL.BAT, compare it with this version. Your logic should be similar, although your messages and comments are probably different:

```
@ECHO OFF
CLS
REM This batch job deletes files given in the command line.
REM Any number of files can be deleted.
:DELLOOP
   ECHO Deleting %1...
   DEL %1
   SHIFT
   IF NOT .%1==. GOTO DELLOOP
ECHO End of %0.BAT
```

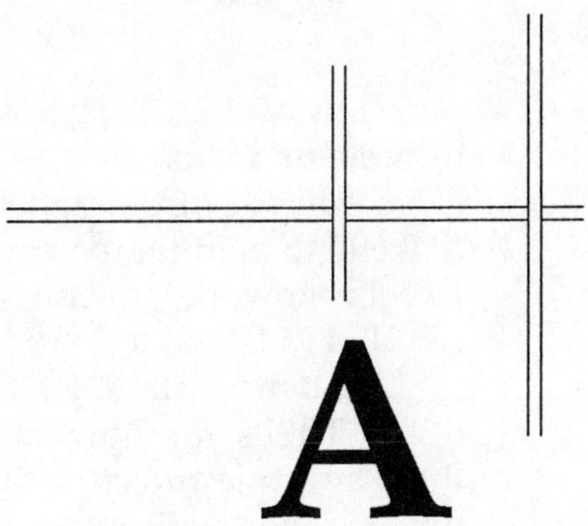

# A

# *Installing DOS 4*

$\mathbf{T}$he installation process consists of four major phases:

1. Select system configuration options (such as whether to install on the fixed disk or on diskettes).
2. Prepare the fixed disk, if appropriate (partition and format it).
3. Make a bootable drive on the fixed disk or make a bootable diskette.
4. Copy all the DOS files to the fixed disk or to a set of diskettes.

The SELECT program, included with your DOS diskettes, performs all these operations automatically. You must do three things: start SELECT, respond to system configuration options, and insert diskettes when told to do so.

## *Getting Ready to Install DOS*

It pays to plan before you start SELECT. First, write-protect all the DOS diskettes. This prevents accidental erasures in case you put the wrong diskette in the wrong drive at the wrong time. If you don't know the methods to write-protect a diskette, see the diagram in Figure 1.1.

You need some blank diskettes. They might be new or they might contain old files you don't need any more. SELECT will completely erase anything on these diskettes, so be sure you don't want to keep any data they currently contain. Do not write-protect these diskettes; SELECT must be able to write on them.

If you are installing DOS on your fixed disk, you need only one blank diskette to hold temporary files. SELECT calls this diskette SELECT COPY. Label it now, before you start the job. You can reuse the diskette after SELECT is finished. It doesn't contain any information you need to save.

If you are installing DOS on diskettes, you need several blank diskettes. SELECT tells you how many and what to label them. SELECT will ask for them by name and copy the DOS system onto them. After the installation is finished, you will put the original DOS diskettes away and use only these copies.

Even if you have a 1.2MB drive, SELECT needs 360K diskettes for the installation process. SELECT will reject high-density diskettes. You'll find it inconvenient to continue working with the lower-capacity diskettes, because the DOS programs span several diskettes. Appendix B: explains how to create your own 1.25MB DOS system diskette. If drive A: is a 3.5" drive, SELECT will work with either 720K or 1.44MB diskettes, as appropriate to the drive.

As the final preparation step, read the rest of this appendix. You'll find out what decisions you have to make during installation. You can prepare for each decision in advance. Then the installation process will be easy.

# System Configuration Options

The following sections detail the options you must respond to while installing with SELECT. Read through the entire section and decide how you will respond to each option, so that when you are at the computer you will be ready to make your choices.

## Specify Function and Workspace

You must choose between these three possibilities:

1. Minimum DOS function; maximum program workspace
2. Balance DOS function with program workspace
3. Maximum DOS function; minimum program workspace

The more memory space you give to the DOS function, the faster it can operate. Since DOS provides input/output services to all your application programs, they function faster too. But huge applications, such as dBase IV and Ventura Publisher, can't get enough memory space to run unless you choose Option 1.

If you have less than 640K of memory, choose Option 1. If you have 640K or more, try Option 3. But if an application says it can't get enough memory space, reinstall DOS using Option 2. If the application still objects, you'll have to reinstall DOS again using Option 1.

## Select Country and Keyboard

The country setting affects the format of dates, times, and numeric values. The keyboard layout affects how DOS interprets each key you type. By default, DOS assumes U.S. formats and keyboard layout. If you want to use different ones, you can select the country of your choice during installation. (The country setting and the keyboard layout do not have to reflect the same country.)

## Select Installation Drive

You can choose to install DOS on your hard disk (drive C:) or on diskettes (drive A: or B:). If you have a hard disk and want to be able to boot DOS from it, choose drive C:. Choose drive A: or B: only if you want to boot some other operating system from drive C: or if you don't have a hard disk.

Choosing drive B: does not mean you will boot from that drive. It simply means SELECT will create your DOS copy in drive B:. You will use the copy in drive A: when you are ready to boot DOS.

## Specify DOS Location

If you install DOS on your hard disk, SELECT will create a subdirectory in which to store all your DOS programs. SELECT suggests the name DOS for this subdirectory. If you want to use some other name, you can override the default. Don't do so without a compelling reason. This book assumes that the subdirectory's name is DOS. (Don't put DOS programs in your root directory. Space in the root directory is limited.)

The same screen lets you choose whether to install all DOS files on the hard disk or to copy only nonsystem files to the specified subdirectory. The second option exists for rare cases. If you want to boot some other operating system from your hard disk and boot DOS only from diskette, then choose the second option. It places all the DOS program files on the hard disk so they are easily accessible whenever you boot DOS, but it will not make the hard disk bootable with DOS. In all likelihood, you will want to boot DOS from your hard disk, if you have one. So take the first option, which is the default.

If you decide to take the second option, use the Tab key to get to the bottom section of the screen so you can select the option. If you want to accept the default option, you do not need to get to the bottom part of the screen.

## Printers

You must tell DOS what printers you have. Your choices on these screens affect all DOS print output. They also affect applications that request printing services from DOS rather than supplying their own printer drivers.

You must tell DOS how many printers you have, what type each one is, and what port each one is attached to. For serial printers, you must tell DOS the communications characteristics of the device: the baud rate, stop bits, parity checking, and data bits. You should be able to get this information from your printer manual.

To indicate the printer type, you select from a menu of standard types. Most of them are IBM models. If your type isn't shown, select the IBM model your printer emulates or select one of the "Other" types. If you're not sure what to do, you might have to retry the installation several times until you select a type that works.

DOS will use the printer attached to LPT1 (the first parallel port) as its primary printer. If you have more than one printer, be sure to attach to LPT1 the printer that will receive DOS output most of the time. If you have only a serial printer, you will need to reroute DOS output to that port. The Serial Printer Port screen has a bottom half where you can do this rerouting. For example, if you have a serial printer on COM1 and no parallel printer, you would reroute LPT1 to COM1.

## The Shell

The DOS shell gives you a graphic interface with DOS that most people find easier to use. SELECT asks if you want the shell installed automatically. If you indicate yes, then DOS inserts a command in your startup file to start up the shell automatically. If you say no, then you start up at the command prompt (the conventional interface) and the shell will not be available to you. Even if you plan not to use the shell most of the time, you should probably indicate yes here so that DOS will copy the shell to your system. Then you can switch back and forth between the shell and the command prompt at will. (Later on, you can remove the DOSSHELL command from the AUTOEXEC.BAT file to eliminate its automatic startup.)

### Predefined Configuration

Based on your answers to the above options, SELECT defines a hardware configuration for you. However, you have the option to view and change your configuration. By the time you complete this book, you will understand the configuration and can realistically view and change it. In the meantime, just accept the predefined configuration and plan to examine it again after you finish the book.

## Starting the Installation

After you have completed your preparation, you're ready to begin. Insert the **Install** diskette in drive A: (the top or left-hand drive) and turn on the power. The system boots. Follow the directions to insert the **Select** diskette, and the SELECT program automatically takes over. Then you will see various introductory screens, which you should read carefully.

Figure A.1 shows the list of keys you can use. The arrow keys and the Enter key are used to select options. The Esc key comes in handy when you

| | |
|---|---|
| Esc | Returns to the previous screen |
| Tab | Proceeds to the next entry |
| Pg Up/Pg Dn | Scrolls pages |
| Up/Down Arrows | Moves highlight bar to next item |
| Left/Right Arrows | Scrolls horizontally |
| F1 | Displays help information |
| F3 | Exits SELECT |
| F9 | Displays key assignments in help section |

Figure A.1. SELECT Control Keys

change your mind after you have already entered a choice. Each time you press Esc, you go back one more screen in the process. This gives you a chance to change your previous answers.

Several screens have two parts. The top part represents one option and the bottom part represents a related option. If you answer the top option and press Enter, the answer to the bottom option is assumed and you go on to the next screen. To enter your own answer to the bottom option, press Tab to move the cursor to the bottom of the screen. Then you can respond to the bottom option before pressing Enter. Backward tab (Shift+Tab) takes you back to the top half again. Only when you are satisfied with both halves of the screen should you press Enter. However, if you accidentally press Enter before selecting both options, simply press Esc to get back to the screen again.

SELECT includes a help system. On any screen, you can highlight an option and press F1 for an explanation of that option.

# Partitioning the Hard Disk

Your hard disk must be partitioned and formatted before it can be used. If you are installing DOS on your hard disk, SELECT will tell you if it needs to be partitioned or formatted. You can choose to let SELECT do it automatically, or you can control the partitioning. This can be a difficult decision to make when you are just starting to use your computer.

The real question is this: Do you want to divide your hard disk into two or more logical drives? If you have less than 20MB of hard disk space, you probably don't want to partition the disk. If you have more than 30MB, you might want to have more than one logical drive. If you have two or more people using the computer, you might want to give each a drive on the hard disk.

If you don't want to subdivide the hard disk into several drives, you can let SELECT partition the hard disk. If you do want to subdivide it, then you should partition the hard disk. When you tell SELECT that you want to do the partitioning, it starts up a program called FDISK for you.

The FDISK program is easy to follow because it is all menus. For example, on the first menu, type 1 to create a primary DOS partition. Then tell FDISK how much space to put in the primary partition. Then type 2 to create an extended DOS partition. Put the rest of the space into the extended partition. Then create logical drives in the extended partition. For each drive you want, tell FDISK how much of the available space to put in that drive.

If you have a 30MB hard disk and want to put 10MB in each of drive C:, drive D:, and drive E:, you would put 33 percent in the primary partition and the rest in the extended partition. Then put 50 percent of the extended partition in drive D: and the rest in drive E:.

After the hard disk is partitioned, you must reboot to continue. Then SELECT formats the primary partition so that it can install DOS on it. You might see the message "Attempting to recover allocation unit *nnnn*." This means DOS has discovered a bad sector on the hard disk. Bad sectors are not fatal. Don't worry about it as long as most of the disk is usable. DOS blocks out the bad sectors so that they won't affect your programs and data.

## Copying DOS

SELECT's final phase is to make a copy of DOS. You will be told what diskettes to insert.

## CONFIG.SYS and AUTOEXEC.BAT

DOS might use two files during the booting process: CONFIG.SYS and AUTOEXEC.BAT. If either or both files are present, they must be in the root directory of the boot drive or diskette. CONFIG.SYS tells DOS the hardware configuration; if there is no CONFIG.SYS, DOS assumes a default configuration. AUTOEXEC.BAT contains DOS commands that should be executed during booting. These commands might do such tasks as setting the date and time, telling DOS what directories to look in for programs, and starting up the shell.

Depending on the options you choose during installation, DOS might generate CONFIG.SYS and AUTOEXEC.BAT for you. If so, these files will go into effect automatically the first time you boot. You will learn how to examine them and add to them in this book. Be sure not to erase them or remove lines from them. Otherwise, your system might stop working properly.

If SELECT installs DOS 4 on a hard disk that has already been in use, it looks for existing copies of CONFIG.SYS and AUTOEXEC.BAT. If SELECT finds them, it does not change these files. Instead, it generates files called CONFIG.400 and AUTOEXEC.400. After you have completed installation and booted with your new version of DOS, examine the root directory with the DIR command. If you have both a CONFIG.SYS and CONFIG.400 file, review them to make sure they do not have conflicting statements. (You'll understand the contents of these files after you have completed this book.)

You can combine them by entering this command:

```
COPY CONFIG.SYS+CONFIG.400
```

If you have both an AUTOEXEC.BAT and an AUTOEXEC.400 file, you can combine them by entering this command:

```
COPY AUTOEXEC.BAT+AUTOEXEC.400
```

This will add the new DOS 4.0 startup commands to the ones you were using with your earlier version of DOS.

# Installing Device Drivers

You might have devices that DOS doesn't know about and SELECT doesn't ask about. For example, you can use a mouse with the shell, but SELECT doesn't give you a chance to install it, as it does with your printers. Extra memory (beyond 1MB) won't be available either until you tell DOS about it.

Such external devices won't work with DOS unless you install a device driver. Usually, this means adding a line to CONFIG.SYS that looks something like this:

```
DEVICE=name.SYS
```

You must look in your device manual to find the appropriate device name to use. You must also copy the named file to the root directory of the boot drive (or include a path with the name in the DEVICE statement).

The best way to add a line to CONFIG.SYS is to edit the file with your ASCII editor. If you don't know how to do this, don't try to add drivers to CONFIG.SYS until you have completed this book. You'll be able to work without your mouse or extra memory until then.

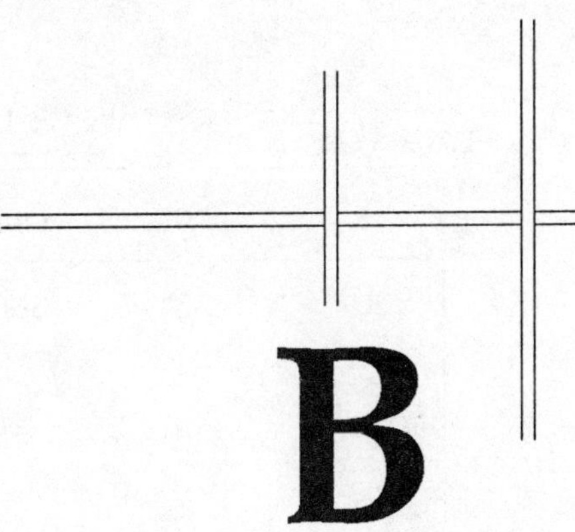

# B

# *Running DOS 4 from Diskettes*

If you didn't install DOS 4 on a fixed disk, you will have to boot from diskette when you want to use DOS 4. Although running DOS from diskette is somewhat awkward, it is quite possible to use most DOS commands and features in this way.

This appendix gives you some guidelines to help you efficiently use your system while running DOS 4 from diskette.

## *Installation*

When you install DOS 4 on diskettes, follow the instructions and prompts you see on the screen for inserting and labeling diskettes. When you are finished, the number of diskettes you have depends on the type of diskettes you'll use to boot the system. Table B.1 shows the number and labeling for each type.

To start DOS, insert the diskette labeled **Startup** into Drive A: and boot or reboot the system. If a separate diskette is labeled **Shell**, you'll have to switch to that diskette before entering DOSSHELL to start the shell.

The diskettes labeled **Working** hold other DOS programs that you may need while working with DOS. Programs that are strictly or primarily for fixed disk use are not copied to diskettes during installation.

Table B.1. Diskettes after Installation

| Size | Capacity | Count | Labels |
| --- | --- | --- | --- |
| 5.25" | 360K | 5 | Startup |
| | | | Working 1 |
| | | | Working 2 |
| | | | Working 3 |
| | | | Shell |
| 3.5" | 720 K | 3 | Startup |
| | | | Working |
| | | | Shell |
| 3.5" | 1.44Mb | 1 | Startup DOS 4 |

# *Consolidation for 1.2MB Diskettes*

During installation, the SELECT program decides which program files to place on which diskettes. You can make some changes later to make the diskettes more convenient for you.

If your diskettes are 5.25", SELECT creates the installed diskettes as 360K. You can combine them if your drive A: can handle 1.2MB diskettes.

The first step is to format a diskette using FORMAT; FORMAT.COM is located on the diskette labeled **Working** 1. Follow these steps:

1. Boot using the 360K **Startup** diskette.
2. Replace the **Startup** diskette with **Working** 1.
3. Type FORMAT A: /S at the command prompt.
4. When you see the message "Insert DOS disk in drive A:", insert the **Startup** diskette into drive A: and press Enter.
5. When you see the message "Insert new diskette for drive A:", insert the diskette to be formatted and press Enter.
6. When you see the message "Volume label . . . ", type a label—such as DOS 4 BOOT— and then press Enter.
7. When you see the message "Format another (Y/N)?", type N.
8. When you see the message "Insert DOS disk to continue", insert the **Startup** diskette again.

The newly formatted diskette is now bootable. The next step is to copy all the files from the **Startup** and **Shell** diskettes to the 1.2MB diskette. Now you can boot from this diskette and enter the shell from it as well. In addition, you can copy the programs you expect to be the most useful from the **Working** diskettes to this diskette, thus making the programs handy.

### Copying Files to and from the Same Drive

Most systems that do not contain a fixed disk have at least two diskette drives. If these are of the same size and type, you can easily use COPY, XCOPY, or DISKCOPY to copy files and diskettes between drives. Details about these DOS programs are covered in the book.

If you have a single diskette drive, the drivenames A: and B: both apply to that drive. A command such as COPY A:FORMAT.COM B: tells DOS that you want to copy a file from one diskette to another; the command will read the file into memory, then prompt you to insert a new diskette into the drive so it can write the file to the diskette.

If your system has two diskette drives of different types, you may have a problem—DOS boots only from drive A:. Table B.2 shows the different combinations you might have. The codes indicate the type of problems that may arise.

A problem arises when you have a diskette on one type of drive and want to copy from it to another diskette of the same type. You can't refer to the same diskette as both A: and B: when a real drive B: exists. You can solve this problem by telling DOS to create a logical drive that matches a real drive and to give it a new drivename. Suppose you have a 1.2MB drive A: and a 360K drive B:. Here's the statement you could include in your CONFIG.SYS file to set up a logical drive C: to match your drive A:

```
DEVICE=DRIVER.SYS /D:0 /F:1 /H:2 /S:15 /T:80
```

Now you can refer to the first drive as both A: and C:, and DOS will prompt you to insert the appropriate diskettes. (If drive B: holds the 1.2MB diskette, use /D:1 in the command instead of /D:0.) Check your documentation for details on how to set up another type of logical diskette.

# File Accessibility

Once you have a method for copying files from one diskette to another, you should examine the directories of your working DOS diskettes. You will use

Table B.2. Diskette Drive Combinations

| | | Drive A: 5.25"<br>360K | 5.25"<br>1.2Mb | 3.5"<br>720K | 3.5"<br>1.44Mb |
|---|---|---|---|---|---|
| Drive B: | 5.25"<br>360K | OK | HL | X | X |
| | 5.25"<br>1.2Mb | LH | OK | X | X |
| | 3.5"<br>720K | X | X | OK | HL |
| | 3.5"<br>1.44Mb | X | X | LH | OK |

OK -- both drives the same
HL -- A is higher density than B
LH -- A is lower density than B
X -- Drive types incompatible

some of the programs much more often than others. For example, the 360K **Working** 1 diskette contains DISKCOPY.COM and FORMAT.COM. The **Working** 2 diskette contains CHKDSK.COM, FC.EXE, SORT.EXE, TREE.COM, and XCOPY.EXE. The programs you often use should be copied to your primary diskette. If you'll be working from the shell, use your **Shell** diskette. If not, use your **Startup** diskette. Even if you boot from a 360K or 720K diskette, there is space on the **Startup** diskette for additional DOS files.

As you continue working with DOS 4, the programs you need a great deal might change. Keep the programs you'll use often on your primary diskette and remove programs you don't use as much.

## Working from the Shell

Working from the shell and diskettes can be a problem if the programs you need aren't available. When you change diskettes, the **File System** won't register the new diskette unless it is forced to reread the diskette. Try not to change diskettes too often while working with the Shell.

The programs listed on the **DOS Utilities** menu won't necessarily be available on your **Shell** diskette. If you want to format diskettes through the shell, you'll have to copy FORMAT.COM to the **Shell** diskette. BACKUP and RESTORE aren't useful in a diskette-based system, so you can delete these programs from the **DOS Utilities** menu if you prefer.

If you leave the shell by selecting **Command prompt** or by pressing Shift+F9, you can remove the diskette in drive A: and insert another. But when you exit a program in this way, you may be prompted to insert the disk containing the batch file. If so, just replace the diskette with the **Shell** diskette and press any key, as prompted.

If you use a program that takes up a great deal of memory, it may overlay the area containing COMMAND.COM. If that happens, you'll be prompted to insert the diskette containing this program. If so, just insert the diskette you boot from, then continue with your session.

## Command Considerations

When you run DOS 4 from diskettes, you'll have to change diskettes fairly often. Some commands, such as FORMAT and DISKCOPY, automatically wait for you to insert the diskette before proceeding with their operations. Others, such as XCOPY and REPLACE, start immediately. You can use the /W switch with either XCOPY or REPLACE to cause the command to pause, allowing you time to insert a new diskette before the operation begins.

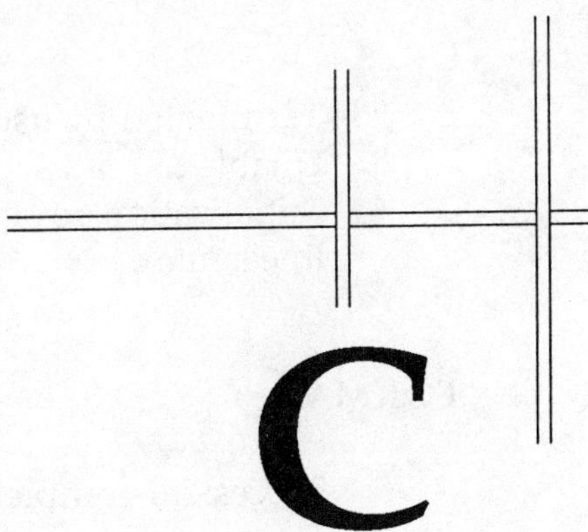

# DOS Exit Codes

## BACKUP

0   Command successful
1   No files found to back up
2   Some files not backed up due to sharing conflict
3   Terminated by user with Ctrl+C
4   Terminated by DOS due to error

## DISKCOMP

0   Compared OK
1   Did not compare; disks not the same
2   Terminated by user with Ctrl+C
3   Did not compare due to hard or unrecoverable error
4   Initialization error; not enough memory, invalid drives, or invalid command-line syntax

## DISKCOPY

0   Copied successfully
1   Unrecoverable but nonfatal read/write error

  2   Terminated by user with Ctrl+C
  3   Unable to read source or format target
  4   Initialization error; not enough memory, invalid drives, or command-
      line syntax

## FORMAT

  0   Successful completion
  3   Terminated by user with Ctrl+C
  4   Fatal error other than 3 or 5
  5   N response to hard disk prompt to proceed with format

## GRAFTABL

  0   Command successful
  1   Table already loaded and replaced by new table
  2   File error occurred
  3   Incorrect parameter, no action taken
  4   Incorrect version of DOS

## KEYB

  0   Command successful
  1   Invalid syntax
  2   Bad or missing keyboard definition file
  3   Could not create keyboard table in resident memory
  4   Error with CON device
  5   Codepage requested not prepared
  6   Table for selected codepage not found
  7   Incorrect DOS version

## REPLACE

  0   Command successful
  2   File not found
  3   Path not found
  5   Access denied

8  Insufficient memory
11  Command-line error
15  Invalid drive

## RESTORE

0  Normal completion
1  No files were found to restore
3  Terminated by user
4  Terminated due to error

## XCOPY

0  Copy without error
1  No files found to copy
2  Terminated by user with Ctrl+C
4  Not enough memory, invalid drive, invalid command-line syntax, file not found, or path not found
5  Aborted with INT 24 error reading or writing

# *Index*

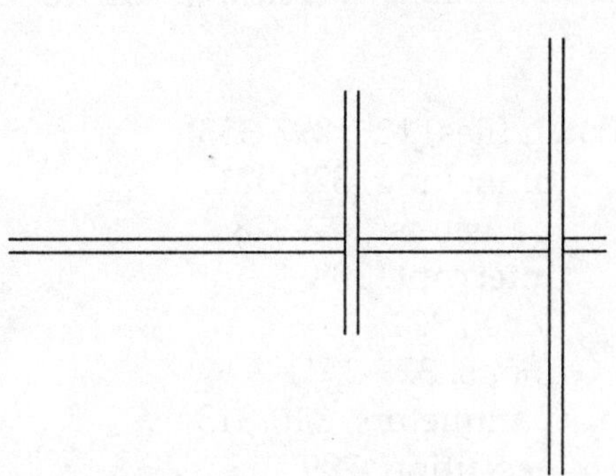